FRIEND OF CHINA – THE MYTH OF REWI ALLEY

Friend of China is a radical and controversial analysis of the life and work of Rewi Alley. Bringing together Chinese and previously unpublished Western source material, this book reveals the policy behind the Chinese Communist Party's 'smiling democracy'. Rather than a biography, this is a revisionist history, encouraging us to re-examine what we know and understand about one of the most famous, or indeed infamous, foreigners in modern China.

Rewi Alley, who arrived in China in 1927 from New Zealand, lived there for the rest of his life. A close associate of Agnes Smedley, Song Quigling and Edgar Snow, Rewi Alley became involved in the underground Chinese Communist Party and was instrumental in setting up the Chinese Industrial Co-operative movement. By the 1940s, he was regarded as a great humanitarian and internationalist. Later he became an outspoken 'foreign friend' of the Chinese Communist regime and a prolific propagandist on the 'new' China. In Deng Xiaoping's China, Alley became the symbol of 'long-standing friendly relations' between China and New Zealand and was presented to the Chinese people as a model foreigner.

Through his efforts, and those of his promoters, Alley became a figure of myth in his own lifetime: a myth that took many forms and meanings. This book examines the myth and reality of Rewi Alley's life, using them to explore the role of foreigners in China's diplomatic relations and their sensitive place in China after 1949, exposing the important role that China's 'foreign friends' played in people-to-people relations as well as in the ideological education of Chinese citizens.

Anne-Marie Brady is Lecturer in the Department of Political Science at the University of Canterbury, Christchurch, New Zealand.

CHINESE WORLDS

Chinese Worlds publishes high-quality scholarship, research monographs and source collections on Chinese history from 1900 to this century.

'Worlds' signals the ethnic, cultural and political multiformity, and the regional diversity of China, the cycles of unity and division through which China's modern history has passed, and recent research trends towards regional studies and local history issues. It also signals that Chineseness is not contained within territorial borders – some migrant communities overseas are also 'Chinese worlds'. Other ethnic Chinese communities throughout the world have evolved new identities that transcend Chineseness in its established senses. They too are covered in this series.

The focus of *Chinese Worlds* is on modern politics, society and history. It includes both history in its broader sweep and specialist monographs on Chinese politics, anthropology, political economy, sociology, education and the social science aspects of culture and religions.

FRIEND OF CHINA – THE MYTH OF REWI ALLEY

Anne-Marie Brady

Routledge
Taylor & Francis Group

LONDON AND NEW YORK

First published 2003
by RoutledgeCurzon

This edition published 2016
by Routledge
2 Park Square, Milton Park, Abingdon,
Oxfordshire OX14 4RN
711 Third Avenue, New York, NY 10017

First issued in paperback 2016

*Routledge is an imprint of the Taylor and Francis Group,
an informa business*

© 2003 Anne-Marie Brady

Typeset in Garamond by Wearset Ltd, Boldon, Tyne and Wear

British Library Cataloguing in Publication Data
A catalogue record for this book is available from the British Library

Library of Congress Cataloging in Publication Data
Brady, Anne-Marie.
Friend of China : The myth of Rewi Alley / Anne-Marie Brady.
p. cm. – (Chinese worlds)
Includes bibliographical references and index.
1. Alley, Rewi, 1897– 2. Alley, Rewi, 1897– Views on China.
3. New Zealanders – China – Biography. 4. Intellectuals – New
Zealand – Biography. 5. China – Foreign relations – 1949–6. China
– Intellectual life – 20th century – Foreign influences. 7. China –
History – 20th century. I. Title: Myth of Rewi Alley. II. Title.
III. Series.
DS731.N48 B73 2002
951.05–dc21
2002069883

ISBN 13: 978-1-138-86337-8 (pbk)

ISBN 13: 978-0-7007-1493-3 (hbk)

He who agrees to be controlled exists; he who does not ceases to exist.

George Konrad[1]

CONTENTS

PLATES

ACKNOWLEDGEMENTS

I first became interested in the subject of Rewi Alley in the wake of debate in my country, New Zealand, surrounding the Tiananmen Massacre of 4 June 1989. At that time, in New Zealand, as in many other Western countries, commentators questioned the nature of our nation's links with China. Throughout the 1980s, as China opened up to the outside world, New Zealand had believed itself to have a 'special relationship' with that country. It was believed that this 'special relationship' in part, if not completely, had much to do with the 'special' affection the Chinese held for New Zealand's own Rewi Alley. Alley, who died in 1987, spent most of his life in China working with the Chinese Communists and is one of the most well-known foreigners there. After 4 June, however, Alley's contribution to the New Zealand–China relationship came under attack. Many commentators stated that New Zealand, like other Western countries, had misunderstood the nature of China's reforms and some blamed Alley for this. They claimed that New Zealand had fallen prey to a romanticised picture of China and added that the idea that New Zealand had a 'special relationship' with China as a result of the Alley connection, or indeed on any terms, was a delusion. Stimulated by these controversial issues I decided to examine the topic for my Masters thesis in Asian Studies at the University of Auckland. This book combines the work I did on the thesis with later research that has since been published in the *China Quarterly*, *Journal of East Asian History*, *China Information* and *Revue Bibliographique de Sinologie*. In the book, as in the original thesis, I have tried to answer the question of Alley's contribution to New Zealand's relationship with China, in addition to examining the role Alley played in China in the sixty years he lived there.

This work could not have been completed without the help of Duncan Campbell, who was the first to foster my interest in China and has continually encouraged and inspired my studies. For encouragement, advice and other crucial assistance I am indebted also to the help of Courtney Archer, Konrad Aron, Franceska Banga, Heather Baigent, Geremie Barmé, Greg Benton, James Charlton, Chris Elder, Mark Elvin, Bill Jenner, Gavan McCormack, Phallon Vaughter-Hossain and Monica Wehner. My thanks

ix

also go to all those who agreed to share their impressions of Rewi Alley with me; the interviewees, whose names are listed in the notes. I am grateful to the various organisations who have provided the funding that has made my research possible; the Ministry of Foreign Affairs and Trade, New Zealand China Exchange Program, the University of Auckland Graduate Scholarship, the University of Waikato Rewi Alley Scholarship in Chinese Studies, the Department of Internal Affairs Historical Branch Bursary, the Freemason Bursary and the Australian National University Vacation Scholarship.

1

INTRODUCTION

> ... this Marco Polo in reverse, who does not carry off the
> secrets of Cathay, but helps the oldest society on earth to dis-
> cover new powers.[1]

Rewi Alley was a man who became a myth in his own lifetime. Alley was by
no means a passive witness to the mythologisation of his own life, indeed he
was an active participant in the process. Although New Zealand-born, Alley
played a prominent role in China from the 1930s, one which continues to
the present day; from relief worker, envoy of Chinese foreign policy, role
model for Chinese youth, to symbol of New Zealand–Chinese relations and
idealised Sino-foreign relations. The persistence of the Alley myth has a lot
to do with his most long-lasting and prominent role, that of 'friend of
China'. The foreign friends of the People's Republic of China (PRC) have an
important role in China's distinctive foreign affairs system, which incorpor-
ates state-to-state diplomacy with so-called 'people's' diplomacy, foreign
propaganda and the management of the foreign presence in China.[2] The
friends are also symbolic of the highly politicised status of the foreigner in
the PRC and the Chinese Communist Party's (CCP) ongoing attempts to
control Sino-foreign relations in the abstract and most literal sense. Alley's
sixty years in China (1927–1987) offer a microcosm of the changing position of foreigners in China from the late Republican period right up until
the current phase of 'reform and opening up' begun in 1978. More than any
other foreigner in this period, beginning in his earliest years in China, Alley
had close involvement in some of the most burning issues of the times, close
contact with the political figures who influenced change, as well as being an
instrument of change himself.

Surprisingly, Rewi Alley's political role in China and the means to which
the myth about him was put has received little scholarly attention in the
past. The myth of Rewi Alley has, however, been thoroughly documented
by his admirers and hagiographers, and the following selection serves as an
introduction to that myth:

> He was a strangely out-of-place figure in that dark, sickly crowd,
> his sunburned face covered with dust beneath a fiery bush of
> upstanding hair. He was of only medium height, but he had

1

tremendous rugged arms and legs. When he stood with those giant's legs spread apart in a characteristic attitude, he seemed somehow rooted to the earth. *But it was the man's great head, with a profile like something carved from Stone Mountain, that struck me.*

Edgar Snow, *Saturday Evening Post*, 1941[3]

Alley had lived and worked in China for 60 years, affecting huge social change and *influencing the thinking of many of the vast nation's leaders, from Mao Tse-tung onwards.* He drew on his early life as a Taranaki back-blocks farmer to shape the programmes and ideologies which were to change China. Always a pragmatist, he used a commonsense, do-it-yourself approach in his early efforts to help create a new order for China's oppressed and exploited workers. Alley was dismayed by the plight of the Chinese workers when he arrived in Shanghai to take up an appointment as factory inspector in 1929.

Auckland Star, 1987[4]

Originally, when he was young, he ran a farm in his motherland New Zealand and he worked really splendidly. At the time, a young lady was very fond of him. Before long, Rewi Alley went to China, the young lady still wrote to him and told him she still wanted to marry him, on condition that he must leave China and come back to New Zealand. Rewi Alley replied to her, 'My work is in China. *China needs me,*' and thus broke the engagement. During the war years, Premier Zhou Enlai was very concerned about [Alley's] lifestyle and suggested he think about getting married. [Alley] disagreed, saying, '*I dash about all the time and it is very dangerous. If I died wouldn't it harm the other person?*'

People's Daily, 1988[5]

About [1931] Alley became *an official member of the Chinese Communist Party* and linked forces with an American communist journalist named Agnes Smedley to become propagandists for the Reds.

New Zealand Herald, 1980[6]

... *more than any other individual* ... responsible for the development of Chinese industry.

New Zealand School Journal, 1946[7]

Rewi Alley, the man mentioned in laudable terms by many writers of books on China: Perhaps we can sum him up by imagining a man of courage and vision and sympathy with the lot of the little people,

2

writer, poet, philosopher, yet practical man all combined; a human dynamo – *one of the world's truly great people.*

CORSO Report, 1947[8]

Rewi contributed in an original way to the development of the New China. The Chinese Industrial Co-operatives, which he initiated and organised, *provided the blue-print for the communes which now exist under the People's Government.* For many, however, *Rewi Alley's greatest contribution has been his literary achievements.* His poems are very personal, close and deeply felt. He is second to none in the translation of Chinese literary works, especially Chinese T'ang poets. . . . His documentary and diary accounts are all first hand . . . these writings are generally good.

National Committee for the Commemoration of Rewi Alley's
Seventy Fifth Birthday, NZ, 1972[9]

To explain China to the world, to take part in conferences including the representatives of people struggling against foreign or local oppression throughout the world; to speak and waken people from the old way of thinking to an awareness of the new hopeful forces – these were his tasks, *a continuation of what he had begun in Shanghai, continued in Gung Ho and in the Sandan school,* and now could share with new comrades not only in China but on a worldwide basis.

Willis Airey, *A Learner in China,* 1970[10]

I went back to my homeland of New Zealand in 1960 for the first time in twenty-three years. This was made possible by Premier Zhou Enlai. At an interview with a visiting New Zealand Labour Party delegation, he said in my presence, 'Why don't you get Alley a passport?' They said, 'Well, we are rather confused. We did not know about that. We did not know he doesn't have one.' Zhou said, *'If you don't get him a passport I'll give him a Chinese one, right now.'* When they went back to New Zealand, I sent in my application for a passport, received it and went on a New Zealand lecture tour.

Rewi Alley, *At 90: Memoirs of My China Years,* 1987[11]

He was one of those few and rare people on earth who move and live for others rather than for themselves. And *at his contact, such was the power that emanated from this colossal faith of his in people, one somehow became better too, one began to understand what it is truly to live within the context of one's own humanity,* which is to care for others.

Han Suyin, *New Argot,* 1974[12]

3

A tour group calls. Rewi is one of Beijing's living monuments, and there are certain command functions he must perform. He talks for half an hour on China and the state of the nation as revealed by a first hand circuit from south to north just completed. At their departure, he is ahead of them. Swiftly, he ducks along the shelves gathering this and that item of pottery, and pictures given him on his travels. Then he is amongst them in the lobby, *a centrifuge dispensing presents until a pink happiness pervades the entire group* . . .

Geoff Chapple, *Rewi Alley of China*, 1980[13]

(Italics added.)

The above series of quotes, culled from a representative sample of writings, are all myth, part of the Rewi Alley myth that flourished during the sixty years he lived and worked in China and continues to the present day. All of the images they present are falsehoods or, at best, present a greatly inflated view of Alley and his life. Edgar Snow promotes Alley to American readers as something akin to their heroic presidents profiled on Mount Rushmore; a New Zealand journalist claims Alley influenced the thinking of China's leaders, including Mao Zedong; Alley's former doctor repeats a myth created by Alley himself that he had never married due to a failed love affair and his commitment to the Chinese revolution; the *New Zealand Herald* tells us Alley is an official member of the Chinese Communist Party; the *New Zealand School Journal* cites Alley as the founder of China's manufacturing sector; the Director of CORSO, formerly New Zealand's leading charity, lauds Alley as 'one of the world's truly greatest people'; other admirers cite him as the inspiration for China's People's Communes; a revolutionary thinker from the very moment he arrived in Shanghai; indeed, so close to the Chinese leadership that he was eligible for instant Chinese citizenship; to Han Suyin, Alley is a Christ-like figure, through contact with him she alleges *'one somehow became better too'*; to New Zealand journalist Geoff Chapple, Alley is a 'centrifuge' dispensing presents and *pink* happiness.

The excerpts present Alley as an heroic figure, yet there is another aspect to his mythologisation that is mostly not available in written form, that is, the way in which Alley was villainised by those who were opposed to him or despised him. It is interesting that most of the hostile claims relate to Alley's sexuality. In these mythic accounts Alley is portrayed as a womaniser who keeps a woman in every Chinese city he visits,[14] a member of the Chinese Communist Party (here it is not meant favourably), a paederast who stayed on to write propaganda in Communist China after 1949 because he was supplied with young boys by the Chinese government; or, alternatively, as someone who was being blackmailed into writing for the Chinese government *because* of these sexual proclivities. As with the favourable versions of the Alley myth, all the above are also untrue.

In Rewi Alley's long and eventful life, a web of often conflicting myths was constructed by Alley and others in order to present him as an iconic symbol, representative of vastly different ideas and objectives. Roland Barthes has written that the efficacy of myth in human life is that it

> abolishes the complexity of human acts, it gives them the simplic-
> ity of essences, it does away with dialectics, with any going back
> beyond what is immediately visible, it organises a world which is
> without contradictions because it is without depth, a world wide
> open and wallowing in the evident, it establishes a blissful clarity:
> things appear to mean something by themselves.[15]

Myth-making smooths out the extraneous aspects of its subjects' lives, since the lives of ordinary humans are too full of inconsistencies to be presented in all their complexity and conflict. Symbolic figures such as Alley have a role in every society. According to Moses Hadas, in authoritarian societies the list of individuals deemed worthy of veneration tends to be rather long, and consists of those persons who have upheld or maintained authoritarianism. In democratic societies, the number of heroes is reduced and their faults are not hidden. Social advances are attributed to society rather than individuals, hence the role of one particular individual is regarded as less significant.[16] Unless there is an organised cult to perpetuate their memory, the eminent figures of one generation easily fall into oblivion. Hadas contends that it is the authorised image of the hero that is always more important than his actual personality. It is this image that will survive, to be revered and remembered, whether in popular tradition or as an organised cult.[17]

To say that Alley was mythologised does not take away from his actual achievements in China: in Shanghai as a factory inspector, in the Chinese Industrial Co-operatives and at the Shandan Bailie School in the 1940s, and in the 1980s, the strength of vision that saw him working to re-establish the co-operative movement and the Shandan Bailie School. To assess the value of his work as propagandist for the Chinese government is more difficult, and perhaps worthy of further study. None the less, most myths have some basis in reality, no matter how remote, and the Rewi Alley myth is no different.

So who was the real Alley? And can we ever know? This study aims to unravel the myth-making that has surrounded the life of Rewi Alley, examining how it was that a self-described 'ordinary New Zealand plug'[18] could become iconised in his own lifetime, a symbol of wide-ranging political objectives, in both his adopted and native countries. While biographical details are a feature, this work is not primarily a biography. There have been three book-length biographies on Alley, all written in Alley's lifetime. They are Willis Airey's *A Learner in China*, Geoff Chapple's *Rewi Alley of China* and Alley's own *At 90: Memoirs of My China Years*. All are useful in different ways, but deeply flawed. Airey's book suffers from having been severely censored by Alley and his editor Shirley Barton (it was written during the

Cultural Revolution). Chapple's book is more honest, but his close relationship with Alley prevented him from revealing everything he knew. Alley's own book, *At 90: Memoirs of My China Years*, is a pastiche of carefully selected excerpts from his earlier writings, interspersed by a few taped interviews with 'the author'. All this was patched together by editors Lu Wanru and Wang Xiaobo, as at the time that the book was being prepared Alley was too ill to do much of it himself. It is at best a picture of the Rewi Alley the Chinese government would like to present to the world: a born supporter of the Chinese Communist Party. In 1997 this memoir was even revised by an unnamed group of Chinese and foreign editors and republished under the title *Rewi Alley: An Autobiography*.[19] In contrast to these earlier hagiographies of Alley, this study is an exercise in historical revisionism, in the sense that it revises what we already know about one of the most famous foreigners to live and work in China and interprets that in terms of the political culture of both his adopted country, China, and his native country, New Zealand.

2

A NEW ZEALAND CHILDHOOD

Rewi Alley was born in Springfield, a rural hamlet in North Canterbury, New Zealand, on 2 December 1897.[1] Alley's family background and other aspects of his upbringing are an important element of his early renown. The following piece, from a school journal of the 1940s, is a sample of the myth-making about Alley's early years essential to the promotion of him both as a symbol of Western humanitarianism in Asia and of New Zealand masculinity:

> Kao Pi-tzu – tall nose, Kun Ho Jen – the work together man or, in English, simply Rewi Alley. This famous brother of former All Black G. T. Alley, Director of the Country Library Service, was born on 2nd December, 1897, at Springfield, Canterbury, and christened Rewi after a courageous Maori chief.
>
> His father – a former schoolteacher was imbued with the advantages of the co-operatives for farmers; his mother, one of a group who won suffrage for N.Z. women. Reared in such an atmosphere, it is scarcely to be wondered at that Rewi saw in rural co-operation the answer to the age old problems of the hinterland Chinese.
>
> When his half share in a farm was lost in the depression following World War 1 – he fought with the ANZACs – he worked his passage to China as a wireless operator on a tramp returning indentured Cantonese from the phosphate islands of Nauru and Ocean. He signed off at Hong Kong in 1926 at the time of the Kuomintang revolution. A job as a fireman with the Shanghai Fire Brigade was followed by 12 years service as a Factory Inspector with the Municipal Council. It was then that he made the horrible discovery that uncontrolled industry still used slave labour. That Chinese boys and girls were bought and sold – hired out – to work under appalling conditions, for long hours with no medical care. That their life expectancy averaged 15 years![2]

The text epitomises all the qualities that made Alley such a ripe choice for mythologisation. First, his good fortune to be named after a famous Maori

7

chief, Rewi Maniapoto, famed for his resolute fight against the British. *Pakeha* New Zealand prided itself on its good race relations with the indigenous Maori, hence to have a *pakeha* hero with the name of a Maori warrior served to enhance that impression.[3] That his brother Geoff was an All Black was an added plus for Alley's popular image; rugby being not just New Zealand's national sport, but a major expression of generally triumphant national identity. National representatives, those selected for the All Blacks, are accorded god-like status in New Zealand. The reference to the Alley parents was also significant. Both were presented as liberal and progressive, part of the tradition of the cherished myth of New Zealand egalitarianism. Alley's service as an ANZAC (the Australian–New Zealand Army Corps that fought in World War I) was further proof of his legitimate place in the New Zealand pantheon, part of the tradition of what historian John McLeod described as the nation's 'egotistical pride' in the military prowess of New Zealand soldiers.[4] And, finally, that a New Zealander had found 'the answer to the age old problems of the hinterland Chinese' bolstered New Zealanders' historical pride in their international role, despite the size of the population and their nation's remoteness from international areas of conflict.

Certainly both parents did have a formative influence on the young Rewi Alley. Frederick Alley, an idealistic schoolmaster, held strong opinions on everything from education to nudity. With regard to education for boys, like the French philosopher Jean-Jacques Rousseau, Frederick Alley believed in combining theoretical knowledge with practical experience. To this end his three sons were despatched to the family farm on school holidays and kept busy with an endless array of jobs in after-school hours. Furthermore, he believed that learning should be combined with need, that children should gravitate through learning as and when they were ready.[5] Like Rousseau he also believed that girls should receive an education, so that they might be good helpmates to their future husbands. Along with many of his generation, Frederick Alley was of the 'spare the rod and spoil the child' school of parenting, an authoritarian style that his son was later to reject at Shandan.

Though Frederick Alley was well known for his progressive educational views, Alley senior did not hold progressive views about sexuality. New Zealand society was extremely conservative; homosexuality was a criminal offence and, hence, a covert activity. Rewi Alley's early years reflect the conservative values of that society; his upbringing was a mixture of repression and illicit liberation. Frederick Alley was extremely puritanical. He had an obsessive fear of anything that could be perceived as sexual behaviour and kept a close watch on the young Rewi and his elder brother Eric. The two boys were frequently beaten and locked in the tool shed for any behaviour perceived as 'abnormal'. In her memoirs *Sunshine and Shadows*, Alley's elder sister Gwen recalled that she used to 'dress Rewi up in a little red smock and call him my little sister "Rosie". Dad objected, especially because Rewi said he was going to grow up to be a lady since they were nicer than men.'[6] Still, at the same time, it is only fair to mention Gwen's comment that 'Rewi was always playing houses with Nora (a local girl), and had arranged to marry her when they grew up.'[7] Although he preferred men and was described by some as a misogynist, Alley was attractive to women. He had a charismatic presence that appealed to both sexes.

Rewi Alley's mother, Clara Buckingham Alley, was one of New Zealand's early suffragettes who helped gain the vote for women in 1893. Clara's family prided themselves on a tradition of philanthropy and good works. Clara was English-born and she was somewhat patronising about the brash young colony of New Zealand. She taught her children to regard England as 'Home', so much so that, according to Gwen, '[England] became the real world, the proper country to Eric, Rewi and me. We had doubts about this upside down country which had no palaces at all, where the weather was summer one day and winter the next.'[8] Rewi Alley's later alienation from his country of birth was encouraged by this upbringing.

The young Alley was inspired by his mother's opinions to an idealistic enthusiasm for the British Empire. A treasured scrapbook dated 1914 indicates his early interest in empire-building; the book's pages are dominated by articles about foreign missionaries and adventurers in exotic locations.[9] In a letter to his brother's biographer Willis Airey, Rewi Alley's younger brother Pip explained this early tendency: 'Rewi has not always been a left-winger. Our father was a Labour supporter later in life but in the early stages they were both glorious Empire-builders and Rewi was a church supporter.' Pip told Airey that at the time of the Russian revolution his brother had written letters home saying 'some very hard things' about the Communists, calling them 'Rotten' and 'Contemptible'.[10]

Clara Alley had to make sure that the children were always fully clothed in their father's presence, though she allowed them to enjoy the freedom of nude swimming when he wasn't around.[11] As a result, as an adult, Rewi Alley became almost obsessive about emphasising the joys of nudity, mentioning it in letters, poems, stories, and frequently in conversation. As in his childhood, it was one of the few ways in which he could express pleasure in the physical. Alley was especially close to his mother; he wrote in his memoirs, 'She was a part of me. I would have told her anything she asked, which she did not. I just did not tell anyone of all the things I learned from village boys.'[12] Exactly what it was that Alley learned from village boys he also neglects to tell his readers. His reluctance to be more specific is common in the writings of gay men from his era. Since homosexuality has for so long been forbidden in many Western societies, homosexual writing in the West is frequently cloaked in nuance and coded images, its true meaning available only, as Robert Aldrich describes, to the 'initiated or the interested.'[13]

All his life Alley managed to keep his sexuality a secret from his family in New Zealand, who speculated amongst themselves as to why he remained single. During the Cultural Revolution both Gwen and Pip wrote enquiring whether he was physically able to have sexual relationships (thinking he might have some old war wound). To this Alley replied 'You could not possibly understand, so please do not labour the subject and do not talk nonsense about my being unfit.... Forget it. Not a subject to be shouted from the housetops either.'[14]

As a public figure, Rewi Alley was always careful to present a sanitised version of his life to the outside world. In New Zealand there is a tradition of deep intolerance towards homosexuality, discrimination on the basis of sexual orientation was only made illegal in 1993, while homosexual acts were not decriminalised until 1987. The stereotype of New Zealand masculinity is always heterosexual; whereas his negative image – characterised by qualities of physical weakness and intellectualism – was under suspicion of being homosexual. The Alley family atmosphere in the years of Rewi Alley's youth was certainly not conducive to openness about sexuality, nor was the social environment in New Zealand in the years before World War I. As a gay man living in an era when homosexuality was a punishable offence, Alley was forced from an early age to play out a role in order to disguise his sexual orientation. His ability to play-act and suppress his natural inclinations would stand him in good stead. Rewi Alley's sexuality is an important key to understanding his ability to act out a part, to be a living myth for much of his life. Disguising his sexual orientation to family and friends was the first role he ever acted out. Many of his closest contacts in China were unaware of his sexuality right up until his death. His ability to keep this a secret for so long demonstrates his skill at role-playing and disguise.

A further theme in Rewi Alley's early years was the need to prove himself to his family. He was the middle child of six, and in a family of overachievers he was the only child not to succeed either academically or in sports: the Alley family's eldest son Eric died a heroic death as a captain in World War I; eldest daughter Gwen became Founding President of the Plunket Society;[15] Geoff was an All Black rugby player and later Head of the Country Library Service; Pip became a lecturer in Soil Engineering at Canterbury University; Kath studied history at university, unusual for a woman in the 1920s; and Joy would eventually become Head of the New Zealand Nursing School. Frederick Alley labelled the young Rewi a 'Norfolk dumbbell' and strapped him for getting his answers wrong or being too slow. Unable to conform to the academic aspirations his father had for the children, Alley grew up believing he was the 'black sheep' of the family. He was very independent from an early age and frequently wandered off on his own to play with boys from the village. His sister Joy described him as always 'a bit of a rebel' who didn't altogether fit with the system.[16]

Plate 2.1 Rewi Alley, World War I.

Source: Kathleen Wright papers, Alexander Turnbull Library, NZ.

This early sense of alienation seems to have inspired an inner rootlessness in the young Rewi Alley. The Alley children did not have a particularly religious upbringing; although their father made them memorise religious texts, they did not have to go to church. Frederick Alley struggled with religion. He had been brought up a strict Anglican but had been influenced by Darwinism as a young man and was no longer able to accept the idea of the divinity of Christ.[17] His son's struggle with religion was a search for something to guide him in life; baptised into the Anglican church by his own choice, he became an altar boy for a time and was a regular churchgoer. His early religious questing led him first of all to look to the missionaries as a solution to the problems of China, and later, when that palled, to the study of Buddhism and Taoism.

In 1917 Alley joined the New Zealand Expeditionary Force and fought in the Somme. Along with many of the young men of his day, he left New Zealand with a sense of fatalism about his future. Sixty years later he wrote: 'One would go and get killed, and that was that.'[18] It was while fighting in France that China first made an impact on his life. By chance, he met and spent the night with some men from Shandong Province, who were part of the Chinese Labour Corps. During the German advance of March 1918, the New Zealand forces fought alongside the Chinese. Alley's experiences with these men had a profound effect on him, revealing a different perspective of sexuality and, ultimately, inspiring a rebellion against his puritanical upbringing. Alley wrote of the meeting: 'It was the first time . . . that I had any inkling of what China meant.'[19] This is his description of his first encounter:

> I was with a friend, out for adventure one evening, just two New Zealander common infantrymen in their late teens. We met two tall men, dressed in blue and with fur hats. They smiled, we smiled, and we went together into a wine shop and had crusty French bread and red wine, talking in snatches of broken French. Then came a struggle as both sides insisted on paying. They were the first Chinese in our lives that we had been able to meet on the level ground of mutual respect.[20]

It should come as no surprise that this narration makes no mention of intimacy. Rewi Alley never publicly admitted his sexuality, he was a very private person who had few confidants in life. Thirty years after the event, however, while in Shandan, he often talked with his close friend Courtney Archer about the Chinese Labour Corps. Both men were gay, and they grew up in neighbouring small South Island towns. Better than most, Archer understood Alley's need to live a double life. Archer worked for six years on Alley's projects in China in the 1940s and afterwards maintained a correspondence with his friend. Archer says, 'Alley was of the generation that didn't talk about sex but would sometimes drop hints.'[21] From these 'hints'

Archer gathered that the evening spent with the men from Shandong was Alley's first significant sexual experience. This encounter certainly made a lasting impression and, as he implies in his memoirs, served as his inspiration for going to China in 1927.[22]

The impact of the Chinese Labour Corps on Alley's thinking was shown in other ways too. Alley's library contains a rare edition of a sardonic, homo-erotic account of the training of the Chinese Labour Corps, written by a foreign officer in one of the battalions. The author, who in many other aspects adopts racist attitudes towards Chinese people typical of his day (hence the book's title *With the Chinks*), praises the beauty of the men's physiques and the golden colour of their skin. He admires them for their obvious comfort and ease with their bodies, and how they walk around together arm and arm, embrace each other affectionately, and bathe and swim naked *en masse* with no sign of shame or awkwardness.[23] In Alley's personal copy those sections of the book that are the most strikingly homoerotic have been heavily underlined and annotated in Alley's own hand.[24] I quote here from one of those underlined sections:

> Nude as mermen they raced over the sand and entered the water with a splash and cry. There was beauty in their shining bodies. The splendour of their physique was suddenly shown. . . . They had no foolish dignity of men. They lived for the sunlit hour. And, like children, they weren't afraid of giving themselves away; they had no false reticence, no false notions of nudity. And that spring morning they seemed to inherit the earth.[25]

The differences in attitudes between the West and China that made such an impression on the young Alley and other foreigners of his day have a long history. Bret Hinsch in *Passions of the Cut Sleeve* writes that the historical tradition of China includes an acceptance of homosexuality 'that dates back to at least the Bronze Age.'[26] According to Hinsch,

> The long duration of tolerance allowed the accumulation of a liter-ature and sense of history that in turn enabled those with strong homosexual desires to arrive at a complex self-understanding. In many periods homosexuality was widely accepted and even respected, had its own formal history, and had a role in shaping Chinese political institutions, modifying social conventions, and spurring artistic creation. A sense of tradition lasted up until this century, when it fell victim to a growing sexual conservatism and the Westernisation of morality.[27]

The Chinese attitude towards homosexuality was distinctly different from Western mores. Hinsch describes the Chinese perspective in terms of

13

'tendencies,' 'actions' and 'preferences,' rather than sexual identity, as in the West, where the distinction between homosexual and heterosexual for a long period tended to be presented as absolute. In the words of Robert Aldrich, 'Western society has for centuries been uncongenial to homosexuality, law considered homosexuality a crime, medicine labelled it a disease, religion called it a sin, psychology analysed it as a perversion or personality disorder and general social mores castigated it as a disgusting deviance.'[28] In China, same-sex love was accepted as a natural expression of human sexuality, and homoerotic as well as homosocial (same-sex non-sexual intimacy such as hand-holding, sleeping in the same bed) behaviour was common. Courtney Archer writes: 'the classical Chinese had no medical or scientific term comparable to "homosexuality" but used metaphors instead. . . . Because homosexuality was so widespread in Chinese society and in all classes there was little need for a special term.'[29] This alternative understanding of the realms of human sexuality was a revelation to Rewi Alley and other foreigners who came in contact with China in the pre-modern era, and they benefited from its ambiguity.

In addition to sexual tolerance, for many gay men there was a further appeal in Chinese society. To Western eyes the Asian male is the epitome of the gay stereotype: effeminate and passive. To some homosexual males Chinese boys are as attractive as the Suzie Wong stereotype of Chinese womanhood is to many heterosexuals. The confession of the fictional Philip Flower in Harold Acton's novel of life in Peking in the 1930s, *Peonies and Ponies*, best illustrates this dual attraction: 'You'll think me a sentimental old duffer,' he confided, 'but I was drawn to Yang the moment I set eyes on him. He appealed to my imagination. I'd do anything for him. Don't ask me why. I hardly know myself! I suppose it's because he is a living symbol of China, and I'm in love with China.'[30]

To some foreign observers the sexual opacity of Chinese society was a reason to despise the Chinese as an immoral and decadent race. The comments of the Jesuit Matteo Ricci, describing what he saw on the streets of Peking, exemplify this attitude: 'There are public streets full of boys got up like prostitutes. And there are people who buy these boys and teach them to play music, sing and dance. And then, gallantly dressed and made up with rouge like women these miserable men are initiated into this terrible vice.'[31] Yet there were a number of less vocal but equally prominent foreigners, exiles from Western puritanism, who chose to live in China at least partly because of the acceptance of their own sexuality that they found there. Rewi Alley was one of these.

At the end of World War I, in 1919, Alley returned to New Zealand, still rootless and still uncertain of what he should do in life. A former schoolmate, Jack Stevens, invited him to become a partner in a block of land in the wilds of Taranaki, in the North Island of New Zealand at Moeawatea. Alley's comment to his sister Gwen at the time was pragmatic at best: 'I guess it is something to do, after all.'[32] His political views continued to be conservative. While in Moeawatea he joined the Legion of Frontiersmen, an organisation of ex-servicemen dedicated to the upholding of the British Empire. According to the Legion's handbook, 'Members must be British by birth or naturalisation, 25 years of age or over. Good citizenship and loyalty to the Throne is an essential qualification.'[33]

Alley spent six back-breaking years at Moeawatea, but the land was not economical to farm. In later accounts, he described these years as a very lonely time in his life. Certainly the loneliness could not have been from a lack of company; in those days the valley was at the peak of settlement. The problem was a lack of soul mates. Pip Alley described his brother's partner Jack Stevens as a 'sex-starved' young man who was fond of gazing at their female neighbour through binoculars in his spare time.[34] Now in his late twenties, Alley seems to have gone through a stage of questioning and searching within himself. A treasured book is one of the few relics that survives from the period; the biography of the mystic Saint Teresa. Alexander Whyte's comment in the introduction to the book was a presage of what was to come. Whyte wrote, 'Those who would be like Saint Teresa today would become missionaries or labour amongst the poor.'[35]

After so many years of hardship, in 1926 Alley gave up his share in the land to his partner and set sail for Australia, the natural point of refuge for many an unsettled New Zealander. Following a series of unsatisfactory jobs he set sail for China, where the prospect of war seemed likely. Rewi told Gwen that war was 'The only thing I know anything about, and I guess I can help a bit.'[36]

3

SHANGHAILANDER

China in the 1920s was a society in chaos. Nominally ruled by the Nationalist government headed by Chiang Kai-shek, it was a battleground for power-hungry warlords and prey to an ever-encroaching foreign presence. Rewi Alley arrived in Shanghai in April 1927, during the 'white terror' – the massacre by Chiang Kai-shek's forces of tens of thousands of Communist supporters in the city. It was a year when foreigners were being made to feel unwelcome in China by the more radical of the Nationalists, and April 1927 marked the end of the first united front between Chiang Kai-shek and the tiny Communist party. Yet Shanghai was still an exhilarating place for a young colonial with imperialist leanings. It was, after all, the Pearl of the Orient, the Paris of the East and, last but not least, a Paradise for Adventurers. Shanghai was a city of great contrasts, heaven for the very rich and a hell-hole for the poor.

Alley had difficulty finding work at first. He wrote to his family that he was contemplating joining either a 'Tommy' regiment (the Shanghai Volunteer Corps) or the Shanghai Municipal Police.[1] Had he done so, his life would have taken a very different turn from the one it eventually did. No ex-member of the Shanghai Police Force, responsible for rounding up thousands of Communist supporters, would have been welcome in post-1949 China. Fortunately he found an occupation that was politically much more respectable. With the help of an associate from a brother regiment to the New Zealand Legion of Frontiersmen, he started work as an officer at the Hongkou Fire Station in the International Settlement in Shanghai.

Shanghai in the 1920s was divided into three cities: the International Settlement, the French Concession, and the Chinese City. The International Settlement was the most important of the three, due to its location and security. It was the commercial, financial, shipping and industrial centre of Shanghai and under the joint control of representatives from Great Britain, the USA and Japan. Located by the Huangpu river, it covered an area of 8.3 square miles.[2] The foreign staff of the International Settlement were well provided for. They were offered adequate pay, long-term contracts and retirement allowances. They were also granted three weeks' annual leave and six months' home leave every sixth year.[3]

The first volunteer fire company was organised in the Settlement in 1866. In 1919 the fire brigade became a municipal department and ceased to be a voluntary body. William Johnstone, reporting on conditions in the International Settlement in the 1930s, wrote of the brigade, 'The absence of a modern fire alarm system and the narrow streets and congested traffic prevent efficient fire control. The department has the difficult task of fire control without adequate powers to enforce inspection laws. Improper storage of flammable goods, for example, has caused many serious explosions and fires, with much unnecessary loss of life.'[4]

The Shanghai Municipal Fire Service was one of the lowlier jobs for the foreign expatriates in Shanghai, akin to working for the police. The foreign community was extremely hierarchical. Most foreigners living in Shanghai had little contact with the Chinese as equals. Many foreigners in China in the 1920s and 1930s took pride in their inability to speak the Chinese language and their indifference to Chinese customs. To do otherwise was regarded as 'going native'. In the International Settlement only foreigners in the police and the fire brigade learned Chinese and they were paid extra for doing so. Trying to earn some extra money after his years of poverty in New Zealand, Alley wrote to his family that he was studying Chinese for the 'language bonus' of NZ$5 per month it earned him. He told them he was learning to drive for the same reason.[5]

Despite being on the lower end of the hierarchy, foreign life in Shanghai in the late 1920s, even for a fire officer, was typified by decadence and privilege. It was a far cry from Alley's hard years in the backblocks of Taranaki. Although in later accounts of his life Alley described how out of place he felt in this environment,[6] photographs and letters from the period tell a different story. Rewi Alley quickly became part of the European élite and he made much of his glamorous lifestyle in letters home. As the family underachiever, he seems to have felt the need to prove that after years of failure he was now moving on to greater things. The fire brigade was famous for fighting in coats and tails, since officers were frequently called out while attending evening functions. Alley wrote to his family after one incident:

> We have had very few [fires] lately. The only notable ones being a few in the bunkers of the 'Sui Wo,' in which I ruined a perfectly good silk shirt, and a block of thirteen Chinese houses and shops which made quite a big blaze. We had to work hard to keep it at that. It is good fun when one learns not to worry about the destitute refugees. They soon get dug in elsewhere anyway.[7]

In this letter Alley exhibits the callous attitudes of the Shanghailanders; the European residents in the International Settlement. These attitudes took some time to undo. When he first arrived in China, Alley took an instant dislike to the Chinese. His admiration was for the orderly and well-organised Japanese. Initially he considered moving on to work in Japan followed by further world travel.[8] After a holiday in Korea he wrote, 'This Japanese dictatorship is the best thing that has happened in Korea. She is dragging the people up to a decent standard of living.'[9] Significantly, this viewpoint was omitted from the published version of Airey's biography and the letter it came from destroyed at Alley's request.[10] Such ideas were not in keeping with his later role as a professional friend of China. They do, however, indicate a liking for authoritarian models of development. On a draft of Airey's biography of him, written at the peak of the Cultural Revolution, Alley crossed out paragraphs that mentioned this early phase of his life in China. His comment was 'not suitable for present reading.'[11]

Rewi Alley had good reason to be afraid of what people might have thought of his early years in China. The contrast between then and his later public image was too great. In the liberal climate of Shanghai in the late 1920s, he was truly able to explore his sexuality for the first time. In the 1920s and 1930s, Shanghai was known as a city where you could do anything if you had money. As Christopher Isherwood wrote:

> You can buy an electric razor, or a French dinner, or a well-cut suit. You can dance at the Tower Restaurant on the roof of the Cathay Hotel, and gossip with Freddie Kaufmann, its charming manager, about the European aristocracy of pre-Hitler Berlin. You can attend race-meetings, baseball games, football matches. You can see the latest American films. If you want girls, or boys, you can have them, at all prices, in the bathhouses and the brothels. If you want opium you can smoke it in the best company, served on a tray, like afternoon tea. Good wine is difficult to obtain in this climate, but there is enough whisky and gin to float a fleet of battleships. The jeweller and the antique-dealer await your orders, and their charges will make you imagine yourself back on Fifth Avenue or Bond Street. Finally, if you ever repent, there are churches and chapels of all denominations.[12]

Shanghai was a city with an active homosexual scene. Male prostitutes were available in the bars and brothels, and in bathhouses where erotic massage was an optional extra. However, it would be a mistake to view this as something separate from the heterosexual sex scene; homosexual activity was simply another option for the sex consumer. In the dance halls and night-clubs where partners could be hired to dance, both female and transsexual dancers were available. Courtney Archer writes of this era:

> Men, and I am not going to call them 'gay,' would find their pleasures in a personal way with say students, soldiers, actors and servants as would the few Europeans. Because there was no

stigma attached there was no need for gay clubs as known in the Western world. . . . As a last resort there were male prostitutes and male brothels in the larger towns. On many occasions in Shanghai when accosted by pimps offering 'nice girls' a refusal always brought forth an offer of a 'nice boy.' This often at 2 p.m. in the middle of a Shanghai summer when one was on the way home for lunch![13]

Nevertheless, for some travellers to China in the 1920s and 1930s, sexual tourism was one of the highlights of a visit to Shanghai. Playwright Noel Coward and his companion Jeffrey Amherst, while staying in Shanghai, were taken by 'some charming new friends . . . three English naval officers, Acherson, Bushell and Guerrier, with whom we visited many of the lower and gayer haunts of the city.'[14] What these 'gayer' haunts might contain is described in fascinating detail in Henry Champly's *The Road to Shanghai: White Slave Traffic in Asia*. While Champly's primary concern is his objection to white prostitutes sleeping with Asian men, he describes an encounter with a White Russian transsexual in a Shanghai nightclub:

At the 'Monica' we were embraced and pawed over by a very pretty Russian blonde, rather plump and pitted, but elegant, scented, eminently desirable. 'That's Schirra. Do you like her?' Katia asked me insidiously. 'I should say so!' They all laughed at my simplemindedness. 'Schirra is a man. His name is Gerald. He does take you in, doesn't he? He's getting a bit fat now, too. If you had seen him when he first arrived from Harbin.' 'From Harbin – he too?' 'And not a single "Taxi girl" had anything like his success when he was dancing at the "*Sun-Sun*" and elsewhere . . .' 'Really?' said I. 'Even with the Chinese?' 'The Chinese are very fond of men disguised as women.'[15]

Christopher Isherwood and W. H. Auden made a point of sampling the delights of the bathhouse scene when they visited Shanghai in 1937, although they omitted to mention this in their travel book of the time, *Journey to a War*. In the 1930s, even openly homosexual writers such as Auden and Isherwood felt it necessary to be discreet about their sexual preferences – in print at least. Isherwood later described the two writers' sexual exploits in his autobiography, *Christopher and his Kind*:

Toward the end of their visit, Wystan and Christopher began taking afternoon holidays from their social consciences in a bathhouse where you were erotically soaped and massaged by young men. You could pick your attendants, and many of them were beautiful. Those who were temporarily disengaged would watch the action, with giggles, through peepholes in the walls of the bathrooms. What made the experience pleasingly exotic was that tea was served to the customer throughout; even in the midst of an embrace, the attendant would disengage one hand, pour a cupful, and raise it tenderly but firmly, to the customer's lips. If you refused the tea at first, the attendant went on offering it until you accepted. It was like a sex fantasy in which a naked nurse makes love to the patient but still insists on giving him his medicine punctually, at the required intervals.[16]

There was a distinctly different community of foreigners in Peking. Peking was renowned, not for decadence, but rather as a cultural centre, and accordingly it attracted gay men whose primary interest was Chinese culture. In contrast to adventurers like Rewi Alley and sexual tourists such as Auden and Isherwood was a separate group of foreign homosexuals whom the writer Harold Acton defined as 'aesthetes.'[17] The aesthetes were an élitist group of cultured and educated Westerners. Not all aesthetes were necessarily gay, but most were. For these men interest in Chinese culture and homosexuality coincided. David Kidd, who lived in Peking in the late 1940s, says that 'Being gay was secondary. It was the lifestyle and the culture which attracted.'[18] George Kates, curator of Oriental Art at the Brooklyn Museum in New York, who lived in Peking for seven years, wrote of his favourite city:

> Peking, in the gentleness of manner of its inhabitants, in their courtesy and good humour, had become for those lucky enough to have found it a sunlit haven difficult to describe, superb for the enjoyment of the mere sweetness of existence, unlike anything they had ever known before or − of course − have ever been able to find since.[19]

The aesthetes amused themselves in appreciating the Chinese arts. They moved in separate circles from the other main groups of foreigners living in Peking at that time − diplomats and missionaries − forming salons of likeminded friends. According to Alistair Morrison, who lived in Peking during the 1940s, the attitude of other foreigners was tolerant, 'although one wouldn't necessarily invite them to dinner.'[20] Sinologist C. P. Fitzgerald gave a less generous account in his book *Why China?*:

> They floated, as it were, halfway between the culture of the West and the civilization of China. They had often virtually withdrawn from active participation in their own culture, largely because they found some aspects of it very little to their own taste.... They were cultured, but unproductive, and mainly un-creative also.... They knew much about Chinese civilization, they studied it with love

and learning, but they did not succeed in interpreting it to the world at large.[21]

But what might have been regarded by hostile Westerners as a foreign 'gay scene' was viewed quite differently by most Chinese. Courtney Archer writes that to the Chinese, sexual preferences were a private matter, and 'homosexuality . . . was widespread and of no concern to society as a whole. As a result there was no "gay scene" as such.'[22] Bob Winter, a fellow professor at Tsinghua University, told David Kidd that as far as the Chinese were concerned, 'You can take anyone you like to bed. Just don't talk about it.'[23]

Not long after his arrival in Shanghai, Alley met Alec Camplin, an English engineer who was to be an important influence during the next ten years. The New Zealand writer James Bertram gave a portrait of Camplin in his book *Shadow of a War*:

> Camplin was an old partner of Rewi Alley's, and an 'original' of the type that is really only happy in places like China. Working as an engineer in the American-owned power plant in Shanghai, he had acquired an amazing collection of university degrees, chiefly by correspondence. He and Alley when they first lived together had one of the best libraries in Shanghai, and both had adopted and educated Chinese youngsters whose parents had become famine victims. Alec's yarns of these days were first-rate entertainment, and sometimes had a pleasant touch of the fantastic.[24]

From 1930 to 1938 the two men shared a house together in the International Settlement. Camplin and Alley had much in common. They were very close friends, though they may not have been lovers. Both were primarily attracted to Chinese men. They shared a love of learning and, unusual amongst the Shanghai community of foreigners, a deep interest in Asian culture. Both had a rather earthy sense of humour that was the mark of an inherent disregard for authority and pomp. Neither was interested in fitting into the British élite that dominated Shanghai society. In contrast to the hedonistic, materialistic pleasures that prevailed amongst this élite, the two men spent their spare time exploring the countryside around Shanghai in the company of young Chinese and European male friends. They made frequent trips to the island of Choshan, site of a Buddhist monastery, where, Alley told Courtney Archer, 'the young monks couldn't keep their hands to themselves.'[25] Both Camplin and Alley adopted Chinese orphans; Alley adopted two boys whom he named Alan and Mike, Alec's adopted son was named Peter. The three children were sent to be educated at Shanghai's prestigious Medhurst College. Alley and Camplin lived together until the outbreak of the Sino-Japanese War, when Camplin returned to England. Alec Camplin died in England in 1939. Significantly, in his autobiography

Plate 3.1 'Vincent, the station officer here'.

Source: PAI-f-148, Kathleen Wright papers, Alexander Turnbull Library, NZ. Reference no.: C20363.

Plate 3.2 'Vincent, "siesta" couch, Shanghai'.
Source: PAI-f-148, Kathleen Wright papers, Alexander Turnbull Library, NZ. Reference no.: C20359.

Plate 3.3 'Out with the gardener, Henli, 1927 (note the grave mounds)'.
Source: PAI-f-148, Kathleen Wright papers, Alexander Turnbull Library, NZ.

Plate 3.4 'After tiffin, August, Henli, 1930'.
Source: Kathleen Wright papers, Alexander Turnbull Library, NZ. Page 75.

Plate 3.5 'My car and driver. I have two cameras now. This is No. 2. September 1931'.
Source: PAI-f-148, Kathleen Wright papers, Alexander Turnbull Library, NZ. Reference no.: C20682.

Alley scarcely mentioned his relationship with Alec Camplin and makes no mention of friends like 'Vincent,' the subject of some suggestively homoerotic photos he took during this period. Such omissions are examples of the self-censorship that was essential to Alley's public life in the Communist era.

Patronage of young men by older homosexuals is a common theme of homosexual life in many cultures. In China, the traditional pattern of patronage in homosexual activity encompassed the adoption of favoured young men. Bret Hinsch writes: 'The creation of fictitious kinship ties was used as a means of organising homosexual relations. The word used to describe such relations is *qi*, which has implications of contractuality, deep friendship and adoption.'[26] The adoption of young boys by Rewi Alley and Alec Camplin was part of this pattern, as it is part of a universal pattern, the desire for family. Throughout his life in China, Rewi Alley surrounded himself with young Chinese men, often referred to by others as 'Rewi's boys.' Alley was a man with a deep need for and love of family. He craved the acceptance and understanding that only family members can give. Yet he both physically and emotionally distanced himself from his New Zealand family. His fear of revealing his sexuality to them meant that he could never find the closeness he needed. Instead he created a Chinese 'family' where he found love and acceptance of who he was.

Alley's political development was slow. In 1929 he described himself as an 'Internationalist', though not in the Communist sense of the word.[27] In 1930 he wrote to his family describing a summer holiday with one of his adopted sons, visiting northern China. He had taken Alan to visit the monument to Japanese soldiers at Mukden (Shenyang), which commemorated the quarter of a million who had died in battle during the Russo-Japanese war in 1895:

> I explained the number impressively to Alan, who, however, was not at all sad. In fact he rather seemed to think it would be a good job if all the other Japs were under the same mound. He is a credit to the school 'Tarn Pu' (Kuomintang Party Rep.) who fills the kids with anti-foreignism and rabid nationalism . . .
>
> Peking . . . On the way to the station we saw a poor beggar being led to execution, trussed up with rope and in a rickshaw. A pitiful poor, object, though the soldiers in charge of him seemed quite happy about it. The rest of the day we spent in buying oddments in curios and visiting an Imperial Park known as the 'North Sea' where we partook of sugared plums, sliced lotus roots in ice, melon seeds and green tea, while cruising around the lotus lake in a barge, in the approved society fashion. We also went to another park in the Forbidden City, where the beauties of the place were somewhat marred by the ridiculous Nationalist slogans in huge blue and unbeautiful characters 'Down with Imperialism' 'Abolish the unequal treaties' 'Guard the Three Principles' were the mildest . . .

In the same letter on the current student unrest in Peking universities he wrote:

> Most of the trouble seems to come from the students who are planted in all Christian Universities by Red organisations to foment trouble. No one is so easily led as the Chinese student.[28]

Both Geoff Chapple's and Willis Airey's biography of Alley as well as Alley's own memoirs cite the witnessing of an execution of silk workers in March 1929 at Wuxi, Jiangsu Province, as the awakening of his political consciousness.[29] In all three works, this is Alley's crucial epiphanal moment; they claim that from this point on he decided to commit himself to the Chinese revolution. Yet as Airey commented in the drafts of his biography, there is 'no mention in letters' of this incident.[30] In the 1930 letter Alley describes the sight of a beggar being led to his execution in Peking as 'pitiful' but is not especially sympathetic. He is scathing of the nationalistic demands of the Kuomintang and those he calls the 'Reds'. Alley's letters to family in the early years of his stay in China were remarkably detailed, quite different in tone to those he would send after 1949. One can only suspect that the description of the incident at Wuxi provided years after the event was, if not apocryphal, written to suit the demands of his public role in the Communist era.

It is unquestionable, however, that at some stage in his first ten years in China Alley decided to make his life there and he took an active interest in the fate of his adopted country. Shanghai in the 1930s was chaotic and corrupt. Not even the most privileged of Shanghailanders could ignore the daily suffering of the poor Chinese. Alley's work as a fire officer for the Shanghai Municipal Fire Brigade brought him into daily contact with the despair of those lives. A friend of the Alley family, the economist J. B. Condliffe, visited Shanghai in late 1927. In his memoirs he described the Shanghai Rewi Alley showed him on that trip:

> I spent my first week in China going the rounds with him as he inspected his district for fire protection. It was like seeing the pages of the early Factory Commission's reports come to life – or the sections of Karl Marx's *Capital* that drew so heavily on these reports. We saw fire traps and insanitary crowding, opium dens, brothels, sweated workshops and slums of incredible degradation – the worst of them in the no-man's land between the foreign settlement and the Chinese city.[31]

The wealth of Shanghai in the twentieth century was built on the labour of these sweatshops. Modern large-scale industry in Shanghai developed after 1914, stimulated by the wartime scarcity of foreign goods. Shanghai's industrialisation was further encouraged by the availability of capital from the foreign settlements and a cheap and plentiful supply of labour from the Chinese countryside. Factories in the foreign settlement areas had the advantage of a more favourable tax system than in the Chinese-controlled city. Moreover, the absence of industrial regulations by either the foreign or Chinese authorities enabled the factory owner to ignore issues of work, wages and labour conditions. Child labour was common in Shanghai; children as young as six were employed. The International Settlement and French Concession possessed limited powers to regulate safety and sanitation in the sweatshops through their licensing system. These regulations applied to the construction of buildings and the elimination of fire hazards. They had no power to control labour conditions, wages or hours.[32] From early on in his career in the fire service, Alley was responsible for safety inspections. What he saw there would gradually influence him to make a commitment to social change in China.

The problems of China in the 1920s and 1930s were not simply those of exploited labour in Shanghai factories. China was split by civil war, and the corruption of the nominal government of the Nationalists was all too obvious, as was its intense anti-foreignism. By the late 1930s, to many, foreign and Chinese alike — not all of them Marxists — the Chinese Communist Party offered the most hopeful alternative to the economic, political and social chaos of the time. Alley's upbringing conditioned him to believe in the righteousness of the British Empire; yet he had also grown up in a family where egalitarianism was valued, as was Christian charity. At first he looked to religion as the solution to China's problems, and his first humanitarian work was with Western missionaries such as Robert Ingram and Joseph Bailie, neither of whom was pro-Communist (Bailie referred to the CCP in letters to Alley as 'bandits'[33]). In 1929 Alley volunteered to do relief work in famine areas in North China and he assisted the League of Nations' relief project in Hubei after the great floods of 1932. Eventually, however, disillusionment with the ineffectiveness and corruption of many of the missionaries led Alley to take a different path. Although initially attracted to Marxism, his philosophical outlook formed into a fundamental belief in humanism, a belief in the equality of all human beings and a desire to improve the lot of the under privileged. In later years, a fellow New Zealander who knew Alley well characterised him as 'a New Zealander of recognisable missionary type.'[34]

Rewi Alley's personal mission in the 1930s was to ameliorate the suffering of China's poor. At first he attempted to do this within the capacity of his job as factory inspector in Shanghai (he became Chief Factory Inspector in the Industrial Division of the Shanghai Municipal Council after 1932) and by his participation in relief work. Alley became friends with Madame Song Qingling, widow of Sun Yat-sen and the only left-leaning member of the famous Song family. (They were on such good terms that he called her by her pet name 'Suzie'.) According to Alley's biographers, from 1934

27

onwards, through his friendship with Madame Song, Alley became involved in the Shanghai Communist underground, providing refuge for Communists on the run and housing a transmitter for CCP radio amongst other activities. They also maintain he was one of the founding members of the only foreigners' Marxist-Leninist Study Group. Claims to membership in this group was one of the means by which Alley and other foreigners who served as post-1949 China's resident foreign friends established their political credibility. However, according to the sole surviving member of that group, Ruth Weiss, there were only four members in the foreigners' Marxist-Leninist Study Group in Shanghai: herself, Comintern agent Heinz Schippe, Trudi Rosenberg and George Hatem. What Alley (and other claimants) participated in, she says, was simply a foreigners' political discussion group, which met regularly to discuss current events.[35] The diary notes of Alley's fellow study-group participant, Maud Russell, now held in the New York Public Library, corroborate her claim.[36] Curiously, Alley's underground activities and participation in the discussion group appear to have been unknown to the Shanghai Municipal Police; at least, what can be found in the archives of that police force record no mention of his name. This is surprising, considering the police files mention virtually all of the other members of the small but active community of left-wing foreigners in Shanghai. Either Alley's file has been deliberately removed from this archive or his activities with the left underground were less significant than his biographers would have us believe. Claims to Alley's important role in the Shanghai underground, though promoted in CCP propaganda, are also disputed by Chinese scholars specialist in this field. While they are not able to write publicly on this matter, in private conversations, some scholars have told me they have found no evidence in Chinese records to back up these claims. This is not to say Alley did not have any contact with left-wing forces. Certainly he wrote for the Comintern-supported Shanghai magazine *Voice of China*, and his home was at times a safe house for a few Communists on the run. He may have engaged in other activities that are not easy to verify because of the secretive nature of underground work. However, the significance and impact of these activities has been greatly exaggerated for the purpose of the political myth that was woven both by Alley himself and those who promoted him after 1949.

The period of the mid-1930s was a dramatic and exciting time for Alley, and his passion for his personal cause was catching. He had the kind of charisma that made other people want to get involved in the things he was interested in: George Hatem, Ruth Weiss, Ida Pruitt and Shirley Barton are just a few of the many within his immediate circle who admitted to being inspired by him at this time or later during his work in the Chinese Industrial Co-operatives. Pruitt, who lived most of her life in China and was already well known for her humanitarian work and writings on China, wrote to him in 1939, 'All my life I have hoped to find a man big enough to follow or a cause big enough to work for wholly. To find both in one is marvellous.'[37] Even the otherwise cynical W. H. Auden and Christopher Isherwood described their encounter with him in 1938 in tones of awe.[38]

Rewi Alley's other life, the sexual freedom he found in the Shanghai years, was unknown to many of those he associated with in left-wing circles. Ruth Weiss reports that it was rumoured that Alley was interested in Maud Russell, an American YWCA official who also attended the political discussion group. When told this, Alley quipped, 'Oh but then I'd never have time for all my other girlfriends.'[39] Weiss says she never met Rewi's close companion Alec.[40] One can only speculate whether it was known by those who invented such rumours that Russell was a lesbian.[41] Like Rewi Alley, she too led a double life in China.

Alley's commitment to living in China was deepened by a sense of alienation from his native land. On his first return home in 1932 his adopted son Alan was abused by racist New Zealanders. Friends from his farming days refused to meet with him because he was travelling with a Chinese boy.[42] In 1937, on his second return to New Zealand for a holiday, he attended a meeting of the Legion of Frontiersmen. What he heard there disgusted him. In a letter to older brother Geoff, written in 1951 to explain some of his reasons for staying on in Communist China, he described what happened: 'I had heard one Vickers by name I think, a territorial Colonel, perhaps, give the most complete Hitler line I had heard outside that country. . . . "If the railwaymen strike knock them on the head". . . . The Legion, an old veterans' fraternal organisation had become fascist.'[43]

His visit home in 1932 was significant as being the first time that his humanitarian work in China received media attention. Wellington's leading paper, the *Dominion*, carried a long article on him and his involvement in famine and flood relief. Yet, after describing this work, the article ended on a note to most insular New Zealanders more relevant than the crisis in China, that Rewi Alley was the brother of All Black rugby player Geoff Alley.[44] The younger Alley's activities overseas were not yet enough on their own to attract public attention in his home country, nor as exciting as his connection to New Zealand's national sport.

Expatriation or exile from one's homeland is a common thread in the lives of gays and lesbians from societies where homosexuality is not tolerated; expatriation enables the traveller to be released from social constraints and psychological inhibitions, from scandal or persecution at home. The traveller is an outsider, free in a foreign society to be whatever he or she wishes to be. A stranger in a strange land, the traveller is free to recreate his or her persona at will. In China, Rewi Alley was able to explore a side of himself that would have been forbidden in his native New Zealand. Moreover, China's chronic political troubles allowed the expression of a latent desire for missionary-type work that had been apparent from his early youth.

4

THE HUMANITARIAN

The 1937 Japanese invasion of China brought about a dramatic change in Rewi Alley's life. During the attack Shanghai was severely bombed, destroying many of the factories he was responsible for inspecting. After the attack, thousands of Shanghainese workers were left without any means of making a living. The Japanese had deliberately targeted industrial areas in an attempt to crush Chinese industry.

Responding to the refugee crisis caused by the bombing, Alley joined with a group of Chinese and foreigners in setting up the Chinese Industrial Co-operatives (CIC). CIC aimed to provide a livelihood for the thousands of refugees who were streaming into the hinterlands away from the Japanese attacks and to maintain China's manufacturing industries. Japanese products were flooding the Chinese market and funding the enemy war machine, the co-ops would be a counter to that. It was hoped that refugee labour, working in the co-operatives, could produce supplies for both the Chinese Nationalist and Chinese Communist armies (by this stage joined in the second united front).

The co-operatives were known variously as CIC, Indusco or, alternatively, *Gung Ho* (in modern *pinyin: gong he*). *Gung Ho* is an abbreviation of the full title in Chinese of the Chinese Industrial Co-operative Movement, *Zhongguo gongye hezuoshe*. The term *gung ho* entered English usage in 1942 after an article was published in the popular American paper the *Saturday Evening Post*. The article reported that US Major Evans Carlson used *gung ho* as a motto to inspire his marines, known as Carlson's Raiders, in the war against the Japanese. Carlson was a close friend of Alley, and he had accompanied him on treks into the interior to visit co-ops. By a strange quirk of intercultural crossbreeding, *gung ho* has taken on a life of its own in the English language, with an Anglicised pronunciation of the original Chinese. The *Collins* dictionary defines 'gung ho' as 'extremely enthusiastic, cooperative and enterprising, sometimes too much so.'

Alley was nominated Field Secretary to CIC. He gave up his luxurious Shanghailander lifestyle for the difficult work of promoting the co-operative movement to refugees in the Chinese interior. It was a very lonely existence.

30

Alley and his companion Alec Camplin differed on their views of the future of China. Camplin left Shanghai to return to his native England, while Alley's two adopted sons elected to join the Communist forces in the north-west of China.

Out on the road trying to drum up support for the co-operatives, Alley wrote in his diary in 1940 how much he missed his 'family'.[1] Here he was not referring to his family back in New Zealand, rather the one he had created for himself in his new life and new identity in exile in China. He listed this family as consisting of adopted sons Alan and Mike, Alec Camplin, K. P. Liu, Frank Lem, Ralph Lapwood, Ed and Peg Snow, Song Qingling, Grace and Manny Granich.[2] Life on the road was not only lonely, it was physically exhausting and dangerous. A New Zealand government report on the co-operative movement in China noted, 'Within two years [Alley] had helped organise over 1,700 manufacturing groups, spread throughout 18 Provinces and embracing 26,000 members. During these two years Alley travelled 18,000 miles, much of the time in or near battle zones. At different stages he suffered from dengue fever, malaria and typhoid.'[3] Not only did Alley travel to set up the co-ops but, having set

Plate 4.1 Rewi Alley and adopted son Mike Alley, Yan'an, 1938.

Source: Helen Foster Snow Papers, Brigham Young University, USA.

them up, he constantly travelled to inspect and encourage the new enterprises. American journalist Graham Peck followed Alley on some of these peregrinations, and he wrote how on the visits Alley would be 'poking, peering, snapping photographs even when there was no film in his camera — it flattered and heartened co-op members to think their effort was being pictured.'[4] This sort of activity provided good preparation for Alley's later career as an official friend of China, where he would be required to tour the factories and communes of New China and report on them for foreign audiences.

Alley seemed to thrive on the difficulties his new life threw up. The part of organiser and motivator of social change suited him. Along with many foreigners both before and after him, Alley worked hard to reform China. At last he was able to become a part of Chinese society in a way he had never been able to when he lived the privileged existence of the Shanghai expatriates. Alley's comment at the time on how he coped with the pressures of this new life is revealing. Taoist Alley told Peck, 'You'll never believe you can change anything unless you think the world is fluid.'[5] Despite his efforts to educate himself in the philosophy of the political left, Alley was ultimately not a Marxist. His writings of this time reveal his views to be a form of what the CCP would, after 1949, scathingly refer to as 'bourgeois humanitarianism' tinged by a whimsical appreciation of the Taoist approach to life's vagaries.

In addition to his practical work as Technical Adviser, Alley had another, even more significant, role as symbolic leader of CIC. Alley became the focus of a publicity campaign that, over the fifteen years of the movement's existence, helped to raise millions of dollars. The plan needed both foreign and Chinese support, and it needed a symbolic leader to unite all forces. Alley was nominated for this role by American journalist Edgar Snow, author of the influential *Red Star Over China*, which promoted the CCP to an international and, in translation, domestic audience. In numerous articles written by Snow, Alley became the focus of both a national and international publicity campaign. The promotion of Alley's leadership role brought in cash and foreign support to the new organisation and, equally important, helped to provide political cover.

Alley had already achieved the beginnings of an international reputation for his relief work and factory inspection. Edgar Snow built on this reputation to create a figure in the great romantic adventurer mould. His articles portrayed Alley as a heroic visionary, setting out to right the wrongs that the Chinese had not been able to right for themselves. One of the most persistent myths as a result of this publicity was that Alley had originated the co-operative idea in China. In fact the potential usefulness of co-operatives in China was first proposed by British academics R. H. Tawney and J. B. Tayler in the early 1930s, and there were many already in existence throughout China.[6]

Snow wrote of Alley's work in CIC, 'Where Lawrence brought to the Arabs the destructive technique of guerrilla war, Alley was to bring China the constructive technique of guerrilla industry. . . . It may yet rank as one of the great human adventures of our time.'[7] The analogy to T. E. Lawrence was significant, for Lawrence was the typical 'Orientalist-as-agent.' Edward Said writes that Lawrence's work, 'symbolises the struggle, first, to stimulate the Orient (lifeless, timeless, forceless) into movement; second, to impose upon that movement an essentially Western shape; third, to contain the new and aroused Orient in a personal vision, whose retrospective mode includes a powerful sense of failure and betrayal.'[8] In Snow's prose Alley became the incarnation of Western superiority over the Chinese. His very body was a symbol of Western dominance over the 'sickly' Chinese.[9] Edgar Snow promoted Alley as someone who could help China in a way that no Chinese was capable of. In a letter to a prominent Chinese politician Snow wrote, 'Alley as a personality should be a good selling point for your talk in America. Don't feel too nationalistic on this point.'[10] According to James Bertram who worked in Hong Kong in the late 1930s with the China Defence League, publicity from the promotion of Rewi Alley as leader of the co-operative movement was 'worth a small fortune in cash support for Indusco.'[11] Charitable donors in the Western world found Alley a particularly appealing symbol of Western humanitarianism in Asia.

The myth of Alley as saviour of China received great support in New Zealand in the 1930s and 1940s. Insular and insecure in this period, New Zealand was eager to claim an international hero as a native son. Once CIC promotional activities began in New Zealand, Alley quickly became a folk hero who, it seemed, could do no wrong. The press competed amongst themselves for the most superlative adjectives to describe Alley. One reporter called him 'one of the world's great men', while another wrote 'So big a man that it is perhaps impossible that he should be appreciated at his true worth in his own generation.'[12] Yet another boasted, 'Rewi Alley is, on his record, among the greatest of New Zealanders. It was he who conceived and built "Indusco", the great Chinese "guerrilla war industry", without which the cause of China – today blockaded – would quite possibly be lost.' Other articles described him as a 'saint' a 'Great New Zealander', and a 'hero in China'.[13]

From the very start, the mythologisation of Rewi Alley emphasised his nationality. Alley's national identity was an important part of his success as symbolic leader of the Chinese co-operatives. Citizen of a young country relatively unknown on the global scene, Alley was able to promote a new attitude towards China free of the exploitation usually associated with other Western nations. As the foreign leader of a Chinese reform movement, he was also free of the traditional social pressures and familial responsibilities of a Chinese bureaucrat. To Western supporters Alley's conservative background, white skin and the fact that he mixed easily in both Chinese and

Western worlds (by this time he had developed some proficiency in both the Mandarin and the Shanghai dialect) made him a much more acceptable leader than a Chinese would have been. Indeed the British Ambassador to China, Sir Archibald Clarke-Kerr, whose support was crucial for getting CIC off the ground, seems to have automatically assumed that the movement would have a Western leader with Chinese staff.[14] To a Chinese audience, Alley could play on his oddness as a foreigner to get away with being innovative and introducing new ideas that were accepted more readily from a foreigner.[15] On a political level, Alley was acceptable to both the Nationalist and the Communist side; though this might not have been the case had the Nationalists been aware of his links with the CCP underground. Finally, as a British subject, Alley was eligible for extraterritoriality, so that while Chinese organisers and workers in CIC were arrested or worse for participating in a movement that the Nationalist government came to regard as 'Communist', Alley went free.

Nevertheless there was some dissension at the emphasis on the personality of Rewi Alley in CIC publicity, and his public persona was not always regarded favourably. Journalist Jacques Marcuse wrote of meeting Alley in 1940 in Chongqing, the wartime capital, 'fresh from his native New Zealand, bustling about in khaki shorts and shirt, physically the very prototype of the scoutmaster, oozing cheerful yet lofty thought, sublimating China of which he knew very little.'[16] This was both unfair and untrue; Alley had already lived in China for fourteen years by the time Marcuse met him and quite probably knew considerably more about China than the journalist did. It is significant, however, as an indication of the disdain by which Alley was held by some foreigners. In contrast to the criticism that 'he knew very little about China', other foreign critics of Alley objected that he had gone 'native' and lost his former respectability as an official of the Shanghai Municipal Council.[17] Alley was derisively known by his foreign detractors in Chongqing as 'Screwy Rewi'.[18] Meanwhile, Chinese critics objected to the foreign dominance of CIC, labelling the International Committee 'imperialist'.[19] In New Zealand it was argued, however, that New Zealanders could never have been inspired to raise the large sums of money for CIC that they did had it not been for national pride in the figure of Alley.[20]

The emphasis on Alley's nationality in CIC publicity not only was useful for the co-operative movement; it had practical benefits for New Zealand too. The New Zealand High Commissioner for Canada described Snow's articles on Alley as 'the best piece of publicity [that] New Zealand ever had.'[21] In a *Listener* article James Bertram analysed why his fellow New Zealanders found Alley's work in China so appealing: 'The motive was of universal interest: help from a little country to a big one in distress (though fighting gamely on our behalf), *help of a kind that only this little country could give* [sic]. And it was a drama with an all New Zealand cast.'[22]

Alley's public image suited New Zealanders' perception of themselves as pioneering, practical types who were willing to get in and lend a hand. A New Zealand children's journal depicted Alley's work in spiritual terms, claiming that he had a 'calling' predetermined by his New Zealand upbringing:

> This then has been the calling – predestined perhaps – of New Zealand's Rewi Alley. First attempting to alleviate the conditions of workers in the suffocating hells of East Coast industry, then directing the new cooperatives into the channels advocated by his father in NZ and latterly, founding a new practical school in the poverty stricken, overpopulated rural town in Shandan. . . . Here, saturated with the humanitarian concepts of the Carpenter, he toils for the good of all in China, with his adopted sons following in his footsteps.[23]

Reports about Alley continually stressed that his ideas and altruism were rooted in qualities that were intrinsic to his place of birth. New Zealand's adoration of Alley in the 1930s and 1940s was tied up with a quest for a place in the world. Geographically isolated, as a Europeanised ex-colonial nation New Zealand was still trying to establish its own sense of culture and identity. Alley's achievements and the international attention they received led to intense patriotism in New Zealand.

Alley recognised early on that New Zealand could be a potentially rich source of support for his activities in China. Indeed he argued that it was in the strategic interests of New Zealand to do so. In a newspaper article published in New Zealand in the late 1930s, Alley urged the New Zealand government to support China against Japan for the sake of its own defence, and provide funding for the co-operative movement to help China build an economic base.[24] Long before most other New Zealanders of his era, Alley recognised that his native land's interests lay not with Europe, but with the countries of Asia and the Pacific. It would be an issue that he was to emphasise for the rest of his life, to not always receptive ears back 'home'.

Alley's insistence on New Zealand's strategic interests in Asia was acknowledged by a 1942 editorial in the influential *Listener*:

> China will either beat off the Japanese and stabilise the East on a new level of civilisation, or it will be conquered and used to uproot the culture of half a hemisphere – the half to which we ourselves belong. Its 'Double Ten' is therefore a day of destiny for New Zealanders as well as for the Chinese themselves, and it is almost incredible that a New Zealander has done more than almost anyone else in the world – far more than any other non-Chinese – to ward off disaster so far. To convey what he has done is difficult if we are to avoid extravagance; but it would come near to the truth to say

that a man who started to cut down a kauri tree with a pocket-knife or move a fair-sized hill with a teaspoon would be showing no more courage and no more faith than the man who set to work five years ago to rebuild the industries that the Japanese were systematically blasting out of existence.[25]

It is noticeable that, despite supporting Alley's views on New Zealand's relationship with Asia, the editors found it necessary to back up those views with claims of Alley's ability to save Chinese industry. At the peak of his fame in New Zealand, to many New Zealanders Alley *was* China and his activities were a lot more comprehensible than the threatened impact of a Japanese victory there.

By his own account, Alley had almost as many enemies as friends during Gung Ho days. In a 1965 letter to Willis Airey, he wrote of his trying experience as spiritual leader of CIC:

> In those years too, I had many enemies, who stuck at nothing in the way of stories to pull me down. I was a British Agent, trying to get hold of Chinese industry; a diabolically clever engineer trying to find out about Chinese resources for foreign interests, a sentimental religious adventurer, out to make a name for himself at the expense of the Chinese people; a sex maniac with a wife in every big city in the countryside, how I took an actress to sleep with me on long journeys, a Japanese agent, spying for the Japanese. A Communist sympathiser. An agent of the Russians. An agent of the Third International, a fool who knew nothing of industry, a gangster who was piling away a fortune in banks in India.[26]

Airey printed this quote almost verbatim in his biography of Alley, though he rearranged the words slightly without informing his readers. Airey's more condensed version gives greater prominence to certain aspects of what certainly were, as Airey wrote, 'fantastic stories.' Airey's quote reads as follows:

> In those years . . . I had many enemies, who stuck at nothing in the way of stories to pull me down. I was a British Agent, trying to get hold of Chinese industry; a diabolically clever engineer . . . a sentimental religious adventurer, out to make a name for himself at the expense of the Chinese people; a sex maniac with a wife in every city. . . . I took an actress to sleep with me on long journeys; a Japanese agent, a Communist sympathiser, an agent of the Russians, an agent of the Third International, a fool who knew nothing of industry, a gangster who was piling away a fortune in banks in India.[27]

In Airey's strategically edited version the reader's attention is drawn to the stories of Alley as a womaniser while those phrases that might imply Alley was a spy, 'trying to find out about Chinese resources for foreign interests' and 'spying on the Japanese,' were removed. By the time Airey's book was being edited in 1969, Alley was under virtual house arrest and allegations of foreign spies in China were being used as a means to bring about the downfall of some of the most powerful leaders in the country.

Alley made a point of publicising rumours that he had 'a woman in every town' to keep off questions about his sexuality. The two most persistent rumours about him – that he was homosexual and that the co-operative movement was a smokescreen for a more subtle form of imperialism – are left off the list of rumours about him he sent to his biographer. Airey's biography, diplomatically titled (at Alley's insistence) A Learner in China, was closely edited by Alley and his faithful friend Shirley Barton who worked for CIC in the 1940s and early 1950s. Alley's ghost-written memoirs At 90: Memoirs of My China Years, written twenty years later, uses exactly the same quote, this time minus the claims that he was 'an agent of the Russians' and 'an agent of the Third International.' In the 1980s when China was still in a state of Cold War with the USSR, the CCP was sensitive about claims of Soviet influence on its revolution. It was not in Alley's interest to let it be known that he was once rumoured to be linked with the Soviet Union. From 1952 on, as he became a fixture of the PRC establishment, Alley tried to keep careful control of what was remembered of him. His personal history was always tailored to fit the ideological needs of the CCP, no matter how much that might change over time. History has an important and central role in Communist China. In the People's Republic, as in George Orwell's fictional totalitarian state, 'Who controls the past, controls the future: who controls the present controls the past.'[28] Ironically, Mao Zedong was to echo this dictum in his directive on how to deal with the corrupt past and decadent foreign in socialist New China: 'Use the past to serve the present, make foreign things serve China.'[29]

In 1942 Alley was fired from all positions of influence in the co-operative movement when it was found he had permitted CIC factories to make guns and blankets for the CCP. Alley decided to devote his attention to technical training in the Bailie schools, centres for refugee children. He still worked under the aegis of CIC, but took a lower profile than before. He wrote forty years later:

> After 1942, I put my time in the main into the Bailie Schools, trying to train people for a better Gung Ho we felt would come in with liberation. The schools were called after Joseph Bailie, an old American who had left the missionary field to try and get young Chinese sent abroad for technical training. Some of our early Gung Ho leaders were those he had managed to get trained, Lu

Guangmian, Lin Foyou, and others. Most of our schools were closed down with the Japanese advance or Kuomintang suppression, until finally we tried to concentrate all that was left in Sandan and carry trainees through liberation. Joseph Bailie I had known well. It was he who had advised me to go to help in Inner Mongolia in 1929, and then worked with me in Wuhan in the flood aftermath of 1932.[30]

Alley's writing style here owes much to the influence of years of writing 'autobiographies' on those who came under political suspicion in Communist China.[31] Much of Alley's writing post-1949 was markedly uninspiring if one compares it to the passion of his output in the 1930s and 1940s. Alley's writing from this earlier period, both personal and public, is quite unlike the writing (again both public and private) for which he was to become renowned. Then he wrote with a passionate, lucid style of prose, writing straight from the heart of the situation in China. In these works alone are we able to catch glimpses of the man who was able to inspire so many into action.

5

REWI'S SCHOOL

Despite the glorious publicity CIC attracted, the scheme to develop a co-operative movement in China never really succeeded, beset as it was by the conflicting objectives of its major participants. A further problem was the lack of suitably motivated people to run the co-operatives; those who had the education to manage them were often unwilling to adopt the hands-on approach to work that they required. Alley's frustration with this situation lead to a whole new role for him, and a period that he would later look back on as a golden era in his life.

After he was fired from his position as Technical Adviser on the CIC Executive, Alley continued to travel throughout the parts of China where co-ops had been set up. Although he had been fired from the executive, he retained his position as Field Secretary to the powerful International Committee, which contributed much of the funding for the movement. Alley had the support of the foreigners in the International Committee, but not of some of the powerful figures in the Nationalist government who were suspicious of CIC's progressive aims. Alley's position within CIC had always been problematic. He had tried hard to maintain a neutral position between the Communist and Nationalist camps, stressing that CIC was a tangible result of the United Front between the two parties. Such a position, however, was untenable and led to Alley being described as a Communist by the Nationalists and an Imperialist by Communists and others opposed to foreign influence in China. In time, however, Alley gave up his organising work for CIC to concentrate his energies on a new project, the Bailie School.

The first Bailie School was established in Shuangshipu, Shaanxi Province, in 1941. At first set up as an orphanage for refugee children, under headmaster George Hogg's leadership it came to be seen as the training ground for future co-operative workers. Hogg hoped to make the Bailie School the focus for a new approach to learning in China, aimed at creating a new generation of educated people who would have both practical and technical skills. The schools owed a great deal to George Hogg's own liberal education and experience, applied to Chinese circumstances. Hogg had an unusual schooling for an upper-middle-class English boy. Though he was an Oxford graduate, his parents had sent him to a secondary school that combined book learning with practical knowledge. Hogg's aunt was the Quaker pacifist Muriel Lester, and it was she who had encouraged him to work in China.

Initially Alley was opposed to the idea of directing CIC funds into education; he believed that the co-operatives were the best way to revitalise China. However, as his personal circumstances changed, this view altered.[1] Alley was closely involved with the school from its inception. He had a cave home built there for him, which he used as his base. He named the school after his former mentor, Joseph Bailie, in part as an innocuous foreign name that might deflect Chinese government suspicions about the school being 'Communistic' and partly to help raise funds in the West through the missionary connection. Bailie's own ideas on training Chinese youth to be future leaders of China were not far off Hogg's aim, so the use of the name was not inappropriate. Peter Townsend, who worked with Alley in CIC from 1942 to 1951, writes that Alley had 'respect and deep admiration' for Bailie and his 'humanistic vision.' According to Townsend, 'Rewi quoted him to me more than any other foreigner in the relief business.'[2]

While the school was at Shuangshipu, Alley continued his trips to inspect the co-ops. Eventually, however, the Bailie School was forced to move because of harassment from Nationalist forces — army officials trying to press-gang staff and older students into service — and the threat of Japanese invasion. Remote Shandan, in Gansu Province, was chosen for the school's new location, but this had some disadvantages. Peter Townsend writes:

> unfortunately the move began the separation of co-ops and school for whereas in Shuangshipu it was located in a 'semi-feudal' area in fairly close proximity to two strong co-operative centres, Baochi to the North and Hanchung to the South, both of which would have provided practical co-op examples to the students, Shandan was an essentially 'feudal' district, far removed from any co-operatives. Shandan was a pretty isolated desolate spot and it was difficult to get good Chinese teachers to go there. So Hogg and from 1945, Rewi Alley, came to depend increasingly on foreigners, permanent or temporary, supported by CORSO, sent by Indusco, provided by the Friends Ambulance Unit, and so on.[3]

When the school moved to Shandan, and particularly after Hogg's death, Alley travelled relatively little and visited few co-operatives; from this time he 'in thought and deed began to separate himself from the requirements and requests of the co-ops'.[4]

George Hogg died of tetanus on 22 July 1945 after a small injury that occurred while he was playing basketball became infected. The school had only limited medical facilities at this time, and the nearest doctor was a day away. Visiting the school at the time, Alley felt a strong sense of responsibility for Hogg's death from such a minor illness. He mourned the death for a long time. He and Hogg had been close. Hogg had been dedicated to the ideals of the school, and Alley committed himself to keep the school going as a memorial to him. Alley had no previous background in education; unlike Hogg, he had not even graduated from high school. However, in lieu of any other suitable options, Alley took on the responsibilities of the Shandan Bailie School. He also took on the care of a family of four young boys, the Nie brothers, whom Hogg had fostered after their mother died.

Taking on the headmastership was an opportunity for Alley to explore his own educational ideas. One of his particular obsessions was that the Bailie School boys should not have to wear more clothes than was necessary. Years afterward he wrote,

> One of our old Sandan School ideas was to get all the sunlight possible on to growing students to make up for the deficiency of long cold winters and help with bone growth. So we wore short clothes as soon as we could from mid-spring on through mid-autumn, while the old swimming pool was immensely popular, with no taboos being imposed on the trainees necessitating bathing clothes.[5]

Alley's preoccupation with nudity was very much a reflection of his rebellion against the repressive Victorian upbringing he had suffered. But it was a preoccupation that would be misunderstood by those who spread unflattering rumours about him in his later years.

The Shandan Bailie School was very different from other educational institutions in China. The students were trained both in intellectual knowledge and technical skills, and they were given responsibility for much of the running of the school. Some teachers at the school found this difficult to get used to. Outside observers, however, were impressed by what they found. One report stated admiringly, 'the students learn by practice the principle of maintaining order through mutual understanding rather than by superimposed rules. The students govern themselves in all matters regarding food, extracurricular activities, maintenance of order, rewards and punishments, administrative duties of the school, and so on.'[6]

Despite its internal upheavals, CIC still had international support and the focus was still on Alley as the symbolic leader of the movement. After 1945, Alley directed this focus as much as possible on the activities at Shandan, which many came to believe was, as British Ambassador to China Sir Ralph Stevenson said, 'one of the most constructive and helpful pieces of work in the whole of China.'[7] In contrast to the success of the Bailie School, by the late 1940s, the co-operative movement was perceived as a failure. CIC officials embezzled funds, used their position to get jobs for relatives, and hired out transportation facilities to private interests. A 1948 Canadian government report commented that the co-ops only function in areas 'where their activities do not compete with commercial interest of influential officials' – in south-east Shaanxi and eastern Gansu.[8]

The Shandan Bailie School was totally dependent on foreign aid for its survival. After the end of World War Two, the United Nations Relief and Rehabilitation Administration (UNRRA) provided a large proportion of the funding for the school and other CIC activities. However, after 1947, this ended when the UNRRA program closed down in China. By 1948, 40 per cent of the school's funding came from New Zealand, 40 per cent from the Agricultural Industries Service (using residual UNRRA funds) and 20 per cent from supporters in the USA, Britain and Canada.[9] As interest in CIC declined in these three countries, the New Zealand aid organisation CORSO (Council of Organisations for Relief Services Overseas) became the major source of funds for the Shandan Bailie School. This was directly a result of Alley's high public standing in his native land. Though CORSO channelled its funding to China through CIC, the money raised was targeted specifically for Alley's school at Shandan. This naturally led to some considerable resentment from the rest of the co-operative movement, which was still dependent on foreign aid.

CORSO persuaded the New Zealand government to provide financial support for the school by stressing that New Zealand's work in China was good for its international image.[10] With CORSO's help, the school was able to attract New Zealand technicians and even a doctor to help run the school. Alley's high international profile attracted a number of workers from other countries too – from a Canadian engineer to a Japanese potter.

Alley was promoted by his supporters in New Zealand as a missionary of New Zealand technical expertise who would save the Chinese through industrial modernisation. The work of Alley was touted not just as a triumph for New Zealand, but for the whole of the British Empire. The leader of a Rewi Alley fundraising group wrote, 'There can be no doubt that the small colony of New Zealanders which works at the present time in Shandan is doing more to maintain British prestige in China than anything else could.'[11] Alley himself adopted the language of the missionary to convince the New Zealand public of the need to send assistance to the Shandan school:

> Sure the whole thing is a gamble. But it is a gamble that would be for the good for us here and for the people of New Zealand to play for the sake of the good of their own souls. Here we shall never cease trying to abolish this poverty which, if it stays, will be the breeding ground of so many new wars, so much human distress. There you have to realise there are other countries in the world besides New Zealand and its Commonwealth neighbours.[12]

In the post-war era, as the sources for humanitarian aid in China were drying up, Alley was well aware of the value of the New Zealand connection to his work. CORSO's funding, though partly raised from donations from the New Zealand public, was underwritten by the New Zealand government. In a confidential report, an official explained why the government believed aiding Alley's work in China was desirable:

> a gift of POUNDS 10,000 was recently made to CORSO for Rewi Alley. It is understood from CORSO and several interested individuals who have from time to time asked the Government for financial assistance for Alley, that his financial position has been increasingly difficult but, while the PM feels that he is doing a valuable work which reflects credit on New Zealand and that public opinion in this country would fully support a substantial grant, it is considered that it would be unwise for international political reasons for the Government to authorise a direct grant. As you are no doubt aware, Alley's relations with the Chinese authorities are often rather difficult. The PM therefore decided, in consultation with the Ministry of Internal Affairs, to make available the sum of POUNDS 10,000 from Art Union monies for relief work in China. This was paid indirectly to CORSO on the understanding that an equivalent sum would be made available by CORSO to Alley. The whole transaction remains confidential.[13]

While the government emphasised the political ends to be gained from supporting the school, CORSO stressed that Alley's work was 'entirely non-political' and should be supported on purely humanitarian grounds:[14]

> New Zealand's name stands high today in China. Our non-selfseeking and non-partisan aid has been received with gratitude. With the great need for help still there, there is surely a responsibility to continue that act of succour and friendship. Were the Western democracies to turn their backs on China, it would be an act against the ideals of 'One World', and could precipitate another step which might make still remoter that 'One World'.[15]

The New Zealand connection was strong at the school: foreign staff, sturdy New Zealand Corriedale sheep sent over to be bred with Chinese sheep, and loads of fertiliser and sheep dip. To many in New Zealand in the 1940s, the Shandan Bailie School was simply 'Rewi's school,' a tangible link with an otherwise alien land and culture. A representative headline from the day reads: 'Corriedale Sheep in Chinese Farm Experiment, Rewi Alley's School on the Old Silk Road.'[16] The image is both exotic and familiar; the mysterious East exemplified by the Old Silk Road, and what to New Zealanders is merely prosaic, New Zealand's own breed of sheep. By 1946 Alley had become such an established figure in New Zealand's pantheon of national heroes that he featured in the *School Journal*, the primer of political socialisation for generations of New Zealand children.[17] The following year, as funding for the school became scarce, New Zealand children were asked to collect money, clothes, toys and other goods for 'Rewi Alley's school in China.'[18]

As it was throughout most of Chinese society at this time, homosexual activity was accepted at the school. According to Courtney Archer:

> From comments that they made it was quite common for boys to sleep together. . . . Saturday night was sauna night. It became a great social occasion when sleeping partners would be chosen. . . . All the pretty young boys at the school were spoken for by the older boys at the school. Nobody thought anything of Rewi sleeping with the boys. It just happened. It was very innocent. Very matter of fact. Rewi used to joke about how all the pretty boys of the school were spoken for: 'There goes so and so with his pretty legs.' For most of the students the [sexual] experiences were ephemeral and didn't really affect their later lives. They all went off and married and had kids and so on. I don't think there was the same black and white attitude which seems to apply in Western societies – I mean either you are or you aren't.[19]

Archer first found out Alley was gay when some of the other students told him Alley had slept with them. When Archer and Alley were alone, Alley felt free to be more uninhibited: 'for example the boys' shorts would get shorter and shorter, with holes etc., the boys would come in to see Alley [while Archer was there] and he would put his hand on their thighs and up their trousers.'[20] Here it is important to define the terms 'boys' and 'students': Archer and other foreign workers in the CIC whom I interviewed always referred to the students of the Bailie School as 'boys' regardless of their age; 'students' included those who had graduated from the school and had taken up teaching positions. Alley was not a paedophile – he was attracted to young Chinese men in their late teens and early twenties, not children. But it is undeniable that Alley had sexual relations with some of his students, and while this is anathema to contemporary Western mores as an abuse of a fiduciary relationship, in the social climate of China in those times it was not at all unusual. According to Courtney Archer, 'Homosexuality in China was a mixture of "agape" and "eros", hence the use of the word "favourite" which had overtones of both. Certainly this was the situation as far as Rewi was concerned – there was a deep bond of affection between him and the students which was life-long even if many of them had just slept in his bed or taken things further.'[21]

Alley was not the only member of the foreign staff to be having such affairs. The heterosexual foreigners at the school turned a blind eye. According to Archer, 'During those years at the school I am sure most of the European staff were aware of the situation as far as Rewi's sexual orientation was concerned. I think the fact attracted a number of Europeans to come and work at the school. Of those who were not homosexual, one was ex-public school and familiar with homosexuality. It was a subject never talked about, although Rewi would refer to it in a very oblique way from time to time. But it was there. It was accepted.'[22]

Alley's sexual preferences were known by many of those who worked with him in the co-operatives, though it was seldom discussed openly.[23] Max Bickerton, a fellow New Zealander working in CIC's Shanghai office, who was himself a homosexual of 'the more outrageous sort,' joked to Courtney Archer in 1946: 'Think of Rewi Alley out there in the Gobi Desert with 300 boys!'[24] The response of most foreigners in China at this time towards homosexual activities was to take on the Chinese attitude and politely ignore it. Archer comments: 'In China in those days, homosexuality was something that was not talked about openly, but was taken for granted. It was casually mentioned in the way you would say someone was a Roman Catholic or a Presbyterian or whatever.'[25] Dr Bob Spencer and his wife Barbara, a nurse, ran the school clinic for three years. According to Spencer, 'We were vaguely aware of Rewi Alley's proclivities and sexual activities. It didn't appear to be affecting the boys in any way. We just did our jobs; it wasn't an issue. I'm surprised now that we weren't more shocked at the time.' When he was in Shandan, however, Spencer felt that 'If they want to live that way, what harm is it doing?'[26] Alley's closeness and affection for the boys was admired and respected by those who worked with him. George Hogg's comments in his book *I See a New China* are representative both of the acceptance Alley retained from his peers in China and of an innocence about relations between adults and children that seems out of place in our prurient times:

The main distinctive feature of Rewi's cave in Shuangshipu is exactly the same as that of his former house in Shanghai – that at any time out of school hours it is filled with boys. Boys looking at picture magazines and asking millions of questions. Boys playing the gramophone and singing out of tune. Boys doing gymnastics off Rewi's shoulders or being held upside down. Boys being given enemas, or rubbing sulphur ointment into each other's scabies. Boys standing in brass wash-basins and splashing soapy water about. Boys toasting bare bottoms against the stove (the scar against Rewi's own nether portions testifies to his own indulgence in this form of amusement). Boys pulling the hairs on Rewi's legs, or fingering the generous portions of the foreigner's nose. 'Boys are just

45

the same anywhere,' says Rewi. 'Wouldn't these kids have a swell time in New Zealand.'[27]

While Alley's sexuality was not an issue for those Westerners and Chinese who knew of it in China, it would unquestionably have been anathema to his supporters in New Zealand and other Western countries who provided the funding for his humanitarian work. It was fortunate for Alley that because it never was a concern in China, he was able to keep it a secret from less sympathetic individuals in the West.

Alley's writings about the school both before and after 1949 resonate with a strong sense of 'us' (Alley and Hogg) against 'them' (the Nationalists, CIC workers, teachers and the superstitious Chinese peasants of Shandan) with the 'Shandan boys' (the students) in the middle. Alley presents himself in his writings of the time as ultra-progressive, while the Chinese community is depicted as ignorant and hidebound by tradition. Foreign staff at the school describe feeling encircled; besieged by ignorance, corruption and poverty.[28] Misunderstandings between the local community and the school were inevitable since, despite its good intentions, the school was like any other missionary-type effort – a rich enclave in the midst of an ocean of human suffering.[29] Colin Morrison, President of CORSO, reported on what he saw on a visit to Shandan in 1948:

> Most of the land is owned by wealthy landlords, many of whom own two to six wives and smoke opium. Most of the people live at bare subsistence level and no more. To buy a little girl of 16 costs quarter the price of a donkey. They are taken home as slaves. . . . The majority of the people are engaged in agriculture and raising sheep and goats, but there are about 1,000 mine shafts in the district. The people are very poor. Children have only one garment which covers the upper half of the body; in winter the temperature at night frequently falls to -40 degrees F. Those who have no bedding (and many do not) pile sand on the *kang* and burrow into it for warmth.'[30]

Although the school had a mainly Chinese staff, the foreign staff held the most influential positions. There was some mistrust of the ability of the Chinese staff to run things for themselves. Up until the time of the Communist forces arriving in Shandan in 1949, Alley held all power at the school. Both in myth and reality, it was very much 'Rewi's school.'

Shandan became for Alley a golden era that he would increasingly look back to as a simpler, more moral time. Constantly looking back to past days is an implied criticism with the present. In a piece written after the Cultural Revolution Alley reflected, 'At Sandan, we all learnt together, I as much as anyone else. Those were wonderful years, and both I and many of the old boys look nostalgically back on them, for the struggles then were very real, and everyone had a full dose of practice to go along with his or her class work.'[31] The Bailie School and CIC were radical, independent programs that could only operate in a chaotic society such as China was in the 1940s. The essentially democratic ideals of the co-operative movement did not fit well into life in China after 1949 any more than the creative and practical ideals of the Bailie School fitted into the education system of 'New China,' based on a symbiosis of the rigid Chinese education tradition and the Soviet model. Once order was restored to the country there was no place for such organisations, nor was it permissible for an innovative, independent foreigner such as Rewi Alley to take charge. Gone were the days of the foreign adventurer in China or the Lord Jims, capable of enlightening the masses with their superior culture. China was entering a new era and if there was to be a part for Alley in that future, it would require a totally different tack.

6

THE 'FAUSTIAN CHOICE'

1 October 1949, the founding of the People's Republic of China, heralded a new era in China for Chinese and foreigners alike, regardless of their political views. The change in the status of foreigners in China necessitated a search for a new role for Alley. After 1949, it was no longer acceptable for a foreigner to head a Chinese school. Alley had no desire to return to New Zealand; he felt he was too old to make a new beginning there and he turned down offers to set up Shandan-style schools elsewhere.[1] As the Communist victory approached, he made a crucial decision, one that Courtney Archer would later describe as a 'Faustian choice.'[2] Alley decided that whatever happened after the Communist take-over he would try to stay on in China. The decision to stay was neither for ideological nor humanitarian reasons, but simply a personal decision: China was the country where he would like to spend the rest of his life. This 'Faustian choice' meant that he would do anything that was required to stay on. At the time this could not have been an easy choice to make. Though Alley had supported the CCP since the mid-1930s, no one could be sure how foreigners would be treated under the new regime. None the less, it was with great optimism and relief that the staff and students of the Shandan Bailie School greeted the arrival of the Communist soldiers at their remote outpost.

The Chinese Communists refer to 1949 as 'Liberation' – liberation from the feudal and corrupt rule of the Nationalist government and liberation from foreign colonialism. Liberation symbolised everything Alley had been working for in China for the previous ten years. Yet on a personal level Communist rule did not mean liberation for Alley and other gay men in China. Now that civil order was being restored, the Communist authorities were able to enforce their moral attitudes. Centuries of relative sexual tolerance came to an end as the new government began to close down the brothels and bathhouses that were the outward manifestation of an entrenched sexual culture. At the same time, by harassment and in some cases imprisonment or expulsion, the government made it clear that Western capitalist influence was no longer welcome in China. The days of hedonism for sexual tourists in Shanghai were definitely over, while the Peking the aesthetes so loved and admired was a symbol of a feudal past that the new regime sought to eradicate. The era of foreign adventurers and aesthetes in China had ended.

Homosexual activity became a crime in the People's Republic of China, categorised, though not formally listed, under the regulations regarding 'hooliganism,' in Chinese *liumang*. Homosexual activity certainly continued, but went underground. The puritanism of the government brought about a dramatic change in social attitudes towards sexuality.[3] A shift in sexual terms reflected this social change: Chinese official usage began to adopt the Western dichotomy of heterosexual/homosexual (*yixinglian/tongxinglian*). Homosexuality came to be seen as an illness that needed curing and a crime that should be punished. Gays and lesbians could be arrested and sent to a labour-reform camp or prison. They might be sent to a clinic to receive treatments such as 'hate therapy' and 'electric therapy' to 'cure' them. They might even be shot if it was thought they were unredeemable. Former CIC worker Max Bickerton, who took up a job teaching English at Peking University, was asked to leave China because of his homosexual activities. Yet a few other foreign gay men were allowed to stay on, perhaps because they were more discreet than Bickerton. But all this was yet to come. In 1949, in remote Gansu, no one could be certain how the Communist policies would affect their lives. None the less, just before liberation, Alley called a meeting of men who were gay at Shandan, mostly Europeans, and told them to be a little more circumspect because, he said, the Red Army was very puritanical about sex.[4]

When the Communist forces arrived in Gansu, as elsewhere, they began the long process of reorganising the society along Communist lines. In what was to become a pattern of Chinese political life, the cadres used political campaigns (*yundong*) as a focus for thought reform. One of the first acts of the new regime was to require all Chinese citizens as well as foreigners to register with the police. The background of every individual was investigated. Any who had worked for the Nationalist government were immediately under suspicion.

Alley and the foreign workers at Shandan had not only had contact with the former regime, they had received financial assistance from the US-dominated United Nations Relief and Rehabilitation Administration (UNRRA) and were thus suspected of being spies for the USA and other Western countries. If Alley was to be permitted to stay it would be necessary to establish credibility with the new regime, break links with the old regime and to make this position clear both in China and New Zealand. Therefore in 1949 Alley announced his support for the new Chinese government and this was widely reported in Western newspapers. Whereas in the past he had been discreet about his political views, he now openly stated that he was a CCP supporter.

Within months of the CCP victory, the Korean War broke out, when the armed forces of the North Korean People's Army launched a surprise against

South Korea. Within twenty-four hours the USA decided to send a massive military force to back up the South Korean side and, soon after, pushed through a resolution in the UN condemning the North Korean attack and authorising a UN military force to fight against the North Koreans. A US-dominated international force quickly routed the North Korean forces from South Korea and advanced beyond the 38th parallel, the dividing line between the two sides. The PRC had already been providing military assistance to the Korean Communists and the UN forces' attacks beyond the 38th parallel gave the government the excuse it needed to engage openly in battle. Fought as much for pyschological as for strategic reasons, the Chinese participation in the war – at enormous cost – gave extra impetus to the CCP's attempts to remould Chinese society and cast off the influences of the semi-feudal, semi-colonial past.

In China the war was officially known by the slogan 'Oppose America Support Korea' (*kang Mei yuan Chao*). Support for the war was channelled with the help of a massive propaganda campaign, stirring up patriotic and internationalist fervour. In December 1950, the CCP Central Committee Department of Propaganda published a secret directive on developing 'anti-American patriotic propaganda.' The goal of the campaign was to 'eradicate a section of the population's (especially people in the cities) feelings of affection, admiration or fear towards the USA, and establish a standpoint of hostility towards US imperialism, disdaining and scorning it.'[5]

The outbreak of the war undoubtedly intensified antagonism within China towards foreigners, even those known to be sympathetic to the new regime. Alley and his foreign co-workers had to work extra hard at this time to demonstrate their support. In January 1951 Alley joined with the other foreigner teachers at the Bailie School in writing an open letter of support for American prisoners of war in Korea who had publicly denounced 'the American invasion in Korea' (the Communist side maintained that South Korea had started the war) and this received much publicity both inside and outside China.[6] He later spoke out in support of Chinese allegations that the USA was using germ warfare in Korea and Northern China. Alley asked friends and family to send him copies of all articles that reported his political views. He wrote to brother Pip,

> Please send me some copies of PV [*People's Voice*, the New Zealand Communist Party paper] with my lines in. And any other old papers that have carried. I must keep a file of such, so as to have everything clear. It is important to know what people write and say, especially as things become as awkward as they are in Korea. One tries to help in keeping things as clear as possible.[7]

Other foreigners at the school resorted to similar tactics to stay on. On the strength of a front-page article in the New Zealand Communist Party newspaper declaring her support for the Chinese Communists, Alley's co-worker Shirley Barton was able to get her visa extended.[8]

Copies of everything that Alley had published were kept on his security file at the school.[9] This was important as evidence of his stance on what the government was calling 'New China.' In addition to the letters and articles he sent to be published in New Zealand, Alley had pro-CCP poems written before Liberation published in order to convince his supporters that he genuinely approved of the CCP and had done so for some time.[10] It was important to his future credibility to prove that this dramatic change in political profile was not a recent one.

Alley and the Australian journalist Wilfred Burchett spoke on Peking Radio on 13 April 1951 in a shortwave message broadcast to New Zealand and Australia. Alley and Burchett's broadcasts were recorded and passed on to the New Zealand Ministry of Defence by 'concerned citizens.'[11] Both New Zealand and Australia had adopted the US policy of the non-recognition of the PRC, both had sent forces to Korea and both were closely allied to the USA in a series of just-signed treaties. Alley warned New Zealanders of the 'disastrous results' if New Zealand continued to be an American puppet: 'Slavish following of America would mean being dragged into one adventure after another, all for the purpose of enslaving foreign people on the Hitler pattern to American commercial power.'[12] Regarding an editorial in the Christchurch newspaper the *Press* on recent purges in China he railed,

> It is interesting to see the disregard for truth and relative facts it displays. In all the years of the imperialist-supported KMT there was no note of anger in the big papers of solid, comfortable countries like New Zealand. The probable 10 million progressive people who perished in the 23 years political struggle for China's liberation, the thousands of millions who died in often man-made famines did not evoke your disgust and indignation.[13]

Notwithstanding Alley's support for the Chinese Communist government, the Shandan Bailie School's main aid donor, CORSO, continued to assert that Alley was not a Communist and indeed had strong links to the former Nationalist government and to missionary activity in China. In 1951, 20 per cent of all CORSO funds were directed towards Alley's school; it could not afford to alienate New Zealand donors. In a newspaper report the chairman of CORSO stated,

> He was appointed national organiser of the Villages Co-op ... by General Chiang Kaishek himself, and still remains chief adviser to the Government on co-ops. The school for training leaders, to which Mr Alley is now giving his whole time, was conceived by one missionary, begun by another, and corresponds closely to missionary

initiated co-op enterprises in India and elsewhere ... the idea of permanently raising the standard of living of China's millions of farmers by helping them to form small-scale industries is regarded in some quarters as a barrier to Communism, in that it transforms misery and unemployment into security and shared ownership.[14]

It was hardly the sort of publicity Alley wanted on his security file back in China. But after the Communist victory, the objectives of Alley and the New Zealand establishment were increasingly at odds. The break between the two sides did not become immediately apparent. In the meantime, CORSO continued to reassure its donors.

Despite Alley's efforts to prove his political credibility overseas and in China, he still faced problems at the local level. The cadres who came to investigate the school after the liberation of Shandan were new recruits who were determined to prove their loyalty. Hence they found it easy to conclude that a foreign-run school in China must be imperialist. These assumptions were encouraged still further by teachers and students who resented Alley's power. These various groups made use of the evaluation of the school to cast aspersions on the intent of Alley and others in working there.

The first challenge to Alley's authority at the school after 1949 was led by K. L. Wu, former head of the Lanzhou Bailie School, which had been closed down in 1946 to save money and its staff and students relocated to Shandan.[15] Wu and his ambitious wife were opportunists who hoped to seize control of the Shandan Bailie School themselves. Though they associated with the Communists after 1949, when the Lanzhou school was closed down they had informed the Nationalist authorities that the teachers at the Shandan were Communists in the hope that they would be arrested. Soon after the Communist forces took over Shandan, Wu and his wife arrived at the school in the company of the newly appointed representative of the Bureau of Co-operatives in Lanzhou, under whose auspices the school was loosely controlled. Wu claimed that Alley had usurped his rightful position as headmaster of the Shandan Bailie School. His wife spread rumours that the foreign teachers there were agents of the US State Department. This attempt to gain power was unsuccessful as the Department of Co-operatives cadre ultimately supported Alley, but the allegations and machinations for power set a damaging precedent.

Other individuals at the school soon realised that the revolution offered chances of advancement. Once again the charge that the foreign teachers were agents was heard, when a group of what Shandan teacher Walter Illsley described as 'super revolutionary' students attempted a coup at the school.[16] The coup was defused by a sympathetic CCP cadre. Some of the teachers also took advantage of the new circumstances to improve their lot. Although immediately after the Communist victory teachers had voted as a patriotic gesture to take only subsistence wages, when the Department of

Co-operatives ordered staff to hold meetings to set a new pay scale, a large number voted themselves a huge pay rise. This led to a large deficit in the school's already limited accounts.

Even more serious was the discovery of Nationalist agents working amongst the Chinese teachers to stir up trouble at the school. After a petition was sent to the authorities in Peking complaining about the management of the school, Alley's adopted son Mike (Li Xue), by then a middle-level cadre in the CCP, was sent out from Peking to investigate. As a result of the investigation, two of the teachers confessed to being KMT agents and one hanged himself. That Alley was able to get his own son sent out to investigate the matter, rather than some unknown and possibly hostile cadre, shows that he was not without connections to assist him in his aim of staying on at Shandan and keeping the school going.

The dissension and fighting for advantage that the school suffered after 1949 was accentuated by Alley's frequent absences from this time on. The future of the Shandan Bailie School and those who worked for it went into limbo after the Communist take-over. Whereas during the state of chaos of the civil-war period the school was able to operate virtually independent of governmental control, with the stability of the new government came a need for the school to find an appropriate bureaucratic niche. Alley spent long periods in 1949, 1950 and 1951 in Peking trying to arrange a sponsor for the school. He hoped that the ideals of the school and its working style would be left intact by whichever government agency would agree to take it over. At the same time he was trying to renegotiate his own status in New China. Both tasks were made difficult by the fact that, since the school's status was in limbo, nobody was willing to guarantee Alley and his relationship with the school — even to allow him into the capital to negotiate his position.[17] Alley was forced to rely on connections made in his time in Shanghai in the 1930s to acquire a guarantee for his safe passage.

Alley's supporters in New Zealand, who since the withdrawal of UNRRA in 1947 had been providing most of the funding for the school, were simply told that he had gone to Peking to get urgent treatment for skin cancer. In fact he did need treatment for this complaint, but it by no means necessitated all the time he spent in Peking. Alley did not think it wise for his foreign supporters to be aware that he and his school were suffering under the new regime.

Contrary to the rosy version he portrayed in his public writing both during this time and later, the first few years after Liberation were a depressing time for Alley, particularly on a personal level. His two adopted sons did not share his views on the importance of Shandan-style education for China's future modernisation. The four sons of the Nie family, whom he had fostered since 1945, returned to live with their father in the north-east of China. Alley found that the new government was as bureaucratic, cruel and petty-minded as the last had been. It seemed that the work he had done for

Chinese people in the last fifteen years went unappreciated by China's new rulers, and was even resented in some quarters.

In addition to these personal woes, the new government was clearly uninterested in continuing the Bailie School's education programme. It was too closely associated with missionary activity, foreigners and the Nationalists to be a desirable model for New China. After much lobbying and making use of former connections, Alley was able to persuade the Oil Ministry to take over the school's facilities; but it insisted on relocating them to Lanzhou, the capital of Gansu Province. Though he was relieved that the Oil Ministry had decided to take over the school, Alley was hurt that all that he had worked for was not valued and was seen as imperialist by some. He felt particularly grieved by the attitude of his adopted sons to the school. He wrote to Alan (then assistant headmaster at the school) on what he described as the 'scuttling of Shandan':

> You must think me quite fanatical on this subject. But the single
> mind in following a thing through, is important, and I have tried to
> give up personal life in the past, and to put all into making this one
> idea come true . . . this will be a headache for you to read, as you do
> not believe in any of it I guess.[18]

He wrote with sadness to his friend Shirley Barton, 'I have not the faintest idea what I do next. Mike does not want me to go back to Shandan, nor does Alan, for the time being. They don't know much about the idea of Shandan though, I fear.'[19] On the subject of what he would always regard as his greatest achievement in life Alley wrote, 'The international group will not stay in Shandan, but will all go elsewhere to work, soon. The idea of a productive school has not come through – I have failed in trying to get this idea accepted. It is best to accept this all. There will be other struggles in other places.'[20]

For years afterwards Alley mourned the loss of what he still clearly saw as 'his' school, frustrated with the directions the Chinese government was taking in its economic and educational policies in the years after 1949. Though in his propaganda on behalf of the government he extolled the virtues of whatever the current line was, in private, and even in his earlier publications in the 1950s, his constant reference to the golden era of his days in Shandan reveal his inner dissatisfaction.

Shirley Barton, who was based in Shanghai at this time with the co-operative movement, was Alley's trusted intimate in the immediate years after Liberation. Reading through their correspondence of this period is an interesting preview to the schizophrenic style with which Alley would conduct his personal and public life after 1949. Alley trusted Barton, at least while she was still living in China. (Barton left in 1952 when it became clear that like most foreigners there at the time, there was no longer a role for her. She settled in Auckland where she became active in the New Zealand–China Friendship Society.) It was to Barton alone that Alley shared his true feelings at this time. Barton both consoled him and advised him on how he should adapt to the new government, making the most of his international fame to secure a new role. She was particularly concerned about the necessary reconstruction of Alley's public image – from apolitical humanitarian to outspoken supporter of Communism. She advised him,

> I would agree that you should continue the blunt, outspoken line which is natural to you and which you have already started, but merely cut out in your writings anything which would suggest that you have been an underground Communist all along and deceived those who gave support to CIC and Shandan by pretending you were a neutral humanitarian and not 'political'. This idea, that you deceived them into 'aiding Communism', (in their language) would antagonise many.[21]

Barton was concerned that Alley's supporters overseas might believe that he had become a Communist under duress or for opportunist reasons. She encouraged him to write that 'your experience through these many years of working in China and seeing the evils under colonial-imperialism . . . has led you bit by bit to realise that a radical change had to come.'[22] The new tack in his public image did not come easily to Alley and his letters at this time reflect the despair he felt. Still, he managed to write what was to become his most famous book, *Yo Banfa!* (*We Have a Way!*) during this period. In the introduction to the book, a glowing account of the miraculous changes occurring under the new government, he writes,

> So many achievements have been made in these last three years that the chroniclers of events find it hard to keep pace with them. But to one who has lived so long under the old, the thing that gets one is to see the light in two lads' eyes when, as they complete a job, they look at each other and say, almost with one voice, 'Yo banfa!' In this lies a whole new world of respect for themselves, for one another, for the endless potentialities of their people and for the glorious future that now faces their country.[23]

Yet at the same time as he composed this paean Shirley Barton wrote to him, 'It was apparent you had a hard time sticking to writing in that depressing hold time in Peking where most of book one was done.'[24] Barton was one of the few people to whom he showed his true feelings about the changes in China after 1949, and even then his comments were veiled. Alley was a compulsive letter writer, as much from loneliness as to promote his various causes. He was very conscious that even letters were a form of public statement, especially for someone like himself with a public reputation. A letter written in August 1952 to Shandan-worker Hugh Elliott demonstrates his awareness of the constraints he and other foreigners were under if they wished to stay on in New China. A letter of Elliott's having just been published in Canada, Alley wrote:

> Kind of nervous when I read the bit in the Canadian peace journal. People are liable to get hold of anything and give it a horrid twist that makes it into something else. The man who would write of things in China today, has to think of every kind of twist that every kind of person can give – the sheer distortion of the foreign press are shocking on most everything. So one can hardly say anything except sheer fact or progress when we have it, and no comment when it dallies at all. Such is the nature of these shite hawks that anything else is seized upon and made into something else. So in letters, I think we should remember this very carefully.[25]

Alley was very aware that his position under the new regime was precarious. The antagonism towards Alley and those associated with him at the school came to a head when the *Sanfan* movement began in early 1952. *Sanfan yundong*, known in English as the Three Antis Movement, was 'to oppose corruption, waste and bureaucracy inside the Party and state organs.'[26] During *Sanfan* Alley was accused of being an agent of Western powers, authoritarian and overbearing, a reactionary spy and an anti-revolutionary. Curiously, among the many things that he was accused of during this campaign and later when he became a target in the Cultural Revolution, he was never criticised for his homosexual affairs. It was simply not regarded as a crime by those who were aware of it; and, perhaps because so many at Shandan were themselves homosexually inclined, there was no incentive to publicise the matter. Moreover, as Alley became useful to the Chinese Communist Government as a public figure, it was in everyone's interest that his 'clean' image be maintained. That it was not regarded as a crime by those in the know is an indication that despite the public harassment of homosexuals in China after 1949, social tolerance continued on some level.

Alley was fortunate that the accusations against him were simply invective – a number of cadres known to be his supporters were falsely accused of corruption, accused by others with a grudge against them. They received harsh punishments, undoubtedly as examples to the citizens of Shandan of the line the new regime intended to take on opponents to its rule. Alley felt particularly responsible about one of the accusations because he had originally approved the man's actions. The former school official was accused of taking a load of Friends Service Unit-donated clothes for himself though, as Alley wrote guiltily to adopted son Alan, 'He reported that he had them to me on arrival ... I thought it alright for him to keep them.'[27] Alley did not protest publicly about the injustice; to do so would have added to his own troubles. Though they too knew better than to speak out, some of the other foreign workers were scathing in their comments on the affair in their letters. Hugh Elliott wrote to Alley in Beijing, 'Sanfan was finally wound up the other day. Fan Wenhai [student manager of the school coal mine] to pay back 13,000 [sic], Gao Qianti 10,000. FWH [sic] thought before it was going to be 7 million. He's out at San Ba working on the farm where he'll be, theoretically, for many years. The whole business stinks and is stupid.'[28] Both Elliott and Alley knew that the days of foreigners having extraterritorial privilege in China were long gone and it was safer, both for the foreigner and the accused Chinese, if they kept their opinions to themselves in the hope that justice would be done in the long run.

The mud that was thrown during the Sanfan movement stuck, and Rewi Alley and the students who had attended the Bailie School were never quite trusted by the new regime. These allegations were to stay on Alley's file and those of the other teachers and students at the school until 1977, when they were finally cleared in the period after the Cultural Revolution.[29]

Following Sanfan, Alley's position at Shandan was untenable. Alley was very reluctant to leave the school and it was hard for him to accept that he was no longer wanted there. Nevertheless, it was clear he could not stay on, even in retirement.[30] Mike Alley, who stayed on at the school for a period after completing the investigation into the school's political problems, wrote to Liu Ding (a senior Communist cadre who had known Alley in Shanghai) asking for his father to be assigned a position in the new government.[31] As a result of Mike's letter and good connections, Alley and Courtney Archer received a telegram in June 1952 inviting then to come immediately to Peking to act as New Zealand's representatives at the preparatory conference for the Asia–Pacific Peace Conference, China's contribution to the Soviet-dominated international peace movement. It was the beginning of a new role for Alley in China, that of propagandist for the CCP and New China.

With some relief, Shirley Barton wrote to Mike, 'I was so thankful Rewi was called to Peking to attend the preparatory conference for the Asia–Pacific Peace Conference. He and Courtney have done and will do good work for New Zealand and international peace relations. Rewi is a famous name still in New Zealand and is also well known in other countries, so can have a good influence on many people overseas.'[32] Barton advised that it should be put about that Rewi Alley and the other foreigners left the school because they were no longer required in peacetime, not that they had left unwillingly.[33] The other foreigners at the school were also relieved at news of the invitation, since it bode well for their own acceptance by the government. Max Wilkinson wrote to Shirley Barton soon after Alley and Archer's departure, 'We were all frightfully bucked at Rewi and Courtney being asked to go to Peking. It proves that Rewi is not the imperialist or Social

Democrat that many people would like to make out. His going was very dramatic – 18 hours after the telegram arrived they were off.'[34]

Mike Alley was relieved at the departures for another reason, since it resolved the issue of what was to be done about Alley's future after the bitterness of *Sanfan*. His letter to Shirley Barton reveals the extent of the hostility towards Alley:

> I think that all of us think that [Rewi] should not come back here. The task of rooting out the prejudices would be a long job. It would be better if he, and us for that matter, were working somewhere else where this suspicion and hate does not exist. Besides nearly all the constructive elements with whom Rewi or we others could work are sent away so that the remaining group would be difficult to say the least.[35]

As it became clear to Alley after this final departure from the school that he would not be allowed to return, he tried to make the best of it in letters to those of the Chinese staff who still supported him. In September 1952 he told them,

> It has been a thrill to try and make Shandan work, and to turn out creative technicians. However, the stage in which we could help a bit seems to have passed by and more people come. . . . It will never be easy to think of Shandan without emotion. There has been so much that has been rich in that seemingly poorest of all places.[36]

He was more truthful about how he really felt to the foreigners with whom he had worked at the school. To Don Kemp he wrote from Peking,

> I'm not doing anything much at the moment, except eating and sleeping and seeing friends at times. Not exactly an inspiring time for me, but it seems to be my fate to live an uneventful sort of existence like this – so what? No word yet of permission to come back to Shandan. . . . Naturally I think of Shandan a lot.[37]

To Wolf Rosenberg, a supporter in New Zealand, he gave yet another version of events:

> I myself am on long leave from Shandan in order to make what small contribution I can to the success of the great meeting of peace fighters here in September . . . in the matter of AID, it is now felt that China's need is not so great as the needs of the struggling peace and friendly relations movements which are doing such valuable work in those countries, and that the best way for friends overseas to

help the Chinese people now is to put all their efforts into maintenance and furthering of these friendly relations and the cause of
world peace ... as to activities for the future, may I venture to
suggest that your group form the nucleus of a New Zealand China
Friendship association, with which I should feel honoured to keep
in contact and give any help in my power.[38]

The letter marked the beginnings of Alley's efforts to transform the support
base in New Zealand that had generously funded his activities in CIC into
support for Communist China and its cause for international recognition.

In 1954 the Bailie School was shifted to Lanzhou, the capital of Gansu
Province, and renamed the Lanzhou Oil School. 'Rewi's School' was a thing
of the past. Not only was there no longer a role for Alley and the other foreigners at the school, the whole philosophy of the school – of combining
work and study – were rejected by the Chinese education authorities. In the
1950s China adopted the Soviet model for education, stressing theory and
rote-learning over practice. Alley's educational views were regarded as out-
dated,[39] not least because they originated from a foreigner coming from a
capitalist country. The school was renamed since, as Alan wrote in a letter to
his father, it was thought that the original name, the Bailie School, was 'apt
to make people think of religion.'[40] Both of Alley's adopted Chinese sons
assisted in sorting out the problems of the Shandan Bailie School. Alan
eventually became the headmaster of the school after it was moved to
Lanzhou, while Mike worked in the Oil Ministry responsible for overseeing
the school. Alley and those who had supported him at Shandan tried to persuade the new government to continue his connection with the school in the
interests of good publicity, to no avail. Courtney Archer wrote that maintaining Alley's connection with the Bailie school would be a 'concrete
example of the respect the People's Government has for Rewi's work in the
last 25 years.'[41] As a palliative to this view, Alley's foreign supporters were
informed that he was now the 'honorary headmaster' of the Lanzhou School,
though this had no meaning in real terms. In practice, he had little more to
do with the school than the information he received through his adopted son
Alan Alley. After 1966, when the Cultural Revolution began, even this title
was taken away from Alley.

7

FRIEND OF CHINA

Following his urgent summons to Peking to act as New Zealand's representative at the preparatory meeting for the Asia–Pacific Peace Conference, Alley was immediately put to work on China's 'peace' propagandising. On 11 and 12 June 1952 he read a speech on Peking Radio criticising New Zealand's participation in the Korean War. This speech was broadcast to both Australia and New Zealand:

> New Zealand, as part of Australasia, can have only one real interest, and that interest must be for peace, and the security she needs to develop herself. To have a lasting peace in New Zealand there must be a just peace in Asia. Factual, geographical links of our country with Asia makes that an imperative necessity. Yet the recognition of that necessity is too often obliterated by considerations that would link New Zealand only with the old Europe, instead of with our immediate neighbours whose destiny must finally be our destiny.... There are economic and cultural links that can be forged to bring the peoples of Asia and Pacific together and make for a new base for understanding.... New Zealanders must ask themselves: 'Why have the old militarists been brought back in Japan? Why are the Japanese peoples' organisations suppressed? What may that mean to New Zealand? Why do Americans oppose a settlement in Korea, while giving it lip service? Who wants to kill whom? Who wants to make money by war?'[1]

To the present-day reader, Alley's comments on New Zealand's relationship with Asia might seem quite reasonable in the current political and economic climate, when even conservative governments make the claim that New Zealand is a part of Asia. Indeed, his views seem almost visionary when one considers how intertwined the New Zealand economy has become with its Asian partners. But this shift came about only when New Zealand's prized favoured relationship with British markets was cut off, after the UK entered the European Union. In 1952, Alley's comments were regarded by the New

Zealand government as radical and dangerous: for in that year New Zealand was closely tied to the USA and its foreign policy through the UKUSA and ANZUS security agreements and was soon to sign SEATO (South-East Asia Treaty Organisation); was engaged in an undeclared war against the Communist countries of China and North Korea through its participation in the UN force in Korea; and the anti-Communist hysteria of McCarthyism was in full swing in the USA. As an obedient member of the Western alliance New Zealand could not afford to step out of line and publicly question why former Japanese militarists were being rearmed or why New Zealand was fighting a war in Korea.[2] A few days after his broadcast urging New Zealand to rethink its strategic relationship with the USA, Alley also broadcast a message to New Zealand supporting Chinese and North Korean claims that the USA was using germ warfare in the Korean War (reported in the New Zealand press on 17 June 1952).[3] The message reiterated earlier statements Alley had made regarding the allegations, which had initially been reported in 1951, to emphatic denials of the USA and the UN.

Alley's opinions on China and New Zealand–China relations held great weight in New Zealand at this time and his views on the Korean War were regarded extremely seriously by both the government and ordinary people. Many New Zealanders did not feel comfortable with the idea of being part of a close military alliance with the US government. They believed that US militarism was as much a threat as Soviet militarism. A writer to the *Press*, signing him/herself 'Not a Communist,' wrote in response to Alley's comments,

> It is a relief to see that some New Zealanders and men of other countries have the common sense and broad outlook to 'denounce the American invasion of Korea.' Who can grasp the Korean campaign better than the world famous Rewi Alley?.... And for those who will say that this Chinese report [on germ warfare] is propaganda, it is no more propaganda than any exhortatory American report.[4]

Another writer commented, 'To this student of current affairs most of the news we get about China is obviously influenced by the Dollar Barbarians and such as Rewi Alley can put fresh air into the sewer gas.'[5] Years later, Alley's biographer Willis Airey wrote to him summing up the conflicting views in New Zealand on Alley's status in New China and the reasons for his pro-Communist statements: 'I remember how people wondered how you would get on when the Communists were in control. You were either saving China from Communism as it was understood by some – Stalin tyranny and all that – or you were not free to talk and anything that emerged you said with a pistol at your back.'[6] Airey's comments reflect the deep awe and patriotism Alley stirred in his fellow-countrymen, to the extent that some of them believed he could even influence the political behaviour of the new Chinese government.

Letters in New Zealand papers supporting Alley's viewpoint on China and the Korean War far outweighed those opposing it. If he was to have a role under the new regime, this was just the sort of support that would help him to achieve it. Shirley Barton was among those who tried to persuade him to return to New Zealand, if not permanently, at least for a speaking tour before the peace conference to strengthen New Zealand–China relations. She coaxed him, 'While you still remain in the public eye and are a controversial figure, crowds would flock to hear you speak all over New Zealand, even if many came only out of curiosity. It would be a great opportunity to tell them what you stand for and what New China means and give lie to the enemy who try to make you out a puppet mouthpiece buying residence in China by "voicing the Communist line" etc.'[7]

The allegations of those Barton called 'the enemy' were painfully close to the truth. As Alley and Barton had discussed in their letters, Alley's public support for the official Communist line was indeed part of his bid to stay on in the country where he had lived for twenty-two years. Despite the urging of Barton and others, Alley refused to leave China while his position there was still undecided. Instead, Alley's friend and co-worker Courtney Archer travelled back to New Zealand in mid 1952 to drum up support for the peace conference. At the same time, he did his best to introduce Alley's new image to the New Zealand public. Archer's views were reported favourably by the New Zealand Communist Party (NZCP) newspaper *People's Voice*, less so by other papers. Archer wrote to Barton, 'We asked the Auckland papers if they were interested in a story and they said NO. There is a blanket of silence over all peace work in this country.'[8] Archer stated publicly that 'Rewi Alley's 25 year struggle for the betterment of the Chinese race has found embodiment in the present People's Government,'[9] and this was reported in *People's Voice*. This stance fitted in well with standard Communist Party tactics to get apolitical public figures to espouse shared points of interest with the revolutionary cause. Alley and his perceived close links with the CCP would be an important connection for the NZCP in the future.

The New Zealand government was very concerned about Alley's influence on New Zealand public opinion and acted to oppose his views. His criticism of New Zealand's participation in the Korean War and support for allegations of the use of germ warfare in Korea were a threat to the nation's new security arrangements. Yet, the government could not afford to oppose him directly since, as late as December 1951, it had allocated £4,000 to the Shandan school and on many occasions had endorsed Alley's work in China. In mid 1952 the government was still debating whether or not to send more money to the school.[10] As a sanction against Chinese participation in the Korean War, all other international support to the school had stopped soon after the war began.[11] Yet New Zealand's CORSO, which received much of its funding from the New Zealand government, only stopped sending money when its representative in China informed it that the school was now being fully supported by the Chinese government. In fact the Oil Ministry of the new government had merely agreed to take over the most valuable equipment of the school, relocating it to Lanzhou; and most of the former teachers had been dispersed, many of them under severe political suspicion for their links with a Western-funded school. It did not suit CORSO to make its donors aware of the pressure foreigners were under in China and that the massive amounts of aid New Zealand had given went unappreciated and was in fact a problem for the school.

The New Zealand government had benefited from the favourable international attention 'Rewi's school' at Shandan and his work with CIC had brought to New Zealand in the past fifteen years. It had no official representative in the PRC and relied on Alley and CORSO for information about was happening at the school. It too had no desire to stir up criticism of public funding of Rewi Alley's activities in China. In 1951, a senior diplomat advised the government that with regard to the CORSO assistance to Alley, and Alley's criticism of germ warfare in Korea, 'I don't think there is anything we can do, unless it be discourage CORSO activities in China, and I don't see why we should do that.'[12] New Zealand politicians had to be mindful of the popular support that Alley enjoyed in his home country. In the 1940s and 1950s, Alley was a folk hero and his work in China had tremendous support and prestige.

In addition to the government's need to appear to be lenient on Alley for reasons of public image, compared to some of the extremist politicians in Australia and the United States, the New Zealand government took a more relaxed attitude to the threat of international Communism. The comments of R. M. Algie, Minister in Charge of Broadcasting, to F. P. Walsh, President of the New Zealand Federation of Labour, in a 1953 letter are typical of the government's position. Algie wrote, 'the best way I know for helping our people to reject Communist philosophy is not to turn one's back upon it but to get it out into the open and meet it with the better way of life we have been lucky enough to inherit.'[13]

The claim that US forces in Korea had used germ warfare received worldwide attention. The USA and the UN emphatically denied the allegations. Whether they were true or not, the claims were a major blow to Western propaganda in the Cold War. Recent research seems to prove conclusively that the germ-warfare allegations were a hoax.[14] At the time that the accusations were made, the USA needed to convince its allies and its own people that the war in Korea, where millions of lives were lost, was a just cause, a necessary war in the face of a potential tide of Communist aggression worldwide. According to this line of rhetoric, the West represented democracy, freedom of speech and a just cause, while the Communist forces symbolised totalitarianism, inhumanity and oppression. Hence to slur this righteous crusade with the taint of germ warfare, which, as would have been fresh in the memory of many in the 1950s, previously only the Nazis had attempted, was a major blow to the West's credibility.[15] What the USA did not want publicly known is that, from around 1942, it was probably the leading country engaged in the research and development of bacteriological and chemical weapons. After World War Two, when it pardoned germ-warfare researchers in Japan and Germany in return for their expertise and research, the USA became the greatest repository for knowledge about germ warfare in the world. Indeed, as we now know, the Americans had even conducted experiments on their own people.

Shirley Barton described the attitude of many New Zealanders to Rewi Alley's support for the germ-warfare allegations in a letter to a New Zealand fundraiser. First, she said, a Peace Council member in Christchurch had written to her that 'Rewi is just about worshipped by the workers here.' And the Christchurch student newspaper had reprinted a Chinese article on germ warfare on their front page, citing that Rewi Alley, 'the great New Zealander', testified the charge as true. A 'worker at a peace meeting' had said, 'If Rewi Alley believes that germ warfare is being used by the Americans, I believe it too!' Barton concluded that the New Zealand government was

> in rather an amusing spot there, having built up Rewi for years as a 'great humanitarian' and given big material support during the relief years, so cannot very well refuse him a hearing now and still claim to be unprejudiced. Moreover he has a number of very respectable relatives in educational positions and comes of a well-known middle-class pioneering family. Anyhow these contradictions can be made good use of by the peace movement and they are busy making hay.[16]

Commenting on an editorial in the *Press* in 20 June 1952 on Alley's claims of germ warfare in Korea, Barton wrote,

> They are much too clever to denounce you as a 'Communist agitator' as some have done. This might alienate and sow doubt in the minds of many people in New Zealand who have been taught to regard you as a man of integrity. So they leave you your 'humanitarian' reputation, and even 'intelligence'. . . . This attitude would be very convincing to the average New Zealand reader unless he had a factual answer on each point.[17]

Nevertheless, Alley's support for the Chinese intervention in the Korean War and his support for germ-warfare allegations were taken much more seriously by the New Zealand government than his earlier endorsement of

New China had been. At first it was said that Alley had made the statements on germ warfare 'under compulsion.' Some observers speculated that he had been impersonated or brainwashed, or perhaps was not quite in touch with events having been in a remote part of China for so long.[18] All of these claims were emphatically refuted by Alley; he stated publicly that he had not written under any compulsion other than his own heart, and that he was well aware of what was going on in the world.[19] Alley's prestige in New Zealand was so high at this time that even the arch-conservative, pro-British Empire organisation the Legion of Frontiersmen (of which Alley had once been a member) turned down a remit to dissociate itself from Alley's pro-Communist statements because, it said, 'He may think his school is of supreme importance, and we do not know in effect whether he made those broadcasts with a pistol at his back.'[20]

The Publicity and Information Division of the Department of Tourism and Publicity reported to the government the alarming news that a survey conducted in Wellington had demonstrated that many people were more likely to believe Alley's viewpoint on the matter of germ warfare in Korea than they were to accept the denials of the government.[21] The Orwellian 'Publicity and Information Division' was responsible for providing the government with material on Communist Party, Peace Council and other 'subversive-type' activities. It also provided disinformation, often received from British or American sources, on such activities, which New Zealand newspapers were asked to print without the government source being disclosed. The division watched closely the activities of Alley's associate Courtney Archer, who, officials believed, had returned to New Zealand with the purpose of trying to 'build up Rewi Alley and use Rewi Alley's attitude to the Communist government in China, which is one of admiration, as proof of the goodness of the Communists.'[22]

The New Zealand government was seriously concerned by the germ-warfare allegations and the threat they posed to the credibility of New Zealand's involvement in the Korean War. A report was prepared for the government on the allegations entitled 'Germ Warfare: Reasons for Disbelieving Communist Propaganda.' That the New Zealand government found it necessary to commission such a report implied that some within the administration did not completely accept US refutations. The following reasons for disbelieving the allegations were listed:

1   UN denial. Troops of 19 nations are fighting in Korea – would not allow such action.
2   Communist refusal to allow investigation by WHO or Red Cross – plan to include neutral experts in epidemiology, including scientists from Asian countries not participating in the war.
3   Faked evidence by Communists – photos of insects shown as fakes, bombs were those used for propaganda leaflets.

4   Epidemic history of Korea – cholera, plague, and typhus common in
    China and Korea therefore not newly introduced. Self-spreading
    diseases; assisted by environmental factors ie. temperature, presence of
    carriers – not within control of humanity.[23]

The government believed that Rewi Alley's name was being used in the propaganda campaign to promote the germ-warfare allegations as a cover for
the NZCP, which often used important and influential non-political figures
such as Alley to represent Communist Party goals or issues to the general
public. One report concluded that 'In fact, it would be true to say that the
remarkable progress the campaign has made in New Zealand has been
mainly due, first to the build-up given to Rewi Alley, and then to the use
that has been made of him.'[24] Another report commented that Alley's June
broadcast regarding germ warfare on Peking Radio gave considerable
impetus to the campaign, since 'many, relying on Mr Alley's reputation as
an outstanding welfare worker and politically disinterested, believe it
unlikely he will lend himself to further a Communist hoax.'[25]

Although the government's primary concern was with the activities of
the New Zealand Communist Party at this time, Alley became a target
because his name was being used to influence the New Zealand public. The
government was obliged to work to destroy Alley's reputation in order to
counter the germ-warfare allegations. In response to what the Publicity
Division called the 'Communist challenge to democracy,' the New Zealand
government began to take a more forceful approach. The question of
whether Alley and other 'Communists' within New Zealand could be
accused of treason for their support of the forces against the United Nations
in the Korean War was considered.[26] It was rejected, however, probably
because it would have been too unpopular a move. Instead, the government
began a disinformation campaign against Alley and those who were opposed
to the government's foreign policy. Anti-Communist material from the
British Foreign Office was passed on to New Zealand papers without the
source being disclosed.

Editors of New Zealand's major newspapers participated willingly in the
anti-Alley campaign. The main paper in Alley's home city of Christchurch,
where support for him was strongest, likened his activities for the Chinese to
the work of Goebbels for the Nazis and called him 'a Moscow agent on a
propaganda mission.'[27] The conservative paper *Otago Daily Times*, which
printed the student magazine *Critic*, admitted censoring an issue of the magazine that had outlined germ-warfare allegations and included a letter from
Rewi Alley, as well as an editorial that referred to Alley as a 'great New
Zealander.'[28] An unofficial prohibition on mentioning Alley's name on radio
operated for a time, as Shirley Barton discovered when she returned to New
Zealand and tried to publicise Alley's views. She wrote to a friend working
in Peking, 'Rewi Alley's name is banned on the air.'[29]

Alley chafed at the inactivity of his new role as a Peking 'peace activist,' so different from his busy life in Shandan. He told Barton, 'everyone is most considerate and kind. It is just that I feel a bit useless, I guess. However, one does learn a lot.'[30] Along with most Chinese people at this time, Alley took part in political study classes where he read selected works of Marxism-Leninism and a few translations of writings by Chinese Marxist theorists such as Liu Shaoqi. He reported facetiously, 'I'm still going around getting my education attended to. Do learn a lot, as well as have a good rest.'[31] Barton was one of the few people who knew the problems Alley was facing under the new regime. She told him 'I'm trying to take everything quietly as you advise and not get too vehement. It's tough on you having to "hawk your own wares" and one would like to have spared you this cross.'[32]

Alley's position in New China was not secure, and he found it particularly hard to accept that he was not allowed to return to Shandan where he believed he still had useful work to do. Worried about her friend's unsettled state of mind, Barton counselled him:

I do hope you will try to put your full interest and enthusiasm into the present situation and its tasks wherever you go in the next few months. There should be some wonderful things to see in the north and you have the background to understand them. I was painfully conscious of your pre-occupation with Shandan – almost to an obsessional degree – a danger for people of strong feelings and energy. It is no use trying to go into the ins and outs here. I wish very much I could listen to you talk about the whole thing, bit by bit, as I have never been able to do. We should all be able to analyse it correctly and objectively now and put this on record. I don't think you should feel that Shandan was something handed to you as a sacred trust by George Hogg. I don't feel that a young man like George if he had lived and kept progressing in the same direction, as I think he would have, would feel he had the right to say, before Liberation, that you should both determine to spend the rest of your lives there regardless of the completely changed situation when the New China came about. This thinking is too emotional and subjective, and maybe too possessive. Right for that time when holding and protection were essential, but not right to go on holding one's arm in the dyke when the flood is over. . . . Time to . . . assess the new situation and get a wider perspective, and a new view of one's future sphere of usefulness, whether in that place or elsewhere. Whichever it is to be in the future I think the period of going out widely all over New China as you are privileged to do will be a terrific help to your future work and mental and spiritual health if you can really give yourself to it for the time being. Not forget Shandan, but exercise some discipline about worrying and giving only half-hearted attention to the glorious present. This should be an experience of joy and triumph to you. I'm sure it is. Don't spoil it by brooding over what at present can't be helped.[33]

Barton's advice was practical and kind-hearted, but it could not prevent Alley from worrying about the future of the Bailie School and his powerlessness to protect the workers there. In addition to the accusations of corruption against some of the Chinese teachers, Walter Illsley, an American teacher, was expelled on suspicions of being a spy. In some frustration Alley wrote to Barton, 'I cannot do very much, if anything. Mike cannot either. No one will take responsibility. Peace people can only act on home Peace Committee note.'[34]

In addition to study classes and the occasional broadcast, Alley occupied himself by working on writing projects at his new base in Peking. He had been asked by the Chinese Peace Committee to write a book comparing the new China with the old. The book that resulted, *Yo Banfa!*, would become his most famous work. Copies of *Yo Banfa!* were distributed to every delegate at the peace conference.[35] The title *Yo Banfa!* means 'there is a way' (*you banfa* in later Chinese romanisation). Alley claimed that after 1949 people in China began to say '*you banfa*' instead of the fatalistic '*mei banfa*' (nothing can be done), commonly heard in pre-Communist days. *Yo Banfa!* contrasted life in the days of foreign imperialism and civil war with that in New China. It carefully distinguished between the behaviour of exploitative foreigners and international friends of New China such as Alley. For the first time, Alley was required to write about things he had not personally observed, and he initially found this difficult. He wrote cryptically at this time, 'Theory without practice does not act for me, very well.'[36]

Yo Banfa! was the means to reconstruct Alley's public image; in writing it he had to follow a careful line between portraying himself as someone who had been a Communist all along and someone who had recently discovered Communism. The book's editors, Shirley Barton and Bill Powell, removed all references to Alley's early contacts with the CCP because, Barton told Alley, a book published in the USA claimed that 'Agnes Smedley was part of a Shanghai group "conspiring" to set up Communism in China. It would play into their hands if they could say you were part of this group of "conspirators" from the start.'[37] Moreover, the Peace Committee gave a directive that anything in *Yo Banfa!* 'which will make peace work difficult, should be cut.'[38] What this meant, in practice, was that Alley had to appear to be politically neutral, yet also pro-CCP. Barton wrote to Alley that she was 'ruthlessly removing all direct declarations of the "I am a Communist" variety. This made my heart bleed, but now that you are in the peace movement I think it has to be done. People here will understand this. Also where meetings are held in the book to farewell volunteers, discuss arms for Korea etc I've said "they" instead of "we".'[39]

Plate 7.1 Rewi Alley with Asian delegates, Asia–Pacific Peace Conference, near Peking, 1952.

Source: Kathleen Wright papers, Alexander Turnbull Library, NZ. Page 242.

The Chinese-organised Asia–Pacific Peace Conference took place from 2 to 12 October 1952, after a preparatory conference from 3 to 6 June. Although Western observers at the time frequently lumped them together, the peace movement in China was to some extent separate from the Soviet peace movement. Hosting the Asia–Pacific Peace Conference gave China an opportunity to carve out its own sphere of influence, separate from the Soviet Union. The conference also signalled China's willingness to work with, and seek support from, non-Communist countries. The conference began with much fanfare; it was the first major international conference to be held in the PRC and the Peking Hotel was rebuilt just to house its delegates. Topics discussed were 'the Japanese question, the Korean question, cultural exchange, economic exchange, national independence, the Five Power Peace Pact, women's rights and child welfare.'[40] Peace delegates were given spending money while in China, as well as free food, travel and accommodation. Security personnel followed them wherever they went and monitored their conversations with Chinese people.[41] In addition to attending the conference, participants were given tours of select sites to brief them on the improvements of life in the PRC. The conference was the first time that foreigners were allowed to visit China in large numbers since the

Communist victory. Ormond Wilson, a New Zealand Labour Party politician, commented at the time that the conference was 'taken almost universally in the West to have been a propagandist dodge on the part of the Communists to weaken Western opposition to Communism.'[42]

The Western powers watched Chinese peace efforts closely. Sir Lionel Lamb, HM Chargé d'Affaires in Peking, reported to the Foreign Office that the peace conference had been,

> from the Chinese point of view, a resounding success. The Chinese People's Government had spared no effort and expense to make it so; the Diplomatic Corps in Peking had estimated that it must have cost the equivalent of more than £300,000 to stage. There was little doubt that a delegate from, say, Brazil could hardly have failed to be impressed at having his full fare paid both ways, and being invited, on arrival in Peking, to equip himself with a complete wardrobe and anything else he might fancy, all at the expense of the Chinese Government.[43]

A report from the British Foreign Office noted that 1952 marked the emergence of China as a leader in spreading the 'peace movement' to the Far East:

> By the most flattering hospitality the Chinese have converted most of the woolly minded delegates into useful apostles of the 'Peace Movement'. The two conferences and the permanent 'Peace Liaison Committee' that stemmed from them have overhauled the machinery of the 'Peace Movement' in the Far East and left it poised for further activities as requisite, by overt sedition in Japan, Malaya and Indo-China and by 'United Front' infiltration elsewhere.[44]

The timing of the Asia–Pacific Peace Conference in late 1952 was significant in that it was considered that most of the activities to eliminate imperialist influence in China had been completed by this time.[45] Now that the polluting foreign influence was destroyed or at least under control, the PRC focused on increasing its interactions with other countries, seeking diplomatic recognition, trade and technology. In this period only a handful of nations had officially recognised the CCP-led government, most from the Soviet bloc. As a result of the Chinese support for the North Korean side in the Korean War, the USA had imposed an embargo on China trade and most Western countries complied to varying degrees. In order to break through this political and economic blockade, the CCP focused on a strategy that drew on its experiences as a guerrilla force before 1949, that of forming short-term allegiances with organisations or individuals to work towards a common goal or oppose a common enemy. This strategy, known as the United Front (in Chinese *tongyi zhanxian*), originated from the Comintern and was one of the most important elements of the victory of the CCP in the Civil War. A United Front could be at either government-to-government, political-party-to-political-party, or 'people-to-people' level. People-to-people relations (*minjian waijiao*) are what other countries might refer to as 'cultural relations' or second-tier diplomacy. All countries engage in cultural relations as an element of their foreign policy to some degree. However, in what used to be the socialist world, people-to-people relations had an especially significant role; that of influencing public opinion in the non-socialist world.[46]

In part because of the economic and political blockade that the PRC faced in the 1950s and 1960s and as a result of the Soviet system it was modelled on, but also, and most importantly, because CCP senior leaders desired to create a new era of Sino-foreign relations, the PRC developed a much more comprehensive approach to foreign relations than is the norm in other countries. A complex foreign-affairs system (*waishi xitong*) evolved, which included organisations that dealt with both state-to-state and people's diplomacy, laws and guidelines regulating where and how foreigners were allowed to live, do business, marry, give birth and go to school, as well as covering such aspects as foreign propaganda, tourism and trade.[47] The ability to control, rather than be controlled by, foreign relations was one of the key elements for the CCP's claim to legitimacy to rule in China. A speech given by Foreign Minister Zhou Enlai in the mid-1950s to foreign-affairs officials demonstrates the revolutionary tack the PRC aimed to take in its foreign relations in the Mao era. Zhou told the diplomats that a nation must always be ready to defend itself with 'a war of words and a war of swords.' Diplomacy, their role, was concerned with the war of words. China must seek to establish itself in a hostile world that did not yet recognise its existence. Zhou's strategy against this was to use the 'war of words' to influence public opinion in the world towards China. Zhou divided the capitalist world into three forces: the warmongers, those wishing to maintain the *status quo*, and the peacemakers. Zhou's method was to win over the peace forces, influence the forces for the *status quo* and isolate the warmongers, thereby creating a United Front for peace in international relations.[48]

People's diplomacy activities went into a higher gear in China after 1952, with the numbers of visitors increasing considerably. People's diplomacy was an important means for conducting the CCP's foreign relations in the period when most countries recognised the Republic of China (ROC), rather than the People's Republic. In accordance with the strategy known as 'using the people to bring the governments closer together,' *yi min cu guan*,[49] beginning in 1952 a number of Chinese 'people's' organisations were formed to enable China to engage in official 'non-official' trade, political and cultural relations with those countries that did not officially recognise the PRC. By staging the Asia–Pacific Conference in 1952, China tried to forge a United Front with peace activists in the Asia–Pacific region, using their support to subvert the anti-China policies of their governments.

Alley enjoyed high status at the conference: he travelled separately from the other New Zealand delegates in his own chauffeur-driven car while they went around by bus.[50] Some in the New Zealand peace movement questioned his selection as a Kiwi delegate (and indeed the fact he had been selected by the Chinese rather than New Zealand peace groups),[51] for he had never previously participated in peace activities, had not visited his home country for sixteen years and seemed to show no inclination to return there. Nevertheless, Alley's name was well known in New Zealand and he enjoyed high prestige; the conference organisers perceived, quite rightly, that having Alley's name associated with a Chinese-organised peace conference would encourage interest and support for it in New Zealand and other countries where Alley was known.

Although he had never been associated with the peace movement before, after his debut at the Peking conference, the New Zealand delegates asked him to come back to New Zealand with them and participate in peace activities. Alley was reluctant to return. 'The New Zealand delegates say I must go back with them,' he told brother Pip. 'This does not seem very wise, for after a month or so I am finished and then have to start and find a way to earn a living there – which at 55, with various kinds of troubles, is not so easy. Don't expect that I shall get back to Shandan ever – but we have done our work there and it stands, so never mind. Maybe it is best to make a break, though I have felt that perhaps my best function was working in trying to interpret from this end.'[52]

Before the conference had even begun, Alley's New Zealand family had been pressuring him to return, especially because Alley's mother Clara was sick with cancer and close to death. Alley still refused to go, afraid that he would not be given a passport by the New Zealand government and would be stuck there with no funds to move, while his position in China was still uncertain.[53] Having spent the previous fifteen years working in the Chinese hinterland, Alley knew virtually nothing about contemporary New Zealand society at that time and even less about New Zealand activities. During the preparatory peace conference he wrote, 'Wish I knew more about the New Zealand peace movement. I have just had the press in asking about it.'[54] Nor was he particularly patriotic. Indeed Shirley Barton scolded Alley for his patronising attitude to New Zealand:

> I feel a little ashamed of you when you make slighting remarks about your native country.... I think you just mean the smug middle-class in New Zealand who exaggerate their importance in the world scene, but you should take care to make this plainer. As for the working-class (and the more decent intellectuals) many of them are still unawakened, it is true, but they need patriots, not people glad to shake the dust off their heels in contempt.[55]

Plate 7.2 Rewi Alley, Peking, 1950s.
Source: Photograph courtesy of Joy Alley.

After the conference, Alley was invited to become a 'peace worker,' nominally representing New Zealand on the Chinese-run Asian and Pacific Peace Liaison Committee, part of the Chinese Peace Committee. His official status in China was as a 'permanent guest' of the Chinese Peace Committee, a reward given to a handful of other foreigners who had been helpful to the CCP and were not needed in any other capacity. The Asian and Pacific Peace Liaison Committee was funded and organised by the Chinese Government, although officially it was an independent 'people's organisation.' It had representatives from the Soviet Union, the USA, North Korea, Thailand, Japan, New Zealand, Chile and China. Alley's duties were light; it was a symbolic appointment rather than an activist's one. Committee members kept in touch with peace groups world-wide, held occasional meetings to discuss national liberation movements in other countries and took part in peace demonstrations in China. Had Alley wanted to, he could have led a quiet, comfortable life in Peking with only minimal responsibilities. But Alley soon began to direct as much energy to his new role as he had to his work in Shandan.

Alley's new role involved taking an active part in the 'war of words,' a role that would require more than ever before an effort on his own part to maintain his status as a public persona whose opinions others would be willing to listen to. Up until 1966, when the Peace Committee was closed down, despite having only marginal contact with the New Zealand peace movement, Alley regularly attended international peace conferences as a self-described New Zealand delegate. Alley had such limited contact with New Zealand peace activists that he was forced to write to friends and family for news. He urged Barton, 'Do encourage all and sundry to write to me on their views on peace and the Pacific – otherwise I'm pretty cut off. Liaison means that lots of people must write.'[56] The mere two lines he rated in the authoritative history of the New Zealand peace movement summed up the attitude of New Zealand peace campaigners to Alley's peace work.[57] Alley was a New Zealand representative in name only.

Alley was also useful in propaganda aimed at Chinese citizens in China in the 1950s. His words of support for the new regime helped to mitigate the sense of international isolation. Alley was one of many 'personages' marshalled to lend their support to the new regime at this time. Articles by and about Alley appeared in Chinese magazines, endorsing the new government's policies. This type of propaganda work for domestic purposes stopped by the end of the decade and did not resume again until 1977, when he was officially cleared of all political suspicions.[58]

Along with other foreigners working for the Chinese government at this time, Alley was initially on the 'supply system,' whereby his basic necessities were provided for, as well as being given a small living allowance. He reported to Pip Alley, 'Quite busy with this and that, reading and writing and so on. On living – one does not worry much. If there is work, there will be food. I have some books and some shirts and shorts for summer, cadre uniform for the winter, and a room to live in. A typewriter and some paper.'[59] As the economy stabilised, Alley was given a generous salary and a comfortable apartment.

Alley was one of only a small number of foreigners who were allowed to stay on in China after 1949. These foreigners were initially known as 'international friends' (guoji youren) to distinguish them from the majority of foreigners who were no longer welcome in China.[60] Apart from diplomats, the only other foreigners welcome to live and work in China in this period were Soviet advisers who came to help the CCP modernise China. Officially, CCP proclamations on the position of foreigners in China after 1949 stated that foreigners were welcome to stay on, live and do business there. But in fact, as we have seen, between 1949 and 1952 even pro-CCP foreigners like Alley and the other foreign personnel at Shandan had been harassed and intimidated in accordance with an internal policy aimed at 'squeezing out' foreigners.[61] Foreign residents were not officially forced to leave, but their presence in China was made increasingly difficult by means of crippling taxes, travel restrictions and the insubordination of formerly trusted Chinese staff, who were encouraged to establish a distance between themselves and their foreign employers or colleagues. A number of foreigners were actually imprisoned, sometimes on trumped-up charges, to show to the Chinese people that 'the power of the men from across the ocean is broken.'[62] In July 1949 there had been 120,000 foreign residents living in 'liberated' China, with more than 65,000 of them living in Shanghai alone. Another 54,000 lived in the former Japanese colony of Manchuria.[63] By late 1952, when Alley had moved to live and work in Peking, virtually all of those foreigners had left.

The small number of foreigners who worked for the CCP government after 1949 were given special status to distinguish them from other foreign residents. This group was known as the foreign experts, *waiguo zhuanjia*. Most were sent by their respective national Communist parties to help China modernise and rebuild, but a few, like Alley, had had connections with the CCP before 1949. This group was given special treatment by the Chinese leadership, though it was not necessarily more trusted. The foreign experts worked as propagandists, translators, teachers and technicians. In addition to their practical assistance, the foreigners had an important symbolic role, one of which they were very conscious. They symbolised the new era of equality in Sino-foreign relations and of international support for the Chinese revolution. After 1949 only those foreigners who were willing to show themselves to be sympathetic to the new government were welcome there, and even they sometimes had difficulties in obtaining visas or staying on. In this period, to be a friend entailed adherence to whatever the current political line was in Peking, or at least to that part of it for which their cooperation was needed. Old friends who publicly questioned the Party line were cast out.

Despite being allowed to stay on, Alley's own place in New China was still quite uncertain for a while. In 1953 he reported to Barton the forced departure of a number of foreigners friendly to the regime, speculating:

> it is hardly possible that I be around here for long enough to correct and edit [a book of translations of Chinese poetry he was working on]. . . . I have been badgering friends to send me all kinds of printed matter, cuttings etc. so that I can better assess things and try to keep up better. Whether or not I would do more sitting here

or back at Westcote outside Christchurch I do not quite know. . . . Shall I come and make a school in North Auckland? Or would it be best to try something else? The idea of trying to do such in the old society, is pretty heartbreaking though. Had enough of that in 1942–49 so shall probably sit and do little things on peace and write about the school when I get a bit homesick for the place and people there. . . . Feel that I must do something more than just live a comfortable life, so we shall see what next to try.[64]

Alley was afraid to return to New Zealand, though he had a 'letter from Pip, wanting me to go and reside at Westcote. Then rely on my relatives for their kindness, stand for parliament, and so on. The prospect frightens me to death. Starting learning a new country at 57, after about 30 years of this one, does not make sense to me, but it is very nice of him to suggest it, and I will certainly come back some time, that is sure.'[65]

Nevertheless, by the mid-1950s Alley's position in China became fixed. The role that emerged for Alley post-1949 reflected the political credibility building he had engaged in since the Communist victory and the foreign policy needs of the new government. Particularly from the late 1950s, when Sino-Soviet relations worsened and China became even more diplomatically isolated, high-profile foreign friends like Alley whose loyalty was to the CCP, not Communism *per se*, became useful. Their support demonstrated to Chinese citizens and foreign supporters alike that China was not in fact isolated and still had, as Mao put it, 'friends all over the world.'[66] By the time of the Sino-Soviet split in the early 1960s, Alley had become an official 'friend of China,' a political title with certain obligations. There was no job description as such, and it was a role created as much by Alley and his desire to stay on and be useful in China as it was by any initial perceived need for his assistance from the Chinese authorities. In addition to his minimal activities for the Peace Committee, Alley became a full-time propagandist for the CCP, writing books, articles and letters for foreign readers, presenting the official line about what was happening in New China and meeting with select groups of pro-China foreigners when they visited China.

'Friendship' (*youyi*) became a key word in the CCP's systems and strategy for dealing with the outside world. Deciding 'who friend, who enemy,' as Alley in a poem had paraphrased Mao, was one of the most essential elements of Maoist ideology.[67] Friendship under these terms was political; it did not have the usual meaning of good personal relations between individuals. Friendship terminology was a means to neutralise opposition psychologically and to reorder reality. Even in the current period, Peking continues to describe positive diplomatic relations between itself and other countries in 'friendship' terms and numerous organisations and items associated with foreigners are prefixed with the word 'friendship.' In contrast, foreign leaders or prominent individuals who dare to criticise China are classed as 'unfriendly,' and nations that act against China's interests are lam-basted as hegemonist, imperialists, 'revisionists' and even 'the enemy.'

Alley's involvement in peace work was at first sight incongruous – as I noted earlier, Alley told his sister Gwen that he had gone to China to join a war; even Edgar Snow described him as 'no pacifist.'[68] But CCP-style peace differed from the Western pacifist concept of a 'peace movement,' which implies demilitarisation and disarmament. For the Chinese government, peace meant an acceptance by the West of the Chinese revolution, an acknowledgement that the Chinese Communist Party was the legitimate government of China, and an end to Western aggression against China. Hence, for high-profile friends of China like Alley, public support of China's participation in the Korean War was an obligatory symbol of their friend-ship, as was support for China's efforts to build a nuclear bomb. By no means did CCP-style peace imply demilitarisation or disarmament in the abstract pacifist sense. It is worth quoting a selection here from Alley's writ-ings, which closely follow the Party line on peace at the time. After visiting a weapons factory in the late 1960s, Alley commented:

> Here a group of workers turn out light anti-aircraft tank rocket launchers. To me they seemed a very useful weapon. 'Prepare against war' is not an empty slogan. It is interesting that here, under the shadow of the Great Wall and its most famous gate there should be a plant devoted to the cause of working peoples' Interna-tionalism, their support going to so many parts of the world.[69]

During the 1950s and 1960s, Alley along with other China-based foreign friends promoted Peking's foreign policy, not only to the outside world, but also to the Chinese people. In 1956 Alley told Barton, 'I spoke to a mass meeting of people in Ruijin, the old Red Army capital the other day. It was raining but thousands were there. It was in protest against Suez. Nan [Green] and Elsie [Fairfax-Cholmeley – both British foreign friends] carried banners down past the [British] Embassy [in Peking].'[70]

Ultimately, Alley's peace activities provided an effective focal point by which the already well-known New Zealander could be promoted while publicising Chinese foreign policy to an international audience. Alley became one of the most prominent of China's foreign friends because it was considered by Chinese leaders that he could play a role that few other foreigners could; that of commentator on China and spokesman to help publicise Chinese policies and conditions to the outside world.[71]

Peace work was only one aspect of Alley's role as a friend of China. He also served as *de facto* ambassador of the regime, regularly hosting groups of foreign visitors, mostly from the West, and especially the so-called 'friend-ship delegations,' prior to the late 1970s almost the only way in which foreign tourists could visit China. In the days when China was politically isolated, Alley played a small but significant part in China's people's diplomacy, which aimed at fostering people-to-people links between China and other countries, regardless of whether China had diplomatic links to them. To those who met him, Alley presented a friendly Western face; his view on Chinese affairs was regarded as more believable than that which came from a Chinese official. For many foreign travellers, a visit to Rewi Alley was the highlight of their trip to China. R. M. Fox, a participant in a friendship delegation to China of Irish artists and writers in the 1950s, wrote admiringly, 'I met Rewi Alley, the stolid and solid, grey-haired New Zealander, whose work for the Chinese people has extended over many years. . . . He had that air of quiet satisfaction which belongs to a man who has achieved victory after a tremendous struggle.'[72] In 1971, a New Zealand journalist noted:

> [Alley's] presence is obligatory when many groups of English-speaking foreigners are welcomed to Peking. This year's New Zealand student tour brought Rewi back to Peking from the countryside and according to one member of the party they spent two valuable evenings with him.[73]

Alley never gave up his nationality, though many other long-staying friends did. When Alley applied for Chinese citizenship, he was advised that 'it would be better for travel purposes' if he retained New Zealand citizenship.[74] Becoming a citizen of New China was a token of the friends' commitment to the new society and their desire to work for it. Alley's role, however, was to be a permanent outsider, and to have his otherness constantly emphasised so that he could claim objectivity. His New Zealand passport gained him an element of independence and facilitated his travels round the world as an unofficial representative of China. Alley's peace work necessitated him being able to travel freely to Western countries to attend peace conferences. If he held a Chinese passport, it would have been not only more difficult to travel, but also harder to claim that he was a non-partisan peace worker. Moreover, if it was known he was no longer a New Zealand citizen it would have been harder to influence Western attitudes to China. Unlike many other China-based foreign friends who held official positions within the Chinese bureaucracy, from 1952 until his death in 1987 Alley continued to be, uniquely, officially merely a 'permanent guest' of the Chinese people, first under the responsibility of the Peace Committee and later under the responsibility of the Chinese People's Association for Friendship with Foreign Countries.[75]

Until he applied for a New Zealand passport in 1956, Alley had a 'Peking Citizen's Certificate,' an internal passport that he was able to use as a travelling document.[76] As he had not returned to New Zealand since 1937, his previous travel papers had presumably expired.[77] When he did finally apply for a New Zealand passport, unlike many of the other China-resident foreign friends Alley experienced no difficulty in having his passport renewed by his native country. The New Zealand government position on the issue of passports was stated in a 1955 paper from the Department of Internal Affairs. Internal Affairs opposed a proposal that the Department of External Affairs should make decisions on the issue and renewal of passports. An official commented,

> It is difficult to see why passports should be considered a facet of New Zealand's diplomatic relations with other countries and thus be a proper function of the External Affairs Department. . . . A passport is merely a document purporting to establish identity and nationality of the bearer issued for the purpose of travelling outside New Zealand. . . . It is in no way a certificate of good character . . . the issue of a passport to a New Zealand citizen is not a diplomatic act of the Government of New Zealand, but an act of the New Zealand Government towards a New Zealand citizen to facilitate the private purposes of that citizen.[78]

An earlier test of New Zealand's stance on a citizen's democratic right to hold views different from the government and express them publicly was the 1952 Peking peace conference. While the Australian government banned Australians from attending, the New Zealand government did not attempt to prevent its citizens participating.[79] New Zealand citizens were able to participate in 'friendship' delegations to China with little interference from their government. A 1960 SEATO report noted that in New Zealand, unlike its close allies the USA and Australia, 'no measures exist to restrict or discourage travel to Communist countries.'[80]

Alley's activities as a propagandist of the Chinese government were noted unfavourably by New Zealand's allies the USA and Great Britain. The two countries kept New Zealand officials up to date on Alley's activities both within China and in other countries.[81] A US activist, Alfred Kohlberg, well known for his involvement in the pro-ROC 'China Lobby' and close association with 'red-baiter' Senator Joe McCarthy, wrote to the New Zealand government asking it to put a stop to Alley's propaganda work. Kohlberg complained in particular about two of Alley's poems published in a US magazine, which 'seem to give "Aid and Comfort" [sic] to the enemy of New Zealand, the North Korean Communists.'[82] The New Zealand ambassador to Washington told his superiors in Wellington,

> [Mr Kohlberg] is not the type who appreciates the fact that the New Zealand Government has no control over the utterances of Mr Rewi Alley and much less responsible for them. Mr Kohlberg is quite capable of communicating to some Senate committee the poems of Mr Alley and of alleging, if he receives no further

communication from me, that the Government of New Zealand has taken no steps to repudiate the sentiments of those poems.[83]

The Secretary of External Affairs refused to accept this interference from a representative of the China Lobby. Kohlberg's request was politely replied to with a reminder of New Zealand's full support for, and participation in, the Korean War.[84] In 1956 the British government directly expressed its concern about Alley's activities when he was seen in Hanoi at a meeting of the Peace Liaison Committee of the Asian and Pacific Regions. The New Zealand High Commission in London reported that, in British eyes, 'the significance of this information is that Alley has previously confined his activities to China itself, and now appears to be venturing furthering afield.'[85]

Alley's efforts to bring about closer contact between New Zealand and China were also watched by US embassy officials in Wellington who recorded the formation of New Zealand–China Friendship Societies throughout the country in the 1950s and friendship delegation visits to and from New Zealand, ascribing them both to Alley's influence. In a report to the US State Department, the embassy listed some of Alley's actions in New Zealand and those of the New Zealand–China Friendship Society concluding, 'All of these efforts are intended and have in some measure succeeded in fostering in New Zealand an interest in and greater tolerance for Communist China.'[86] Embassy dispatches described Alley as 'a minor Albert Schweitzer, in New Zealand eyes.'[87]

Certainly there was considerable sympathy for Alley's views in New Zealand government circles, despite official opprobrium. Approval was especially strong in the Labour Party. Labour MPs John A. Lee, Ormond Wilson, Warren Freer and Walter Nash, amongst others, all spoke out in support of Alley and his views on China. The radical and extremely popular John A. Lee wrote,

> Rewi Alley is making amends in part for the stupid New Zealand government which refuses to recognise the New China, as if shutting one's eyes tightly obliterated the fact that a 200 year unalterable has fallen and that a people are building a new normal. This Chinese Revolution is one of the great facts of history; a day which shall be recorded and written of for hundreds of years, and New Zealand knows nothing about the revolution. Officially, we are political pettifoggers. . . . But there is one New Zealander who strives to help and he is a man. While the missionaries of 2,000 years of heavenly crusade tumble out of China, Rewi Alley stays, a missionary of tomorrow, a New Zealander enlisting for Chinese Liberation. . . . One New Zealander is helping and we should be thankful . . . Rewi Alley's work atones for our political stupidity.[88]

Labour MP Ormond Wilson travelled to China with the first 'Friendship Delegation' to visit China from New Zealand and helped Alley to gain a New Zealand passport. Labour MP Warren Freer also travelled to China in the 1950s. Having been sent a copy of Alley's speech to the World Conference for Disarmament by Pip Alley (who shared his older brother's political views and was a vocal critic of New Zealand foreign policy), Freer told him, 'I have read it with considerable interest and agree with the sentiments expressed by him.' He also told Pip in confidence of his plans to develop trade relations with China.[89] Through his brother Geoff, who was Chief Librarian of the National Library and a National Party supporter, Alley also had good connections with National Party governments.[90] A. D. McIntosh, Founding Secretary of the Department of External Affairs, was a close friend of Geoff Alley and, as he wrote in a letter to Rewi Alley, greatly appreciative of Alley's work in China.[91] Notes on the MFAT files on Alley and CORSO reveal strong support and respect for Alley among diplomats in the 1940s and 1950s. Moreover, Sir Joseph Heenan, Under-Secretary in the Department of Internal Affairs (the department responsible for issuing passports) had supported Alley's work in Shandan in the 1940s.[92]

The New Zealand government's leniency towards Alley is even more outstanding when one considers the treatment some of the other Westerners who promoted the Communist side in the Cold War received from their governments. Wilfred Burchett, the Australian journalist who also wrote in support of germ-warfare allegations and spoke out in opposition to Australia's participation in the Korean War, was refused the right to have his passport renewed in 1955 and not given another for the next seventeen years. British journalist Alan Winnington was declared a traitor by his government for activities similar to Burchett's and denied his passport for twenty-odd years. Winnington wrote in his memoirs, 'I hardly needed to be told ... that American rancour was behind this petulant act.'[93] The US government was equally hostile to its own citizens who had criticised US foreign policy – journalists Bill and Sylvia Powell and Julian Schuman were accused of treason for nothing more than publishing the Shanghai-based *China Weekly Review*. After 1949, the *Review* featured idealised portraits of life in New China and both Burchett and Alley wrote articles for it. It was not an influential journal, but the temerity of its editors in opposing US foreign policy was enough to provoke the hostility of the McCarthyites. The charges against the Powells and Schuman were eventually dropped, but only after a lengthy and expensive public trial.[94]

The comments of Ormond Wilson, the Labour Party politician who assisted Alley to renew his New Zealand passport, give some insights into the reasons for the New Zealand government's equivocal stance:

Once we had blindly followed Britain, right or wrong. After the war, it seemed to me, we were blindly following the United States

81

and thus became enmeshed in the hysteria of American anti-Communism which influenced its foreign as well as its domestic policy. I was convinced that Communism was no more monolithic than capitalism or Christianity. I was confident that China would go her own way, not Moscow's. . . . By contrast I saw the policies of Moscow and Washington as mirror images of one another, both obsessed by the theory that political allegiance required an ideological basis, and both convinced that its own security depended on gaining allies with political systems identical with its own.

Outside the United States, in those post-war years, only committed Communists still based their faith on Stalin's Russia. Elsewhere, radicals might turn to such emerging leaders as Fidel Castro, Che Guevara and Ho Chi Minh. For myself, it was from Mao and his China that I hoped the most.[95]

Wilson's criticism of New Zealand 'blindly following' its major allies Britain and the USA is representative of New Zealand public opinion in the Cold War era, though his professed admiration for Mao Zedong may not be.

One of the results of popular frustration within New Zealand with the policy of 'blindly following' the USA in the Cold War era was that the diplomatic recognition of the People's Republic of China became a *cause célèbre*.[96] In the early 1950s, the National Party government had considered recognising Communist China but was thwarted by the USA's intransigence on the issue. Prior to a meeting in 1953 with the US ambassador to New Zealand, the National government's Minister of External Affairs, T. Clifton Webb, wrote that it was better not to delay recognition of the People's Republic as this would 'only serve to strengthen the ties that unhappily exist between Communist China and the USSR.' Clifton Webb advocated 'making every effort to detach Peking from Moscow,' and that the Chinese Communists should be taken 'on trust.' Webb believed it was not safe to assume that the Chinese were completely subservient to Communist Russia. However, after his meeting with the ambassador a foreign ministry memorandum reported that 'The US Government earnestly hopes that the question of Chinese representation in UN bodies will not be raised by countries outside the Soviet bloc.'[97]

Pressure grew on New Zealand's two main political parties to make the recognition of China part of their Party platform. By 1955, Labour Party policy supported both recognition of the People's Republic of China and its right to a seat on the UN. Shirley Barton wrote to Alley that even within the conservative National Party, 'their Minister for External Affairs had already declared in favour of it, a number of individual candidates embraced it and it was clearly too generally popular for the National Party to officially oppose.'[98] In 1958, Labour Prime Minister (1957–1960) Walter Nash wrote to Pip Alley that he was willing to recognise Communist China.[99] In early

1959 the Prime Minister wrote, 'There are some difficulties with regard to the recognition of the mainland government of China but I will do all I can to resolve them at the earliest possible date.'[100] Nash's desire to take a more independent stance in New Zealand's foreign policy was eventually dulled, however, by strong pressure from both Washington and London. Five months after Nash's assurance that New Zealand would soon recognise China his stance had altered:

> The Government has on several occasions stated its belief that the Peking Government should be recognised as the governing authority in China. As I made clear in my New Year message commenting on international affairs, the Government considers that recognition is inevitable. However it is conscious that this issue is now a most complex one, and that the international implications of a decision to accord recognition would be so important that such a step could be taken only after other friendly powers, Asian as well as Western, who might be affected by any New Zealand decision.... It will be appreciated that in considering the appropriate timing of any decision on recognition, New Zealand and other countries will naturally be influenced by the conduct of the Chinese Communist authorities towards other peoples. You will, for example, realise that the manner in which the Chinese Communist authorities dealt with the revolt in Tibet earlier this year has certainly not created a climate of opinion in which recognition could be contemplated in the immediate future.[101]

Ultimately the recognition of the People's Republic of China was not a decision that any New Zealand government in the 1950s and 1960s felt free to make on its own. A 1966 Department of Foreign Affairs memo discussing the recognition of Communist China noted, 'all New Zealand governments since 1950 have recognised that on this question the attitude of the United States is, and must be, the most important factor. And having in the last few years gone to considerable lengths to strengthen our relations with the United States, it would seem to me unwise for us to place those relations in jeopardy by supporting an initiative for which the US was opposed unless our own vital interests required it.'[102] Until 1969, when Nixon and Kissinger would decide for 'geopolitical' reasons that it was time to improve relations with the former foe, New Zealand subordinated its national interest to the domestic concerns of its American ally.

Alley's transition from headmaster to agent of Chinese foreign policy was not easy. In the past, he had opposed the attempts of CIC propagandists to turn him into what he called a 'Living Buddha'; now, he was required to cultivate that image. Moreover, the role of friend of China entailed obedience to the Party line. Alley was by nature an outspoken man, not afraid to point out injustice when he saw it. It was this quality that had motivated him to become involved in relief work and factory inspection during his years in Shanghai. And it was this quality that got him into trouble when he worked with the Nationalist government in the co-operative movement in the 1930s and 1940s. How then was he to square this with a career choice that required him to be a mouthpiece, a symbolic figure, valued for his influence rather than his opinions? A letter written to his New Zealand family in 1952 is revealing of the struggle going on in Alley's mind as he adjusted to this new life:

> My main interest now is in helping the new society, and to do this effectively I must be very objective. To fit into the new society here today, I must correct many organisational faults. I am pig-headed, rather than clever. I like people and production, and to me China is part of my being. But I must struggle for objectivity.[103]

Alley was neither a Marxist nor a Maoist: he was a friend of China. Friendship meant going with the Chinese political tide. His first book on the Chinese revolution, *Yo Banfa!*, contained no references to Mao and many to Liu Shaoqi's *How to be a Good Communist*.[104] Yet later, during the Cultural Revolution, he wrote, 'Liu and Deng [Xiaoping] would have led China steadily toward the revisionists. They will not now be able to do so.'[105] The 1976 edition of *Yo Banfa!* was purged of all its Liu quotes. In his book *Travels in China 1966–1971* (which ends rather conveniently just before the Lin Biao affair), Alley wrote, 'Mao is . . . ever vindicated in the end.'[106] In 1977, however, Alley said that he 'breathed a sigh of relief' when Deng Xiaoping returned to power.[107] Privately he told a friend in 1987 that he thought Mao was a 'prick' for what he did to his comrades in the Cultural Revolution.[108] Alley was like most people living in China in this era, a survivor. Being a survivor meant he had to be pragmatic about political changes and ride the waves as best he could. Alley had a knack that not all foreigners or Chinese shared, that of following the current political line and perhaps even sensing the next one before it became obvious.

Rather than Marxist-Leninism or Mao Zedong thought, Alley was, if anything, more influenced by China's Taoist and Buddhist traditions. A letter written in 1948 to close friend Dr Joseph Needham gives some sense of Alley's mystic beliefs. Responding to some drafts Needham had sent of his writings on China, Alley wrote: '[I] think the influence of Taoism on China, a sort of Tolstoyian peasant anarchist influence, cannot be overestimated. It will have its influence on any progressive movement in China, and will not be easily eradicated. The real Taoist of the village, does help to solve people's problems. How does he gain this intuition? He lives close to nature, maintains a sense of humour that the bureaucrat loses.'[109] Alley's sympathy for the principles of the two traditions engendered in him a sense of the fluidity of life and an empathy for the Chinese sense of time, which would help him through many difficulties in the Communist era as it had in the Republican.

Having established a readership in 1952 with *Yo Banfa!*, Alley had succeeded in persuading the Peace Committee that he should continue to write about the PRC for Western audiences. Alley told the Chinese authorities his aim was to arouse interest about China in Western countries so as 'to excite the imagination and capture the interest of youth and the broad masses' with stories written in as 'simple and human a way as possible.'[110] For the next 35 years, from his position of privilege and comfort, Alley told outsiders (including his New Zealand family) that everything was getting better and better in New China. He frequently spoke of the cruelty of the old society, which he contrasted with the hope and promise of the new. Even in the worst times of political upheaval and natural disaster, Alley accentuated the positive in his writings. During the period of three years of natural disaster in the early 1960s (which even Chinese officials now admit caused the deaths of millions of people from starvation and other related causes), Alley wrote articles and published the booklet *China's Food Problems*,[111] refuting Western reports of China's crisis. It cannot be that Alley was unaware of the problems China faced (though he may have been unaware of the extent). His Chinese family, unable like himself to get extra food rations, struggled during this time. Alley told brother Pip, 'Alan was down [from his home in Lanzhou] the other day and ate steadily for a couple of weeks. Whenever I have extra the kids come around and it all goes in a grand sweep.'[112] Alley, however, had the reverse problem; as millions starved he became obese and he wrote to friends and family asking for suggestions on how to lose weight.[113]

Alley's books were mostly reportage, describing the places he visited and how they implemented current policies. At times Alley did not even visit the places he wrote about. Instead, he reconstructed stories from Chinese official news reports and his own memories of the places described.[114] When he did travel, more often than not it was in tours with other foreign friends or to the holiday resorts of Conghua and Beidaihe. Alley, like other foreigners in China at this time, could not travel freely, he could only go where the authorities wanted him to go and he always had minders in attendance. This did not come across in his writing. Like the ancient Chinese poets who describe their solitude, omitting to mention the servants and family who tended to their needs, Alley always wrote as if he were free to travel alone in China.

Alley reported on what he saw on his travels in Chinese propaganda magazines targeted at foreigners as well as in books published under his own name. All his trips were carefully planned: local authorities would be notified months in advance of Alley's intended arrival, and buildings and people would be spruced up in preparation. He always travelled with an entourage

Plate 7.3 'We are looking up at the monument for the fallen at Hung Hu, Hubei, November 1963'.

Source: Photograph courtesy of Joy Alley.

of several cars. Before at least one such visit to a small village, all the village buildings were whitewashed in preparation for the visit. The local inhabitants were instructed to stand outside their houses to await the great foreign friend, but though the locals waited for hours, the visitors were behind schedule and drove through the village without stopping.[115]

Alley's travels served a further purpose for local consumption, of signalling official approval to the areas he visited. After 1949 and right up until the early 1980s, China was extremely isolated from the outside world. In his capacity as an official friend of China Alley took endless photographs, and admired and took notes on the long lists of village achievements. These would be written up almost verbatim in his literary outpourings. Alley was fortunate to be free to photograph as much as he liked on these trips: many other foreign residents were careful to avoid taking any photos at all for fear of being thought a spy. Alley's writing also served to provide politically correct English-language reading material for foreign language learners in China in the years when foreign literature was banned or limited. In the early 1970s, Alley's *Travels in China 1966–1971* was one of the few new foreign-language books available to Chinese readers.[116]

In his earlier years Alley had been a man of action: as a soldier in World War I, as a farmer, as a fire-fighter and finally as organiser of the co-operative movement and the Shandan Bailie school. In his life after 1952, however, that vigorous energy was thwarted by his cocooned existence in Mao's China. It was a tremendous waste for a man who, in 1949 when the Chinese Communists came to power, was lean, fit and in his prime. In his new relatively sedentary role in Peking, Alley rapidly gained weight and became bored.

Alley's energy was directed instead into words. Only a fraction of his verbose outpourings have ever been published. Not only did he write quantities of apologist literature about China, which at times even the Chinese propaganda system refused to publish, he translated poetry and wrote screeds of his own, wrote newspaper articles, and thousands upon thousands of letters. Thirty-four of Alley's books on contemporary China and the policies of the Chinese Communist Party have been published; still more languish in dusty archives. He also published eighteen collections of poetry on pro-China themes and, with the help of Chinese translators, translated eleven volumes of both classical poetry and revolutionary verse. His poem *What is Sin?*, written in 1967, gives an indication of the uniquely convoluted mix of the themes of Christian morality and the current political line in Alley's poetic works:

> Once more,
> Imperialism escalates
> Today the U.S. bombers spread
> more death from Thailand's bases.
> Tomorrow's death may come instead
> from other chosen places
>
> Once more,
> Revisionism escalates
> into reaction with new ties
> that bind it to the China haters,
> publishing the self-same lies,
> invented for dictators.
>
> In China now,
> We know the friend, we know the foe
> We toss the garbage to the wave.
> Flotsam in the Revolution,
> is washed into the Revisionist grave
> by the People's Ocean.
>
> To rebel, is right.
> Against the imperialist might that grinds
> the poor beneath its iron heel.
> People of the world must win:
> the foe must feel the People's steel —
> not to rebel is mortal sin.[117]

87

Alley's poetry became an integral aspect of his self-fashioned enactment of the part of an official friend of China. Even his closest cohorts admit that, though plentiful, his poetry was never very good. The poems were yet another vehicle for influencing public opinion in the English-speaking world. The poetry was mostly published in New Zealand at Alley's own expense, using money he had inherited from his mother, royalties he earned from his other books, and money left over from the Rewi Alley Aid Group (set up to provide funds for the school at Shandan).[118] Unusually for a poet, there was very little of the personal in Alley's poetic output. His subjects were always political, concerning topics appropriate to current CCP concerns. Even Alley's diaries were politically motivated; they do not, as most journals do, describe the author's inner world. In all of Alley's extensive opus after 1949, whether published or not, from poetry, private letters, fiction or non-fiction, there was a strong awareness on the part of the author that all his writing was potentially public. Hence, he made sure to proclaim the current line at all times.

Alley was always paranoid at being caught out saying the wrong political thing. In 1969, because of growing Sino-Vietnamese tension as Vietnam moved closer to the Soviet Union, Alley asked his brother to reduce the number of pro-Vietnam poems in a book to be published in that year. He advised Pip, 'Better to hold the book up than make a mistake. People do not forgive mistakes.'[119] To Alley's acute embarrassment, his contemporary and friend Wilfred Burchett mentioned in a 1976 publication, *China: The Quality of Life*, that at the time of the 1958 Great Leap Forward, the mass movement to create people's communes and generate rural industry, Alley had privately opposed some of its most basic policies. Burchett noted, 'I had found him somewhat gloomy about the exclusive emphasis on big modern industry and the tendency to organise the whole of China's productive forces under central ministries.'[120] Yet, in 1958 Alley was in the process of writing *China's Hinterland*, a paean to the 'successes' of those very policies. Even worse, Alley was co-author to Burchett's book, so there was a possibility that negative fallout in China towards Burchett's views might land on him too. The Burchett–Alley friendship deteriorated markedly after this gaffe. The problem was, as Burchett had mischievously demonstrated, that what Rewi Alley said in public, as an unofficial representative of China, was frequently different from what he said in private. Alley reacted equally negatively to New Zealand journalist Geoff Chapple's attempt at political analysis of the changing situation in China in the late 1970s. Chapple wrote in his biography of Alley that Mao's revolutionary line was being changed for a more pragmatic one in the Deng era. In a letter to Shirley Barton, Alley blustered that it was 'Quite wrong to say that Mao's "revolutionary line" is being exchanged for a pragmatic one. The line that held China together till 1964 was one thing. The one that Mao and Zhou instituted in 1970, is quite another – a continuation of what we see today.'[121] Alley's reputation and his high status rested on his faith in the CCP. He was, as he himself admitted, like a doll that could only 'squeak when pushed in the tummy, or when a string is pulled.'[122]

Early on in his writing career, Alley deliberately concentrated on positive aspects of the revolution and turned a blind eye when policies failed or he believed them to be wrong. He was afraid of his future in China were he to act differently. Alley knew enough about political intrigues in China to understand the consequences for any foreigner who was publicly critical of the regime. In a candid moment he told biographer Geoff Chapple, 'To present only the positive things is a little bit self-destructive because people don't necessarily believe it can all be like that. . . . But if you do present negative things along with the good, people in China seize on that, and say that's what you're talking about.'[123] The comment is interesting both for its honesty about Alley's situation in China and because it is an example of the difference between Alley's public voice and private opinions, which were often bitter, as many others in whom he confided would attest.[124]

Alley made periodic broadcasts to New Zealand and Australia throughout the 1950s, promoting the positive developments in New China. Little was known in China about New Zealand at this time; perhaps this is the reason Chinese broadcasters referred to Alley in a letter as 'a symbol of the friendship between China and Australia.'[125] As well as writing under his own name, Alley frequently wrote under a number of assumed names for such pro-China papers as Hong Kong's *Da Gong Bao*.[126]

Alley's translations of Chinese poetry were a hobby he had engaged in before 1949.[127] His translations were 'assisted' by Chinese cadres, although he could read classical Chinese quite well. The cadres' role was more as insurance policy than linguistic advisers. All Alley's writings were vetted by his work unit in China before publication even though many were published in New Zealand. For this reason he told his brother to quote only things he had said in these published items, not letters or conversation.[128]

Alley was always conscious that as a public and controversial figure his letters were being read by others than those they were intended for. He lamented to his brother that because of this he was not able to say what he really thought.[129] In 1967 he wrote, 'Sorry my letters are torn. Perhaps not surprising. So many people seem interested, don't they!'[130] Even in conversation with foreigners to whom he had formerly been close in the pre-1949 era, Alley was careful to be circumspect in his comments about Chinese politics. The strain of living such a life must have been immense. At times Alley would write up to two times a day to some of his closest supporters and family in New Zealand, yet the letters seldom contain anything but the most banal of observations.

Having established himself as an official friend of China, Alley had to be very careful to maintain a public image that was commensurate with that status. At the same time, he was conscious of the contradictions of his role;

although he needed to have a high profile, he was well aware that this could be turned against him. He wrote to his brother in 1962 begging him to remove a photograph from the front cover of his latest book of poetry to be published in New Zealand:

> Please, oh please, do not put me in that speaking attitude in the poetry book. I would hate it and the people here would see it as self-advertising. Best to put in a picture of child or children – the next generation of Chinese, that the world has to get along with.[131]

In a later letter Alley told Pip, 'Thanks for the picture removal. I'm nervous of such.'[132] Willis Airey, writing Alley's biography in the late 1960s, was asked to pass the manuscript on to Shirley Barton to make any necessary alterations that did not fit the image, such as Alley's earlier desire to join the Shanghai police force.[133] Alley was concerned as to how the biography would be regarded in China and asked Airey to make cuts that would bring it closer to the current political line, which by the late 1960s was both radical and anti-foreign.

Nevertheless, many of Rewi Alley's confidants whom I interviewed asserted that he *did* criticise policies and problems he saw in China, but he did so by writing letters or speaking directly to the appropriate officials. In the 1950s, he even inserted criticisms into his publications. In *Shandan: An Adventure in Creative Education* (published during the Great Leap Forward), Alley criticised the struggle sessions and mental punishment favoured by the Chinese government as a tool of thought reform (*sixiang gaizao*), which he had seen enacted at the Shandan school in the early 1950s:

> Different kinds of youth will always need different kinds of treat-ment; and no measure must be taken that will leave a mental scar and destroy the spirit. Too heavy a pressure, such as some kinds of mass meetings might give, is sometimes crippling to the sensitive and may cause a lasting mental injury.[134]

However, such qualms were absent in Alley's account of the Cultural Revolution, *Travels in China 1966–1971*, where he quoted Mao Zedong thought: 'if we want to correct a social wrong we must set up the absolute authority of the masses and not be scared of violence.'[135] Alley wrote to Shirley Barton of the severe drought conditions and other natural disasters occurring in China after the Great Leap Forward but made no comment about the severe food shortages. In all his letters to Barton, the closest he came to admitting there were problems was the vague comment, 'Not many visitors are being asked these dry years when there is so much to be done on the home front.'[136] A diary article written for publication compared the present day conditions with what had happened during drought years in the pre-1949 era, concluding 'Now all share struggle and victory together.'[137] This was not strictly true, however; Alley and the other foreign friends were entitled to receive special rations far in advance of what was available to Chinese people. Alley was very circumspect to give public support of CCP policy. He wrote to Shirley Barton with regard to the Hungarian uprising, 'many will side against the Communist Party because in many cases the COMMUNIST PARTY [sic] sets standards that they dislike – they do not want to have the realities of class struggle. I hope that you read the Chinese news release that contained the Chinese statement on all of this. It seemed to me to be an excellent one.'[138]

Despite not having lived in New Zealand for any length of time since 1927, Rewi Alley had always looked to New Zealand for support in his other ventures in China, and after 1952 he continued to make use of sympathetic forces in New Zealand for his new cause of supporting Communist China. Alley's utilisation of his natural audience in New Zealand coincided with the United Front strategies of the Chinese government towards New Zealand and other nations that refused it official recognition. These tactics were aimed at garnering popular support for the CCP government, in the hope that public pressure would eventually force governments to change their diplomatic recognition from the ROC to the PRC.

The New Zealand–China Friendship Society (NZCFS) was an important channel for PRC United Front activity and the promotion of Rewi Alley. It was set up under the instigation of Alley, although the less political China Society already existed. Much of the admiration that had supported Alley as a great humanitarian was successfully transferred to the New Zealand–China Friendship Society. For left-wing intellectuals in New Zealand in the 1950s, recognition of China was the burning issue of the era. Meetings of the NZCFS in the 1950s were packed. According to former society president Jack Ewen, many people were members just to be on the mailing list and find out what was happening in the Chinese revolution.[139] In the 1950s and 1960s, many believed Alley's official views on China provided a balance against the strident anti-Communism of the times. In more conservative circles, although he was thought to be misguided, respect for Alley was still high, as shown by the gentle review in 1955 of Alley's follow up to *Yo Banfa!*, *The People Have Strength*, in the conservative paper the *Press*:

Mr Alley's book is unquestionably interesting: his sincerity is not doubted – indeed he is sincere to the point of fanaticism in his admiration for the new China. But he fails to be convincing because his book is so obviously a product of thought relentless in determination to see only good in the service of China. The clearest proof of this is that a man of deep human sympathies fails to perceive the sadness of the many examples he gives of young minds being systematically emptied of individual thought and filled with ideas of undeviating service to the State, and that he sees nothing wrong in being an instrument of this process.[140]

With the help of the society, Alley's books were made available to the New Zealand public. Until the early 1990s, the society had its own tiny bookshop in every major city in the country. At least half of its stock consisted of Alley's publications; the rest was Chinese government propaganda aimed at foreign readers and basic materials for studying Chinese language. Rewi Alley's three visits to New Zealand prior to the establishment of diplomatic relations (1960, 1965, 1971) were sponsored by the New Zealand–China Friendship Society and supported (discreetly) by the New Zealand Communist Party. Until tourism in China became open to all, the lucrative monopoly of New Zealand–China tourism was controlled by the New Zealand–China Friendship Society. Regular 'friendship' tours were arranged to China by society members (they still are today but it is no longer a monopoly) with the assistance of Thomas Cook Travel, who in 1974 supplied a list of all those who attended such tours to the New Zealand government.[141] Thomas Cook continued to supply the names of tour participants to the New Zealand government until October 1982, when the SIS (Security

Plate 7.4 Poster for a talk given by Alley in Dunedin, NZ, 1971.

Source: Kathleen Wright papers, Alexander Turnbull Library, NZ
Note: The inset shows Alley with Chinese Foreign Minister Zhou Enlai, 1970.

Intelligence Services) removed the NZCFS from its list of suspicious organisations.[142] By this time the New Zealand Embassy in Peking had taken to inviting visitors on friendship tours to have tea with embassy staff. Not everyone was happy to be part of such a politically orientated group. One participant of a tour organised during the Cultural Revolution complained in a letter to then Prime Minister Bill Rowling and Leader of the Opposition, Rob Muldoon, that other members on the tour had formed political 'study groups' on arrival in China and been 'openly supportive of Communism.'[143]

The New Zealand–China Friendship Society became the keeper of the Rewi Alley myth in New Zealand.[144] Rewi Alley was the official patron of the society and remains the patron saint. Alley was a source of inspiration and guidance to many society members, and his faith in China bolstered their own. Members wrote to him for advice on the vagaries of Chinese politics or to complain about fellow members when there were political problems within the society. Soon after Alley's death, the New Zealand–China Friendship Society even proposed to the Chinese government that the anniversary of Alley's arrival in China should be made a national holiday.[145] This request was politely declined. The society continues to hold regular memorial meetings and fund-raising activities in Alley's name. In 1997, an important year for Rewi Alley acolytes since it was the hundredth year since his birth, seventy years since his arrival in China and ten years since his death, the society organised a well-attended tour-cum-pilgrimage to visit sites in China associated with Alley's life.

The New Zealand Communist Party's support of Alley in his position as its *de facto* New Zealand representative in China was very useful, particularly after the Sino-Soviet split when the NZCP was one of the few parties to support the Chinese side. The CCP supported the NZCP's 'fraternal relationship' by ordering large quantities of the party paper *People's Voice* and inviting NZCP members on lavish tours to China; unlike the USSR, which was more frugal in its relations with brother Communist parties. According to former NZCP member and ex-Shandan worker Max Wilkinson, the NZCP's support of the Chinese line in the Sino-Soviet split was more opportunism than anything else; what he calls the 'China franchise.' He says Alley's presence in China was more a bonus for the NZCP than a reason for supporting the Chinese side.[146] As late as 1975 the Chinese government published articles from *People's Voice* in the CCP organ *People's Daily* as a means to criticise the New Zealand government.[147]

Alley joined the NZCP in 1960, on his return to New Zealand, though his membership was regarded as a symbolic gesture rather than a genuine political conviction. It was agreed by the NZCP that it would be good for Alley to join at this time, since he supported the Chinese Communist government and followed the same line as the New Zealand party.[148] During subsequent visits to New Zealand, Alley made a point of emphasising his

NZCP membership and wore the party's badge prominently displayed on his lapel.[149] He did this as a deliberate provocation to the anti-Communist Returned Servicemen's Association (RSA), whose badge, as an ex-World-War-One veteran he would normally have worn.

Alley had a good relationship with NZCP secretary Vic Wilcox, and described Wilcox's support of his role in China as 'essential'.[150] In the 1960s and early 1970s Party Secretary Wilcox was the most well-known New Zealander in China because of his support for the CCP line in the Sino-Soviet struggle.[151] Because of the NZCP's support for the CCP, Wilcox's statements on issues of importance to Chinese politics, such as the dispute between India and Pakistan in 1965, were published in Chinese papers.[152] Long before Alley's writings were, Wilcox's articles were translated into Chinese and published. When he visited China, Wilcox was met by Kang Sheng and other top leaders and their meetings were written up on the front page of the leading Chinese papers. The support of Wilcox was especially helpful to Alley in the Cultural Revolution period when the position of foreigners in China became difficult.

The NZCP made much of Alley's connections with senior leaders such as Mao Zedong and Zhou Enlai to boost support for its stance on China. In a less than subtle hint, articles in *People's Voice* discussing the visit of NZCP members to Peking featured a picture of Mao shaking hands with Alley. In the late 1960s when Alley's position was under threat, such endorsements, from both Mao and the NZCP, were important.[153] In 1970 when factions within the New Zealand party criticised the Cultural Revolution, Alley's advice on the 'correct Line' ensured that the NZCP supported Peking. An article in *People's Voice* proclaimed: 'Rewi Alley commends N.Zers [sic] who beat counter-revolutionaries.' The article featured a photo of Zhou Enlai talking with Alley at the Workers' Stadium in Peking, adding extra weight to the credibility of his words. Alley's stance swayed most NZCP members to continue to support China (those who disagreed were expelled).

However, in 1978, the NZCP opposed Deng Xiaoping's new economic policies of opening up to Western investment, labelling them 'revisionist.' Rewi Alley, Vic Wilcox and a number of other New Zealand Communists who supported the Chinese position were thrown out of the NZCP.[154] That Alley's membership of the New Zealand Communist Party was a token gesture rather than a reflection of a deeply held belief in Marxism was illustrated after Alley refused to join the NZCP in criticising the CCP. As a good party member, Alley's loyalty should have been to the line of the NZCP.

Rewi Alley's people's diplomacy work in New Zealand also included activities involving a wider, less partisan audience. Alley donated Chinese antiques and curios to the Canterbury and Auckland Museums, and this received favourable press coverage in the 1950s.[155] Under the guise of visiting friends and family back home, in the 1960s and early 1970s, Alley returned to New Zealand and held carefully orchestrated public meetings to promote the Chinese government's view on diplomatic recognition. The Chinese authorities decided to support his trips to New Zealand after the 1956 visit of the first 'friendship' delegation to China from New Zealand, when the possibility of New Zealand recognising Communist China was discussed. After this meeting, Alley told Shirley Barton, Zhou Enlai advised him to 'go for a holiday to New Zealand for a while'.[156]

Alley did not in fact return to New Zealand until four years later. Alley's visit home came at a time when China was working hard to improve relations with Western countries. The Sino-Soviet split was public knowledge and the NZCP had announced its support for the Chinese position. His first visit home in twenty-three years was initially low key. Alley's old friend from CIC days, James Bertram, now a professor at Victoria University, advised him to feel things out before seeking publicity. Alley presented his visit to New Zealand as if it was for personal reasons only. He wrote to Pip, 'Hope you will be home around the 8th, as I will probably drop in on you for a couple of weeks for a quiet, I hope, and restful rest and to get away from the winter here. Hope that there will be no embarrassing splash, and I will be able to go to the Museum for a few days and look over things there.'[157] Nevertheless, though his stay was still promoted as a 'rest,' Alley held sixty meetings during this five-week visit from 19 February to 29 March 1960.[158] He travelled throughout the country giving speeches in trade union halls, schools, factories, wherever he was welcome. The New Zealand government did not prohibit the meetings, though New Zealand's Security Intelligence Service (SIS) sent agents to follow Alley wherever he went. Indeed while the SIS kept tabs on him, the Head of Foreign Affairs, A. D. McIntosh, invited Alley to give a private talk on China to foreign-affairs officials.[159] Alley also met with Prime Minister Nash on this trip. Alley's knowledge of conditions in China both before and after 1949 was still appreciated in his home country, even if his political views were not. This was symptomatic of the mixed signals the New Zealand government continued to give Alley and those who advocated the cause of recognising Communist China throughout the 1950s and 1960s, reflecting the tensions beneath its outward support for the US stance on this issue.

Although the unofficial ban in New Zealand on mentioning Alley's name publicly had been lifted by this stage, the media response to Alley's activities was still hostile. Whangarei paper the *Northern Advocate* paraphrased Alley's remarks from an interview, making clear its own disapproval. Readers were informed that Alley believed New Zealand should recognise what the paper preferred to call 'Red China': 'Although Red China couldn't care less about the matter, as it had a self-contained economy, it would be to New Zealand's economic advantage to have trade relations with a country whose standard of living was rising so much.'[160] The *Listener* reported sarcastically on Alley's work to increase understanding of China: 'To this work he brings as weapons neither the rapier nor the bludgeon, but rather a soft pillow in which the harsh questions asked of China abroad are quietly and ever so politely smothered.'[161]

A further visit in 1965 covered much the same activities as in 1960, with a similar mixed response in public and private support for Alley's views. Alley's 1971 visit home was timed to coincide with the announcement that the PRC was at last to be given China's seat at the United Nations. Alley was on the spot to benefit from the huge public interest in China that ensued. This time round, the *Listener*'s account of Alley's 1971 visit was jubilant and awestruck:

> Public meetings in Wellington and Auckland have drawn nearly 2,000 to hear him read a short address and answer questions until he tires after nearly 100 minutes. Unbending, with the knowledge that he speaks for China on the public platform, he holds an audience spellbound with moralistic parables on his life. The audience is mostly interested in education, the family and social services in China. A question on Pakistan draws a sharp 'No comment'.[162]

Shirley Barton told Alley, 'You certainly impressed the press here. I think there is a real longing to hear truth spoken (though a fear of words that can be called "propagandist") and they are so sickened of professional politicians – the Holyoakes, the Muldoons and Marshalls, and disappointed by the Kirks.'[163] During this trip, Alley publicly denied that he had ever attempted to apply for Chinese citizenship;[164] more than ever, at this stage in his career, it was essential to stress his New Zealand origins. Alley's last visit to New Zealand was in 1972–1973. It was timed to coincide with New Zealand and Australia's diplomatic recognition of the PRC, and this trip too was extremely successful. Alley wrote to Jim Wong of the New Zealand–China Friendship Association, 'Tell them I'm coming to visit friends and family if anybody asks.'[165] Wong's report of the trip was fulsome:

> In contrast to his earlier visits, Rewi, on this occasion, was constantly besieged by the mass media – TV, daily newspapers, radio, student papers, literary and other journals, and of course the Communist Party of New Zealand's weekly paper 'People's Voice', for interviews. For the first time Rewi Alley was regarded as an authority on New Zealand's Pacific neighbour, China.... The prime object of Rewi's visit was a holiday, a period to see his family and friends, and to meet again comrades of the CPNZ of which he is proud to be a member.[166]

Though its response to his activities had mellowed over time, the New Zealand government still kept a watchful eye on Alley, since he continued to make much of his New Zealand citizenship and New Zealand continued to be an important target for his propaganda. Lacking the resources of its richer allies, New Zealand still had one valuable resource in espionage: its citizens. On many occasions on more than matters relating to Rewi Alley, New Zealanders showed themselves willing to assist in the 'fight against Communism.' Shortwave aficionados provided the government with the time and content of Alley's broadcasts from China.[167] Visitors to the PRC in pre-recognition days not only provided the government with their impressions of the country, they provided up-to-date reports on Alley's life and state of mind. Brian Shaw, who went to China as a member of a 'study group' tour of New Zealand and Australian students in 1968 reported that Alley was reluctant to comment on the power struggles of the Cultural Revolution 'but I got the impression he was rather unhappy about some aspects.'[168] Once New Zealand established its own embassy in China in 1973, 'Rewi Alley-watching' became one of the many tasks of its diplomats.

For some who had known and supported him in his work for CIC, Alley's wholesale public support for germ-warfare allegations in the Korean War and all other aspects of CCP foreign policy was a disappointment.[169] Before long, Alley came to be seen by many as simply an apologist for the Chinese Communists. Some academics and journalists even regarded Alley as a traitor to the ideal of the Western intellectual as the loyal opposition. They believed he was morally corrupt for writing propaganda for the Chinese Communist government and participating in the guiding of foreign perceptions of China. Alley's activities as both publicist and representative of the CCP made him a subject of disdain among those whose job it was to explain China to the outside world. Canadian journalist John Fraser wrote of Alley, 'He is a fantasist who sees only what he wants to see, he is fixated with a vision of revolutionary China that rarely differs from the propaganda department. . . . [Alley] gave all foreign experts in China a bad name . . . they seemed to be toadies to whatever faction or party had power in Peking.'[170] Paul Hollander listed Alley in his fools gallery of fellow travellers, *Political Pilgrims*, as a 'prominent propagandist of the regime . . . playing an active part in the guidance of important foreigners [in China].'[171] Alley's unpopularity with Sinologists and Western journalists is not surprising, given that he publicised a vision of China that many of them had once believed in and since turned against. Some who disliked Alley may have been irritated at his seeming ability to travel freely about China, while they, the 'true' experts, were not even allowed into the country. Alley and other foreign friends writing on the PRC were criticised by Western China watchers because they expected them, as Western intellectuals living in China, to be a social conscience, to point out anomaly and injustice, rather than supporting the Communist social structure unquestioningly. Western critics could accept the silence and complaisance of Chinese intellectuals, but they expected foreigners to take on a more adversary role.

Though Alley was regarded by some as a traitor and apologist, to someone of Alley's background and understanding, not to betray the cause he had committed himself to was the most honourable course. In the context of the West's extreme anti-Communism in the 1950s and 1960s, Alley's partisanship does not seem out of place, however history might judge his pronouncements. By Alley's standards, his behaviour was moral and reasonable, while Western observers of China were immoral or at best misguided. He at least was loyal to a cause that he regarded as just: the improvement of the standard of living of Chinese people. Alley did not think much of many Western commentators on China; he wrote, 'I read the often naive, sometimes insulting reports of so-called China experts, marvelling at their blindness as they cook up the pap a self-satisfied readership will lap up because it gives them such a feeling of superiority. And then I think of China.'[172] Finally, as I have discussed earlier, Alley was a survivor. He did not criticise by speaking out to Western journalists and other visitors, in part because of his strong antagonism against the Western media, but primarily because of his awareness of the personal consequences had he done so.

8

PEKING'S MAN

After Rewi Alley's relocation to Peking in 1952, more than ever before his public persona required a high degree of conformity. His behaviour, both past and present, had to be believed to be beyond reproach. The friendship role would allow no hint of scandal; it required a spartan and wholesome image. Homosexual activities were punishable in New China by imprisonment or even death, and public attitudes turned hostile. Although Alley had originally found freedom and acceptance for his lifestyle, now he was required to go back into the closet and present himself as a bachelor who had never married because of his commitment to the Chinese revolution.[1] Alley was anxious to keep his sexuality a secret in Mao's China; he refused to discuss it, even with his own family.[2]

From this time on, Alley made a clear choice between his personal life and the right to stay on in China. Years later, in response to the questions of brother Pip as to why he had never married, he answered somewhat disingenuously, 'With me after coming to China and getting into the revolution, it was either revolution or family life. Not both.'[3] What China's revolution prevented Rewi Alley from having was not a family in the traditional sense, rather the family he had created for himself in the years when he lived with Alec Camplin and their adopted sons, or the larger family of the Shandan boys and like-minded teachers. Under the puritanism and anti-foreignism of the CCP government, it was not possible for Alley to continue in this former lifestyle. Instead, he focused his energies on his new occupation. He continued to form close attachments to a number of young Chinese men, though it seems that these relationships were platonic. Even this was restricted; depending on the political climate, Chinese citizens were frequently forbidden contact with foreigners, even friendly ones like Alley. Most of those who knew Alley only after this time had no idea that he was gay; even some of the Chinese men with whom he formed close relationships were not aware of his sexual orientation. Two of those men whom I interviewed flatly denied that Alley was homosexual. Those who were aware of his sexual preferences kept silent.

It is probable that Alley chose to be celibate after he moved to Peking.

However, his bachelor status was an anomaly in a society that regards marriage as a social duty. Biographical articles invariably state that he did not marry because of his political commitment.[4] While the Chinese attitude towards Alley's homosexuality was to deny it, Western observers after 1949 were less tolerant. Foreigners in China after the 1950s were divided between those who, like Alley, were pro-CCP and those who were there simply for work or study purposes. There was little mixing of the two groups, and this led to a mutual distrust. Alley was a well-known figure amongst the foreign friends, and he attracted unfavourable attention on account of his pro-China writings. Rumours circulated that he was a paedophile who liked Chinese little boys and that the Chinese government supplied him with these in return for his propaganda activities. An alternative rumour was that the Chinese government was blackmailing him because of his proclivities, forcing him to continue to write and speak favourably about China in exchange for not exposing the 'truth.' The evidence given in support of these allegations was that he was regularly seen at the summer resort of Beidaihe in the company of pre-adolescent Chinese boys and other Chinese men, and that some of his secretaries were good-looking males; also that Alley's annual Christmas cards, composed of shots taken with his own camera of Chinese children, were examples of Alley's paedophilia. The cards sometimes contained pictures of children playing in the nude. To those inclined to believe rumours this might seem interesting if one did not know that the boys were the children of his adopted Chinese son Alan Alley whom he took with him on holiday every year to get them away from the pollution of their home city, Lanzhou. Nor does it seem particularly remarkable that some of his secretaries were good-looking Chinese men; some of them were also good-looking Chinese women and no one thought to comment on that. Moreover, Alley's innocent Christmas cards reveal little more than a sentimental attachment to children. The occasional shot of a Chinese child's bottom in split pants could only seem salacious to puritanical, sex-saturated Western eyes unfamiliar with Chinese sartorial custom. What is interesting about these rumours is what they reveal about the homophobia of many in the West, who could not accept the validity of a non-heterosexual lifestyle, always associating it with 'dirty old men' and paedophilia.

Alley's role as a 'peace worker' and friend of China put him under the responsibility of the Chinese Foreign Ministry. He was initially quartered in the glamorous Peking Hotel, which had been requisitioned by the Ministry. From the beginning, he was a high-status, high-profile figure. Alley became one of the most important members of the expatriate community of foreign friends. This came about neither because of his length of time in China, nor his good relationship with certain CCP officials, though this was helpful. Rather, Alley came to be valued for his propaganda skills and his ability to perform as an ostensibly independent supporter of New China. Unlike other foreign friends who stayed in China for a few years before moving on, or came for high-profile short-term visits, Alley was committed to living in China and working for its interests, and this too was esteemed by the relationship (*guanxi*) and sentiment (*ganqing*)[5] conscious Chinese who even above politics stress personal relationships.

The status of friend of China in residence guaranteed a high standard of living by local standards. Despite the spartan image that the Communist government chose to project to the world, Rewi Alley's lifestyle was far from austere. He was given free accommodation, at first in the Peking Hotel and later a luxurious apartment in the former Italian Legation. He had a driver and car at his disposal, and a secretary and cook to look after his needs. As a resident friend in the early days of the People's Republic he was initially on the 'supply system,' whereby all basic needs including food, clothing, accommodation and transport were paid for. Later he was granted an allowance well in excess of the average income. His travels around the countryside and overseas as a peace representative were paid for by the Chinese government, as were his holidays at the resort of Beidaihe in the summer, and Hainan and Conghua in the winter. This situation lasted until the early 1980s when, as China's economic policies changed to become more market-oriented, Alley was required to pay for some of the costs of his holidays. In the early years of the People's Republic he had more money than he required for his personal needs, using it to acquire a valuable collection of Chinese antiques. One of his favourite activities in Peking was to visit the antiques market at Liulichang. In the 1950s this was filled with valuable artefacts sold at bargain-basement prices by the besieged, formerly privileged Chinese bourgeoisie. In the austere first decade of New China, foreigners like Alley were among the few who could afford, either financially or politically, to collect Chinese antiques.

Alley was a devoted Sinophile — to his last days his house was filled with exquisite art objects of ancient China, not revolutionary art works. The exotic ancient culture of the East was extremely appealing to him; the peasant culture the CCP promoted was not. Alley's library was filled with the writings of fellow travellers and books about ancient China. Though he kept the obligatory copy of the collected works of Mao Zedong, Stalin and Lenin, little other evidence of an interest in revolutionary thought could be found there.[6] Political rhetoric aside, Alley's Peking life more closely resembled that of a privileged colonial than a revolutionary.

Alley's closest friends after he moved to Peking were George Hatem and Hans Mueller. Hatem, more commonly known by his Chinese name Ma Haide, was an American doctor who first came to China in 1933 and settled in Shanghai. Hatem soon became involved in the activities of the small group of pro-CCP foreigners in Shanghai, and he assisted Alley's work to improve conditions in Shanghai factories with a study on chrome dermatitis among child chromium-plating workers. In 1936, Hatem travelled up to China's north-west with American journalist Edgar Snow to visit the CCP base. In the CCP-base area, Hatem learned to speak fluent Chinese, adopted a Chinese name, married a Chinese woman and was admitted to membership of the CCP. After 1949 he became a citizen in the new People's Republic, though he did not relinquish his US citizenship. For a time, Hatem served as Mao's personal doctor. After 1949, Hatem settled in Peking and worked in the Ministry of Health. He was responsible for organising campaigns to eradicate leprosy and venereal diseases. Like Alley, he too had a small part to play in people's diplomacy, acting as host to visiting foreign delegations. Alley's other close friend, Hans Mueller, was a German doctor who came to Yan'an in 1939. He worked on the Chinese Red Army frontline in the Taihang Mountains and at hospitals in the north-east until 1949, when he too settled in Peking. After the Communist take-over, Mueller worked at Peking Union Medical College. Like Hatem, he also married a Chinese woman. Unlike the other two men, he did not have a political role. The three friends met at least once a week for dinner, usually at Alley's house.

The small number of foreigners living in Peking in the 1950s tended to stick together, meeting regularly for parties at a mutton restaurant near Beihai Park they called 'The Dump.' One of the other focus points for inter-action among the pro-CCP foreigners living in Peking in the 1950s was the political study groups. Unlike for Chinese citizens, attendance at a political study group was not compulsory, but there was a certain amount of peer pressure and most of the foreign friends attended. In the study groups the foreigners read translations of basic works of Marxism and discussed contemporary political issues. Alley described his particular group in a diary entry intended for publication:

> Today is Saturday. It is the afternoon when we have our study group in the English language for those people who use it. Some, like the American married to the Chinese, have been born abroad. All have a great interest in keeping up with the times and in study-ing those events that have led up to the present. We are anxious at the moment to get forward, and to finish with the outline of Chinese revolutionary history, and get on to the present five year plan which is a really thrilling epic. In China today everyone almost [sic] studies politics, and the understanding grows deeper and deeper as the years go on. Our three hours together pass swiftly; for one question leads to another and all the while nine of us are deeply interested.[7]

Alley told Shirley Barton the gatherings were 'rather fun, as well as being instructive and helpful.'[8] For the Peking-based friends, the study groups were as much a social activity as they were an opportunity to discuss the dra-matic changes their adopted country was going through.

Despite Alley's high-profile status in the PRC, he was never quite trusted

by the Chinese authorities. In the paranoid atmosphere of Mao's China, foreigners, no matter how loyal to the regime, were always suspect isolates.
This was shown in numerous small ways. One of the most obvious and dis-
turbing to some of Alley's former associates who visited him from abroad
was that he was almost never left alone with a guest. His secretaries made a
point of listening in to conversations, and when Alley wished to visit
Chinese acquaintances he always had to have a translator with him – though
Alley spoke fluent Chinese and many of his contacts spoke English. Alley
was even forced to be guarded when talking with or writing to his New
Zealand family. Pip Alley visited his brother in the 1960s, and after seeing
some children playing in the street asked him why they weren't in school.
To Pip's discomfort, his brother launched into a fifteen-minute diatribe,
mostly for the benefit of the servant who was listening in.[9] Alex Yang, a
New Zealand-born Chinese man who visited Alley regularly from his arrival
in the mid-1950s to the mid-1980s, knew Alley was under surveillance and
censored his interactions with him accordingly. When he visited Alley, he
did not dare talk openly with him about what was happening in China. He
knew he could have been accused of sedition for telling Alley the truth
about campaigns such as the Great Leap Forward. Because of this isolation,
according to Yang, Alley was 'gradually weaned away from reality after
1949,' since he became separated from the lives of ordinary Chinese people
and as a foreigner there was always a wall between him and them.[10] As a
Chinese citizen, Yang had to write a report for his superiors every time he
visited Alley and needed a letter from his work unit to get permission to
visit him regularly. Alley never visited Yang's cramped quarters at the
Foreign Languages Press: to do so would have embarrassed the cadres who
would be required to accompany Alley on his visit. Even in the relatively
relaxed 1980s, the surveillance on Alley continued. Alley's youngest sister
Joy was particularly upset that she was not given a single moment alone
with her brother when she visited him for the last time in 1985.[11] Despite
living sixty years in China and committing his life to supporting the
Chinese Communist regime, Alley was always an outsider in his country of
adoption.

Compared to Chinese citizens, the privileged foreign friends lived well in
Mao's China. During the famine years after the Great Leap Forward the
foreign friends were provided with all the food they needed (though a small
number refused to take full advantage of these privileges). They were given
access to special shops, which provided goods unavailable to ordinary
Chinese citizens. In the period from 1959 to 1961, tens of millions of
Chinese people died from starvation or related causes and many more who
survived suffered permanent damage from the famine conditions. China's
foreign supporters were deeply involved in the propaganda campaign conducted to refute Western reports of famine in China during this period. A
small number of politically reliable foreigners were invited to give witness

to the Chinese government's claims that it was managing to feed its people despite three years of what it stated were 'natural disasters.' The American journalist Edgar Snow visited and wrote that he found no trace of famine after a six-month visit.[12] The 'Red Dean of Canterbury,' Hewlett Johnson, who was well known in the 1950s and 1960s for his involvement in the international peace movement, visited in the same period. Ignoring the rumours of famine completely, he described how he had supped on 'an excellent Chinese dinner' while China-based foreign propagandists Anna Louise Strong and Israel Epstein entertained the guests with stories of the lamaseries in Tibet, 'which consumed quantities of butter in lamps, while the people starved on herbs.'[13] Foreign visitors on short-term stays in China could perhaps be excused for being unable to break through the system of political hospitality that kept foreigners and the Chinese apart. But old hands like Alley knew about the famine while deliberately denying it both in public writings and private letters to correspondents abroad. Throughout the famine period Alley insisted that all was well. He wrote to his brother Pip in New Zealand in 1960, 'Mike [Alley's adopted son living in Beijing] sends you a card. He is well, and the kids are better than they have been. More vitamins in the coarse grain they are having now than in the polished rice of before.'[14] According to recent research, the greatest numbers of people died from starvation in 1960.[15] A year later he wrote, 'Yes of course people who do not want to struggle run to Hong Kong – that is the same in all revolutions. The magnificent thing about present day's China is the way she has gotten over three years of fantastically bad weather and kept on going.'[16] Pip was still not convinced, so Alley was forced to assure him still further: 'Don't worry about HK. The $3\frac{1}{2}$ million there all have relatives in Guangdong, and they come and go. . . . In the off season many people like to go there to stay with friends and relatives, and so on. Don't worry. No one is starving.'[17] Alley himself certainly faced no threat of starvation; he wrote plaintively during this time, 'How does one get weight down? I am 200 and should be 170. Only one way I suppose. That strong push away from the table!!'[18]

In 1960 Soviet Premier Khrushchev ordered the Soviet experts working in China to return to the Soviet Union immediately, taking their blueprints with them. This rupture was the first outward manifestation of the great tensions that had been developing between the erstwhile Socialist allies in the 1950s. The Sino-Soviet split brought significant changes in the make-up of China's foreign community, as those who were from pro-Soviet Communist parties were ordered home. The remaining pro-China foreigners were known by their detractors as 'Sunshiners' and 'Three-hundred percenters' for their unswerving support of Mao. A new group of foreigners were invited to replace those who had left and they tended to be less political than their predecessors were. The swift change in China's political alliances was confusing to many, even for someone on the spot like Alley. At first he discouraged his correspondents from discussing the affair. He told his brother, 'Should not write on the political differences between China and USSR's K [K stood for Khrushchev]. The two peoples are very close friends. K is a politician, a pygmy beside Mao. He will have his little day, but the Soviet people will stay. I have followed this since 1957, and it is too complicated to get over unless there is a lot of time and a good deal of background taken in. Best to just go along and take things in their stride.'[19] However, as the split became more obvious Alley wrote to Shirley Barton, 'It is now important to take a firm positive stand with things having developed as they have. China needs to be backed in a direct strong way, and the older concepts must bow before the newer ones.'[20] A few months later he told Barton, 'Everyone is studying politics these days, and one needs one's wits about one to keep up.'[21]

The Sino-Soviet split had a major effect on unity in the international Communist movement. In New Zealand the NZCP supported the Chinese, but some of its members dissented and split away to form their own group. As we have mentioned, Alley joined the NZCP in 1960, the year when the Sino-Soviet split occurred. The factionalism affected Alley's ability to be published in New Zealand as the mainstream Leftist publication *New Zealand Monthly Review* began to reject his articles. According to Pip Alley this was because 'Winston [Rhodes, editor of the *Monthly Review* and Professor in Economics at Canterbury University] had sided with the USSR and is a revisionist.'[22] However, the fact that the bulk of the NZCP took China's side in the dispute, and that Alley was now a member of that party, would prove extremely useful for bolstering the security of his position in China as anti-foreignism grew in the 1960s.

Regardless of the Sino-Soviet split, throughout the 1960s Alley continued his role of publicising China's political spin on events for a worldwide audience, incorporating and responding to the propaganda trends of the day. Increasingly, throughout the mid to late 1960s, Alley's writings reflected the growing Mao fever in China. His comments on what was known in the West as the Cult of Mao now seem remarkably prescient and accurate, though he was writing to deny its existence. 'Amongst ordinary people there have grown up myths surrounding this or that historical personage,' he wrote, 'with the tendency to lift him out of historical context and use him as a justification for what is essentially a reactionary position.'[23] Not only did his description fit the situation in China in the late 1960s, it came uncomfortably close to explaining Alley's own prominence.

The tumultuous upheaval known as the Great Proletarian Cultural Revolution (*Wuchanjieji wenhua dageming*) began in a seemingly innocuous way. On 10 November 1965, the Shanghai newspaper *Wenhui bao* published a piece of literary criticism on the play *The Dismissal of Hai Rui*, an article we now know as the first salvo in the revolt. In the same month, also in Shanghai, Chairman Mao met with a select group of foreign friends, flown in from their homes in Peking to celebrate American journalist and

105

well-known friend of China Anna Louise Strong's eightieth birthday.[24] The foreigners invited to attend the meeting with Mao were: Strong, Sid and Yulin Rittenberg, Rewi Alley, George Hatem, Israel Epstein, Frank Coe, Sol Adler, Julian and Donna Schuman, David and Nancy Dall Milton, and Chileans Jose and Delia Venturelli.[25] Significantly, at this meeting Mao, in typical casual style, revealed the major shift in policy signalled by the article: the launching of the Cultural Revolution. Mao told the foreigners that world revolution was in decline and in need of a vanguard party to lead it, and that the Chinese Communist Party would be that force. Mao's assessment of the international scene was that the US threat to China would decrease, while the threat of the USSR was likely to grow. He stated his desire to continue the struggle to reform Chinese society, regardless of what he described as his 'minority' in the Party.

As they had been in the past, the group of foreigners were proxies at that moment, for their governments and for world opinion. They were symbols of Mao's theoretical position that China's revolution was more than a nationalist struggle and in fact was part of a greater international movement. At the time, most of them did not understand the significance of Mao's comments, nor the meaning of their presence at the meeting. Within a few months, however, the popular movement was launched and the foreign friends could not avoid becoming participants.

Many of the foreign friends wanted more than just a symbolic role in the Cultural Revolution, they wanted the right to rebel too. Many of them believed their role as internationalist supporters of China entitled them to take an active role in political activities there. In June 1966 four American foreign experts wrote a *dazi bao* (big character poster) entitled 'What Monster is Driving us on the Road to Revisionism?', which they pasted up at the Foreign Experts Bureau in Peking.[26] The *dazi bao* criticised cadres within the bureau for imposing high salaries, élite living conditions and other privileges on foreign experts, thereby undermining their revolutionary work. To the surprise of the petitioners, a copy of their poster was shown to Mao who wrote a commentary praising it as a revolutionary statement. Mao announced that all 'revolutionary foreign experts' who wished to do so should be allowed to participate in the political movement.[27] A further directive from Mao stated, 'Revolutionary foreign experts and their children should be treated the same as the Chinese. No difference should be allowed. Please discuss this matter. All those who wish to should be treated this way.'[28] Mao's support for the foreigners' participation in the Cultural Revolution was in line with his dictum on intellectuals in New China that they must be both 'red' (have high political consciousness) and 'expert' (knowledgeable in their field). According to this line of thinking, foreigners who wished to work for the Chinese government should also follow these principles.

In January 1967 Chen Yi, Minister of Foreign Affairs, addressed a

Plate 8.1 'Peking, winter 1968' Rewi Alley with close friends George Hatem and Hans Mueller.

Source: Kathleen Wright papers, Alexander Turnbull Library, NZ.

meeting of the foreign friends and gave them approval to form their own rebel group or participate in Chinese ones.[29] The radical foreigners formed their own political organisation, the Bethune-Yan'an Rebel Group (*Baiqi-uen-Yan'an zaofandui*). For some foreigners the motivation to form the group was to support Chinese rebels, rather than to reform their own position in Chinese society. For others it was to fight for the integration of foreigners into Chinese life. The internationalist ideals of Bethune-Yan'an were symbolised by its organisational structure, which had delegates from five continents. The group aimed to unite the disparate group of foreigners around the common cause of support for China's line in the world revolution.

Just as it did in the Chinese community, the Cultural Revolution brought out the tensions and divisions between the foreigners. There was antagonism amongst them, between the old hands and the new. Some of the newer arrivals were jealous of the privileged position enjoyed by old China hands such as Rewi Alley and George Hatem and their apparently close relationship with the Chinese leadership. Meanwhile both Hatem and Alley were firmly opposed to the participation of foreigners in the Cultural Revolution, which they argued was a purely Chinese affair. Their disapproval of foreign participation in the movement was as much a defensive action as it was a principled stance about the role of foreigners in the PRC. Both Hatem and Alley feared that Bethune-Yan'an's criticism of the privileges accrued to the foreigners was meant as a personal attack on their own comfortable lifestyles. Alley wrote bitterly to his brother Pip, 'It seems to have become the fashion to criticise me, because I, now approaching the 70 mark, live quietly in two rooms at the top floor of an old Peking house built at the turn of the century. Because I have collected some small art objects, which give me a great deal of pleasure, as they do those real friends of mine who come and go.'[30] A later letter gives an indication of the difficulties caused by Alley's fractured relations with the Peking-based foreign community:

> Sorry to bring up the matter again, but please do not write me in anger, and above all please do not quote me on anything you feel my letters indicate. Actually, I do not know much about the situation here – no foreigner does – and you can make as good estimates of the world scale as I. You can quote from anything I say in articles or poems, but not in letters. Letters written carelessly, often when tired at the end of the day, are not pontifications. I try to say things as clearly as I can, but always I have much trouble from the chant 'Rewi said . . .' so much so, that I keep clear of most of the permanent foreign community here. If one says 'Good morning' to some people they are liable to rush off and say, 'I met Rewi Alley, and he said good morning in such a funny way. I wonder what is meant by it?' Then the second person enlarges on the tale and bang, bang it

goes around until in the end it dumps back on one! Some people like to complicate everything and to the Chinese, who have high standards of discipline, this all seems unruly, and the people concerned untrustworthy.[31]

Alley not only found himself in disfavour with many of the other foreigners in Peking, he was also attacked by Chinese rebel groups in his work unit. The Peace Committee was closed down for good at the beginning of the Cultural Revolution in 1966, and its cadres engaged themselves in 'making revolution.' *Dazi bao* were pasted up outside Alley's front door accusing him of seeking publicity and personal fame,[32] being an 'imperialist with ulterior motives,' and a 'bourgeois Rightist,' meaning that his writings weren't Leftist enough for his Chinese critics.[33] In Lanzhou, Alley's honorary title as headmaster of the Lanzhou Bailie School was taken away from him. The movement he had inspired and led, Gung Ho, was labelled an imperialist organisation by rebel groups,[34] and all who had been associated with it came under suspicion. The accusations against Alley, which had lain dormant on his personal file since 1952, came back to haunt him in this period. Alley wrote a report based on documents from the earliest days of the co-operatives, proving that they had had the support of Mao Zedong and other Chinese Communist leaders all along, and in fact had been working under their instruction.[35] In answer to the critics of Gung Ho who said it was bourgeois and imperialist, Alley stated that the inspiration for the movement had in fact come from an article written by Mao Zedong that had reached Shanghai in 1937. This, he claimed, led to Edgar Snow writing the first promotional pamphlet for Gung Ho.[36]

It was unfortunate that New Zealand historian Willis Airey was writing his biography of Alley during this period. Though Airey died before the book could be completed, his wife Isobel Airey was able to finish it with the help of Alley's close friend and ally Shirley Barton. In a letter written in 1969, perhaps the low point of all Alley's sixty years in China, Alley told Barton the background to the problems the writing of the biography had brought up:

> Isobel [Airey] wrote me asking me to do a foreword. I said I could not do that, much as I would have liked to be able to say what I feel about Bill in it. One of the criticisms that come to me is that of personal name seeking, publicity loving, etc. In Gung Ho it was necessary to have a name and mine was used. Seeing that it was there, I have tried to use it in the best way possible throughout these later years. That is all. The last half dozen books I have written are stacked up in manuscript form, and most probably will never see the light of day partly because of this, I guess.
>
> It was very good of you to cut out some of the immature things a

young person writes. I am not the type which develops fast. Truths penetrate but slowly, and sometimes quite painfully.

Good that you have family ties. Mine have scattered to the four winds in this movement. The kids are all with communes or state farms, the old people in some development centre. The struggle to change the nature of man, get together and refashion the hinterland, keep off the imperialists, and so on, is a vast enterprise.[37]

As she had with Alley's first book, *Yo Banfa!*, Shirley Barton co-ordinated with him to carefully edit the manuscript of anything that might reflect badly on his position in China. Alley and George Hatem, who also acted as an adviser on the book, had earlier instructed Airey to keep all mention of Chinese names out of the book.[38] Reflecting the xenophobic climate of the times, Alley cut certain sections which he feared gave 'too much emphasis to the New Zealand end of things.'[39] Airey's suggested titles for the biography, 'Warrior' and 'Flanders,' were also problematic, Alley wrote that 'If used [they] would amount to an attack on me at this time.'[40] Eventually the innocuous title *A Learner in China* was adopted. The title aimed to convey a sense that Alley had spent his years in China humbly learning from the Chinese people rather than arriving with any notions of Western superiority. If it didn't quite match with the reality of Alley's experiences in China it was at least politically safe. As I have mentioned earlier, the author Willis Airey had been asked to remove information on such matters as Alley's early political leanings and his desire to join the Shanghai police. Though Airey had access to the full collection of Alley's letters home to his family and other papers in New Zealand, in 1968 the majority of these were burned by Pip Alley at Rewi Alley's instruction. Clearly, as the little that remains of those papers demonstrates, there was too much in them that contradicted the image that Alley and others had carefully constructed of his public persona. In the terror-filled days of China in the late 1960s, Alley could not afford the possibility of the truth about his past being revealed.

During this frightening time, Alley warned his brother Pip on a number of occasions not to talk about him in letters or to ask him what was going on in China. He told him, 'I have no knowledge whatsoever.'[41] Alley refused to specify directly what was happening to him other than mentioning some 'misunderstandings.'[42] He did, however, inform Pip that 'There has been a complete stop to publishing my books here, until the movement finishes, next year I suppose. Even the binding of the Hubei one awaits new assessment of the work. But I am all for the Cultural Revolution. It is important.'[43] Pip invited his brother to come back home to New Zealand and stay with him, an offer Alley was unwilling to take up, no matter what the problems he encountered in China. He was afraid that once he left he would never be allowed back.

As he did with any change in the political current, Alley outwardly supported the movement one hundred per cent. 'You will be hearing a lot of Taiwan, TASS and other stories of the more lurid kind,' Alley told biographer Willis Airey in 1967, 'Struggle there is in plenty, but Chairman Mao is good and the people are good, and it will all work out. . . . On the Liu Shaoqi issue, it is the trend back to revisionism that Chairman Mao is fighting. The picture is one of considerate struggle, but Mao will win easily.'[44] He told Pip, 'Queer that some still think old Liu could do anything else but push for revisionism, which is not revolution, but something else entirely. This fact has now been more than fully shown up.'[45] Alley tried hard to maintain the pretence that everything was normal during the Cultural Revolution. In 1969 he wrote to Pip Alley, 'Glad that the [New Zealand–China Friendship Society] Conference was a success. You got no message from here, as organisations are busy with study etc. just now. Actually, the friendship societies have quite a role to play in enlarging people's understanding so that they look for deeper material later.'[46]

Occasionally an oblique comment in Alley's letters of this time reveals his true feelings about the 'struggle' going on. 'In revolution you always need to have a base in mind,' he told Pip. 'If thugs come to muck up a place though, it does not do them much good in the eyes of the people. Never pays. So do not worry.'[47] The 'thugs' Alley indirectly referred to were the Red Guards who had been instructed by Mao to destroy the traces of China's corrupting past, wrecking ancient monuments and burning private collections of valuable books and antiques in the process. Four of Alley's adopted son Alan's six children and both of Mike's two became Red Guards. Publicly Alley praised the Red Guards' destruction of temples and other vestiges of the past, though in private he worked hard to prevent the destruction of his own and his friends' precious *objets d'art* in the violent years of 1966–1969. A journalist in the 1980s visiting Alley at his home in Peking noted, 'The 500 year old Ming paintings on a screen on the terrace were saved by [Alley] from a temple during the ravages of the Cultural Revolution. . . . Alley always did what he could to collect and preserve art works and historical artefacts. Unlike many ordinary Chinese, Alley and all his collections of Chinese art and literature were protected during the Cultural Revolution by Zhou Enlai.'[48] The interesting question the quote raises is what Alley was doing scavenging from temples during this period. Given the terror of those times, especially for foreigners, Alley's version of how he got the Ming screen is probably incomplete.

At the beginning of the Cultural Revolution, Alley's old friend Song Qingling sent precious paintings and porcelain to Alley to keep for her. Alley's home was a safer location than Song's at that time for such things. By 1968, however, Alley too was under siege, suffering from 'almost universal suspicion.'[49] Song Qingling, who was by this time under the protection of Zhou Enlai, wrote a letter in support of her old friend. As late as 1970, Alley was still not allowed to travel freely around the country to get material for his writing, and he wasn't able to meet with Song Qingling or George Hatem, to avoid being seen as conspiring with them.

Though he would later bitterly denounce the Cultural Revolution and the main scapegoats Lin Biao and the so-called Gang of Four, in this period Alley wrote for and edited Anna Louise Strong's pro-Cultural Revolution, pro-Jiang Qing newsletter *Letter From China*. According to well-known translator Yang Xianyi, 'Rewi behaved very wisely during this time. He remained friends with us [Yang Xianyi and his English wife Gladys Tayler, who were under political suspicion and later imprisoned] and helped Anna Louise because that was the thing to do. But when he talked to us, sometimes he made sarcastic comments. Rewi did not always stand on principle. You could not survive if you did.'[50]

Over the months of 1967, the foreigners' rebel group Bethune-Yan'an became increasingly radical. Although Mao had given permission for revolutionary foreigners to participate in the Cultural Revolution, there was concern from some leaders about the appropriateness of this decision. Jiang Qing and Lin Biao in particular were known to be disapproving of foreign involvement in Chinese political struggle. Tension grew about the foreigners' involvement in the Cultural Revolution, whether as observers or activists. It became increasingly dangerous even for those who supported the 'rebel' position to participate. On 17 October 1967, British friend and foreign expert at the Foreign Languages Institute, David Crook, was imprisoned after trying to intervene in a student dispute.[51] He was held in custody for five years and his wife Isabel Crook was held under house arrest.

A few weeks earlier a new campaign had been announced to root out renegades (old cadres who worked in the CCP underground and had been arrested by the Nationalists), special agents (agents of foreign imperialism) and die-hard 'capitalist roaders' (cadres who weren't revolutionary enough). The revolutionary zeal of Mao's followers had become too dangerous, as they were willing to call the whole system into question. Mao decided to regroup his forces and unite the population by redefining the targets they were to rebel against. The foreign friends became victims of this new line, a line that encouraged already existent anti-foreign feeling.

From January 1968 foreigners were forbidden to participate in the Cultural Revolution. They were to be excluded from Chinese political life because, according to Zhou Enlai speaking five years later, 'Some had supported this faction and some that, and then you have these bad people stirring up trouble.'[52] Most members of Bethune-Yan'an, excluding the leadership and a small band of followers, voted to close down the group after the arrest of their *de facto* leader Sidney Rittenberg; soon after, the Chinese authorities detained the remaining leaders: Israel Epstein, Elsie Fairfax-Cholmeley and Michael Shapiro. These three were held in prison until 1973. A number of other foreigners were arrested at this time, also on trumped-up charges of spying.

There was a deep sense of bewilderment and fear among the resident friends in 1968. Many left China at this time. Anna Louise Strong even asked the visiting Belgian writer Han Suyin (who was not known for her political nous), 'Can you tell me what really happened during the Cultural Revolution?'[53] Despite living in and writing about China for her regular news-sheet *Letters from China*, Strong could not understand the turn the revolution had taken. Both Strong and Rewi Alley were, unusually so, quite outspoken in their criticisms when they spoke to a group of New Zealand and Australian students in January 1968. Alley was scathing of the Shanghai Red Guard zealots, who he said were 'a lot of pseudo-intellectuals, most of whom hadn't the faintest idea of what it meant to work as a peasant.'[54] Of course, by that stage, when the political tide had turned, it was politically acceptable to criticise the so-called Ultra-Leftists who had formed a people's commune in Shanghai. Alley wasn't breaking ranks, it was just that his personal views happened to coincide with the current line.

Pip Alley wrote to his brother asking after the fate of the Peking foreigners during the Cultural Revolution. Alley told him not to discuss them; with the exception of the old hands (like Alley and George Hatem) he thought they were 'rather a class unto themselves,' and dismissed his brother's concerns with the trite slogan, 'The thing that matters always is the people.'[55]

In 1969, Alley was isolated and scared, unable to travel and frightened he might be either arrested or deported from China as so many other foreigners had been. It was at this desperate moment that he turned to his old confidante, Shirley Barton, for comfort. He wrote to thank her for her help in editing Willis Airey's biography:

> You have always been a wonderful full-back. I shall never be able to thank you for all the support in difficult days gone past. Often kicked myself for ever letting you go, but actually did save you many a heartbreak, I am sure. In revolutions one must not give hostages to fate, and for the main part things must be faced alone, if one is in another land where change changes those who know one, etc. And I have always tried to put the Chinese revolution first in everything. How much help I really have been able to give, I do not know. But I hope never to leave it.[56]

Alley was extremely lonely at this time: even his Chinese family kept their distance from him for fear of attracting political trouble. He told Barton, 'Lao 3 and 4 [George Hogg's adopted sons] come in with their kids at times. But for the rest I do not see much of the old Shandan bunch. Alan and Mike I do not see either. Their kids along with their generation will be going back to the villages to become farmers. This will be good.'[57]

Whatever Alley's intentions were in declaring to his old friend that he had 'often kicked [him]self' for letting her go, Barton's reply was definite: she had never thought of herself as 'his' to begin with. 'I can only say that whatever I decided to help was viewed by me as objectively as possible,' she wrote in response to a poem sent by Alley praising her work on his behalf.

> After all, I was not very young when I came to China and I had already learned to distrust emotions and personal attractions as a base for action. I had learned to give help and support not to a person but to a cause – and to 'take cognisance of the objective situation' – an excellent and never failing guide. This sounds a bit smug. I can't say I always succeed, but honestly I have tried. Therefore the male chauvinist idea that the female has no integrity and will simply follow the strongest male personality is peculiarly bitter to me. I backed you Rewi, both at Shandan, and in *Yo Banfa* etc, not for your charms (considerable though these are!) but for what you are and represent – the cause you are identified with – the cause of China and the world.[58]

Though people who knew them both in New Zealand rumoured that Barton was in love with Alley, from this letter and others it is clear that from Barton's point of view the connection was based more on shared political beliefs than any romance (or at least so she proclaimed). One may wonder whether Alley's declaration to her was pure fantasy, born out of desperate loneliness and fear. Described as a misogynist by some of the women who knew him well in Peking, had he been given the choice, it is unlikely he would have amicably shared his life with a woman. Alley's close friendships with women such as Shirley Barton and Song Qingling were 'heterosocial' rather than heterosexual. And in his ambiguous sexuality he conforms to the norms we have already described in Chinese traditions; norms that worked in terms of 'tendencies,' 'actions' and 'preferences,' rather than sexual identity.

None the less, however frightening and difficult this time was for foreigners, the consequences of the xenophobic turn were much more serious for their Chinese families and those who associated with them, whether in a private or professional capacity. Having relatives abroad or associating with foreigners was a criminal offence in the Cultural Revolution. Alley's adopted family suffered badly because of their foreign connections. Alan Alley, who was working at the Lanzhou Oil School, was beaten repeatedly and imprisoned in a 'cow shed' (the term used for the makeshift cells for persons under political suspicion in this era).[59] Alley was forced to be oblique about even this brutality. He told Shirley Barton, 'Alan is having a pretty thin time at the moment. Doing manual labour in the mornings reading Mao in afternoons.'[60]

Not only did Alan Alley have connections with a foreigner; he had been briefly imprisoned by the KMT in the 1940s for his work with the CCP, which in the Cultural Revolution hysteria meant he was also under suspicion of being a KMT spy. Alley wrote to Pip asking him to search amongst the papers he had stored in Christchurch for a letter written by Alan in 1946, when he was arrested by the KMT. Pip told Willis Airey, 'Rewi states that if it is found and presented to the Chinese authorities, Alan's name will be cleared. Evidently the Chinese have never trusted him since the time he was put in gaol by the Nationalists.'[61] Meanwhile, Alley's younger son Mike and his family suffered too for their connection with Alley: Mike was forced to dig ditches for two years.[62] Alley's sister Kath, back from a five-week trip to China, reported that 'some members of the Red Guards had seen Rewi drive up to Mike's place, and thought he was a capitalist. They reacted by breaking up Mike's furniture. However this story is not for publication. . . . Rewi has a guard and has had one for some time.'[63] Alan Alley managed to escape from his imprisonment and found haven with Alley and the Hatems in Beijing. He was finally 'liberated' through the intervention of Zhou Enlai. While Alan was in prison, Alley told Edgar Snow in 1970, 'all around him comrades were dying of beatings, starvation, exposure and suicide.' Snow noted in his diary that Alley was lonely and isolated, he no longer saw his Chinese family, 'He spoke quietly in a mix of nostalgia and loneliness and cautious hope.'[64] The break in normal relations with his Chinese family continued right up until the overthrow of the Gang of Four in 1976. Pip Alley visited China in 1974 and reported to Shirley Barton, 'Rewi . . . went for a walk in the park yesterday after seeing Mike and Li Li [Mike's wife] off to their home (he will not be seen at their actual home).'[65]

Despite the fact that Alley continued to be under political suspicion, the Sino-US *rapprochement*, beginning from the secret visit to China in 1971 of US Secretary of State Henry Kissinger, meant that the foreign friends became useful again to the Chinese authorities. On 5 October 1971 approximately fifty foreigners living in or visiting China met with Zhou Enlai, Guo Moruo and Geng Biao for a 'cordial, friendly conversation.' The group was told of Nixon's impending visit to China and asked to help facilitate Sino-US friendly relations. With the exception of Alley and Hans Mueller, all the other foreign guests were American citizens. Alley's political rehabilitation began from this period. He was allowed to visit New Zealand and was once again frequently on hand to host the increasing numbers of foreign delegations that came to China as a result of the shift in foreign policy. Due to the new stress on 'friendship' rather than ideological goals, the Chinese People's Association for Friendship with Foreign Countries (commonly known as the Friendship Association or by its abbreviated Chinese title *Youxie*) became the main foreign-affairs organisation involved in hosting foreign groups.[66] This organisation took over responsibility for the management of Alley and the handful of other 'permanent guests' who had formerly been looked after by the Peace Committee.

Although Alley's political role was restored from this period on, his personal situation continued to be tense. His letters to friends and family in 1976, during the last months of the Cultural Revolution, were vague and ambiguous. Alley briefly described demonstrations in Tiananmen Square in March and April. The demonstrations, ostensibly in memory of Premier Zhou Enlai who had died on 6 January 1976, were a form of protest against the Chinese leadership. The day before the Tiananmen Incident of 5 April 1976, when scores of people were seriously injured or killed by attacks from militia and armed police, Alley visited the square. 'Probably half a million people on Tiananmen today. Big demonstration,' he told Shirley Barton, though he did not tell her what the demonstration was about.[67]

New Zealand left-wing publishers Progressive Books were in the process of republishing Alley's most successful book, Yo Banfa!, at this time. Shirley Barton, once again in the role of editor-cum-censor asked her old friend what should be removed. Alley told her, 'On cuts leave what you like, hold what you like. Except for references to people like Liu Shaoqi.'[68] Barton accordingly eliminated all mention of Alley's admiration for Liu's book How to Be a Good Communist, which had been in the original Yo Banfa! Alley's foster son Deng Bangzhen, a professional artist, was forbidden by his work unit to draw a cover for the revised version of the book because Alley was still under suspicion.[69] New Zealand reporters asked to interview Alley on the political upheaval going on in China but, as he wrote to Barton, 'The interview business with me at this juncture, believe me, old dear, is quite impossible. The New Zealand Broadcasting [Corporation] also asked me, but I turned them down. Low profile needed at the moment.'[70] In the final paragraph of the revised Yo Banfa!, Alley wrote:

> Vast people's movements like those of the Great Leap Forward, and the Cultural Revolution, have swept the countryside, leading to better livelihood and a deeper political understanding everywhere. Education and the way education will go, is still a hot topic in China. I am very happy that the method of education as used in Shandan, that of a combination of theory and practice, is more and more becoming standard practice in colleges and schools all over China.[71]

All of the above was a fib at best, if not a complete lie, but it was what Alley had to say at the time. In a 1985 interview, in response to the question 'Was the Cultural Revolution a failure?', Alley replied 'I think by and large it was. Of course there were good things that happened at every stage. A lot of people gave up a lot and did a lot of things, but I think you could say it was ten years of growing chaos which came to a culmination toward the end of Mao's life.'[72] After 1981, the CCP officially negated the Cultural Revolution and it was the proper thing to criticise it. In any era, Alley had an answer to fit all viewpoints.

After the death of Mao Zedong in September 1976 and the arrest of the Gang of Four in October of that year, China entered a new phase. Alley wrote to Barton, 'We are all very happy with events in China now, and there will no doubt be a strong movement forward as a result.'[73] A week later he wrote, 'The city is a mass of sound, banners and marching feet. The people are expressing themselves in no uncertain way. . . . They preface a big change all round. We are all very happy. Hans, George and I and friends had a little celebration last evening. All very heady stuff, but heading progress all round.'[74] Shirley Barton wrote in reply, 'It is very reassuring to know you are all "very happy with events in China now." We have to meet the usual lot of questions, some anxious, some malicious, so strengthen our hands please.'[75]

Alley wrote the booklet 'China and the Clear Road Forward' to explain the new political line, copies of which were mimeographed and sent to New Zealand–China Friendship Society branches around the country and published in the national newsletter. As he told Barton, 'It is very important in the next stage for China to have her friends all over the world. Friends who have some understanding and can analyse.'[76] Though Mao was dead and some of his associates had fallen from power, the new leadership, officially led by Hua Guofeng, who presented himself as Mao's designated successor, still faced a power struggle. In 1977 Alley wrote, 'The drums and bugles, gongs and songs are all out on the streets here in Peking today. Everyone pleased that Deng [Xiaoping] has come back into the leadership again. I have written some lines and hope they carry some understanding. The revolutionary force is on the ascendant and that for mad chaos has lost out. . . . The coming back of Deng Xiaoping is momentous. Good news for China indeed.'[77]

As always, the political changes required a rewording and reordering of Alley's written output. A book of poems was being published in New Zealand by Caxton Press at this time:

> With regards to the book of poems, the importance of title. I gave the list to my committee of George and Hans. They thought we ought not to use Gang of Four slogans at this stage. The present stage is in trying to correct the mistakes of the Gang of Four, bringing back confidence to people in the good old cadre leadership, halt any trend to cynicism, and get the whole nation working as it did before the big upsets. 'Why do we live?', is an enduring idea, that needs to be kept in mind. At the moment there needs to be a basic clearing of minds.[78]

After the Cultural Revolution Alley reassessed his views a little – at least in private – about what had happened. He told Barton, 'I send you my collected translation of the poem about Liu Shaoqi which was published here. . . . There are no gods, only people. All leaders especially in chaotic times are liable to make mistakes, but the main thing is to be true to the cause. Liu Shaoqi was framed, and a lot of lies told about him. He did have mistakes like everyone else had, but nothing that deserved the treatment he got. The legacy of the Russian method in dealing with people is a pest.'[79] After Barton replied sympathetically he wrote to her again on the same subject, falling back on the old excuse he used each time the Party line changed: he had not understood before.

> Thanks for the letter about Liu Shaoqi, I did the translation in penance for believing in the frame-up, with no real knowledge of what was going on, though by 1974 I had more idea and by 1976 was fairly awake, though I did not know the extent of the damage. But sometime when you come we can discuss this. I am on the side of the people who keep this part of the world operating, and they are good. Have always been good. There are people who work and those that live on that and scheme.[80]

As always he clung on to his standard line that the CCP system was essentially good, no matter what it did. In an interview in 1976, in response to a question on what would happen to Jiang Qing and company now that Mao was dead, Alley replied,

> The function of a man like myself, a foreigner in China, is to try to make clear what the Chinese people are trying to do. They are trying to make a new world using creative and productive qualities of the back country China. I leave all discussions of politics and intrigue to the China watchers in Hong Kong. That's their job, and it's much safer for them on the periphery than it is for me here.[81]

Alley's claims to be a fool rather than a knave in his reporting on the Cultural Revolution can not go unquestioned. Some of the violence and abuses happened literally right outside his door, as his residence was opposite the Peking Muncipal Government offices, the scene of much Red Guard conflict, and less than five minutes' walk from Tiananmen Square where massive demonstrations were held in 1966–1967. As he complained in private letters, from 1966 to 1968 loudspeakers from opposing factions in the Peking government blared day and night near his home. Unlike most other foreigners in China at this time, Alley was not cloistered in foreigners-only accommodation; his apartment was in the compound of the then Peace Committee, which, as a part of the foreign-affairs establishment, was deeply involved in rebel activity. And unlike the majority of foreign experts in China at this time, Alley spoke and read fluent Chinese and had a wide circle of Chinese friends and acquaintances. Through them he had access to informal news in China as well as having the privilege of being allowed to listen to foreign news broadcasts on his own radio. Members of Alley's own adopted family in China were victimised because of their connection with him, as were those who had worked with him in the Industrial Co-operative Movement. He himself was under considerable pressure, as were his closest foreign associates in China. Alley had lived in China long enough to be sceptical about sudden policy changes and character assassinations. Yet he accepted at face value stories of the cruelty of Liu Shaoqi's wife Wang Guangmei at the model communes she supervised, and published them in his book praising the policies of the Cultural Revolution.

From the mid-1950s on, Alley seems to have adopted a policy of always going along with the dominant political tendency and its propaganda line. Before the Cultural Revolution, if the line changed he switched tack without mentioning the old, for example not questioning the failure of the Great Leap Forward, simply promoting how well China was doing despite 'three years of natural disasters.' After 1978–1979, when the government's political about-face was too drastic to be ignored, he explained his positive accounts of the Cultural Revolution in terms of not knowing the real situation and joined in the chorus of those who publicly denounced Jiang Qing and the rest of the so-called 'Gang of Four.' For someone whose status in post-1949 China rested on his propaganda work for the government, to have taken a critical attitude to government policies would have been suicidal. He risked banishment from China or possible imprisonment. He had nothing to return to in New Zealand, and he knew that if he left China it would be would be seen by many as a rejection of the CCP government. Though he was privately critical of much that went on, Alley had no desire to provide ammunition for China's critics. Alley's self-deception and deception of his foreign readers about what was really going on in China was deliberate and calculated. And under the conditions of the times, at least up until the late 1970s, he was not at all foolish in doing so.

The end of the Cultural Revolution meant a full restoration of status for old friends of China, as well as a reorganising of the government policy towards foreigners. In the Deng era, foreigners were no longer automatically suspect as they had been in the past. They could be useful to China's new policy of opening up to the West. China needed the help of foreign friends both old and new as the nation began to rebuild. Just as Alley wrote in a 1979 article, in this new epoch, the role of foreign friends became more important than ever before to China's development: 'China is a quarter of the world, but in the days of super power rivalry, she is anxious to reach out in a people-to-people relationship that will grow ever stronger and lead to the world without war.'[82] Both Chinese and foreigners needed to be 're-educated' about the new tasks for foreigners in helping China's economic development, and the government stepped up its propaganda on the necessary role of foreign friends accordingly.

China's foreign supporters not only needed to understand that the

Cultural Revolution was over, they had to accept the revolution in economic policy that was to characterise the Deng era. Many former Maoists turned away from China at this time, unwilling to accept the new line. Within the New Zealand Communist Party, debate about Deng's shift in policy caused rifts that almost broke up the party. Naturally Alley supported the new policy direction; he was critical of those within the New Zealand–China Friendship Society who supported the 'Albanian line' and criticised China's repudiation of the 'Gang of Four.' He called them 'imbeciles . . . China must somehow modernise to feed her people. Another year of Gang of Four would have cost millions of lives by starvation. The going in many areas to halt this has been epic in these last two years.'[83]

The end of the Cultural Revolution and of the Mao era led to a nation-wide reassessment of political cases. Thousands of political prisoners were released and many more had trumped-up charges and slurs removed from their personal files. The allegations from Shandan days that had dogged Alley's career and those of the other teachers and students at the school were finally cleared in 1977. Alley received an official letter commending the Shandan Bailie School 'since its inception,' and his two adopted sons were also cleared of accusations against them and allowed to resume their previous jobs.[84] However, the separate allegations against Alan Alley, that he had been a KMT spy, were not completely settled until 1981.[85]

Alley's political rehabilitation was made public by the elaborate celebration at the Great Hall of the People in 1977 for his eightieth birthday, which was attended by Deng Xiaoping as well as most of the other leading figures of the day. The lavish event was in recognition of his long and unswerving service to the CCP. At the banquet held in his honour, Alley acknowledged the compliment being paid him with the modest statement, 'The encouragement given on this occasion will certainly help over all the years to come.'[86] In addition to the political rehabilitation of cadres who had been involved in the Bailie School and other Chinese Industrial Co-operatives activities, the Gung Ho movement itself was re-categorised as a patriotic organisation. Alley's links with the Lanzhou Oil School were also officially re-established in 1982, the fortieth anniversary of the founding of the Bailie Schools. On this date, he was finally reinstated with the title of Honorary Headmaster.

Alley's newly regained prestige in China was marked by privileges usually the exclusive right of China's top leaders. When New Zealand Ambassador Atkins visited Alley at the resort of Beidaihe in 1977, he had difficulty getting in touch with him. He told the New Zealand foreign ministry, 'We were not permitted to contact Mr Alley direct, but had to pass messages to him through the "concerned department" (this hitch I hasten to add was not of Mr Alley's making – it was simply that his guest house was in an area out of bounds for foreigners like us).'[87] Though the New Zealand Embassy included Alley in its social activities, Alley was wary. At a 'Rewi

Alley' film and cocktail evening in Peking, held to show New Zealand journalist Geoff Chapple and film-maker Geoff Stephen's documentary on Alley,
an embassy official noted: 'He is still as canny as ever. Thus it was noticeable
that when asked a question inviting some criticism of economic events in
Mao's "Great Leap Forward", Rewi answered in diplomatic terms of unim-
peachable objectivity.'[88] When he was hospitalised for his numerous ail-
ments, Alley was well looked after, staying at a hospital that New Zealand
diplomats reported was 'clearly used by Chinese leaders. There is no lack of
facilities, comfort or attention.'[89]

Alley clearly had an ability that not all foreigners or Chinese shared: that
of following the current political line and perhaps even sensing the next one
before it became obvious. This ability served him well throughout the
Chinese government's political campaigns, especially during the Cultural
Revolution. While many other foreigners went to jail or had to leave the
country, Alley remained unscathed through his good relations with Song
Qingling and Zhou Enlai and his will to stay out of trouble. But despite the
pragmatism and good connections that helped save his own skin, Alley was
racked by guilt because he had survived while others had not and that he
had even joined in the attacks. For many years after the end of the Cultural
Revolution, Alley frequently wrote to close friends mourning the fate of his
old revolutionary acquaintances such as He Long, Chen Yi, Peng Dehuai,
Liu Shaoqi and others less famous.

Plate 8.2 Rewi Alley on holiday at Beidaihe, 1979.

Source: Photograph courtesy of Eva Siao.

However, Alley's need for penance did not extend to his own adopted family, who suffered during the Cultural Revolution because of their relationship with him. Alley's grandchildren Mao Mao and Bao Bao, children of his adopted son Mike, wrote in 1978, 'In the old days, we suffered a lot from the rule of the Gang of Four. We had been kept from you by them, and injured badly. They took the just relationship between you and us as a unthinkable thing which you were very hard to bear in the past [sic]. So we all have a bitter unforgettable past.'[90] The children were seeking Alley's help to leave China, preferably to go to live in New Zealand and start a new life. Alley refused to help them, on the grounds that they should stay on and work for China. He felt they made use of his name for disreputable ends. 'I am tired of having any good qualities I may have once possessed, exaggerated highly for the purpose of promoting the interests of family members.'[91] A few months later he complained that 'Mike's family are so mad to go to New Zealand it spoils the pleasure of seeing them. I have no way to send them. And do not think it is a good idea, without a definite plan, what to do, what to bring back. Simply to live off people!'[92] Mike's daughter, Bao Bao, even went behind Alley's back to try to make use of his connections to leave China. After he found out what was going on, Alley wrote apologetically to his old friend and confidante, Shirley Barton, 'Do hope you are not bothered with Bao Bao's pressing. She took your letter to me from my desk to her organisation to show them she is welcome in New Zealand. Heaven protect me from the demanding, rather spoilt group of the present college graduate generation. Every place is better than their own, super critical of everything. Thanks be for 800 million Chinese peasants!'[93]

Alley consequently became estranged from the whole family. Their aspirations and demands were alien to him. 'Believe Mike is in Guangdong working in one of those special areas for capitalists from Hong Kong,' he informed Shirley Barton, 'Still trying to get the kids to New Zealand, I have not seen any of them since last July.'[94] Mike was eventually able to get both children to the USA where they worked at low-paid jobs, though both had university qualifications – Bao Bao as a doctor, Mao Mao as a translator. In 1984, Mike Alley tried to publish a biography of his adopted father without his permission. Alley complained, 'Poor Mike – he wants to gain face for his family on my little achievements so badly.'[95]

The crisis with his Chinese 'family' makes one question how genuinely Alley felt the connection with his adopted and fostered children and their extended families and what it meant to them. Though much was made of this connection in the last years of Alley's life and after his death, in actual fact, Alley had only a few years in close proximity with those who were known as his 'Chinese family.' In Shanghai, Alan and Mike, the two boys he adopted, were sent to boarding school, spending only weekends and holidays with Alley. After 1938 both boys went to the north-west to help the CCP resistance while Alley became involved with the co-operatives. He saw little of them until after 1949, when through their connections in the CCP he was able to resolve the problems at the Bailie School. The Nie brothers, whom he looked after in Shandan when George Hogg died, moved to live with their father in the north-east, soon after 1949. Alan Alley eventually settled in Lanzhou to become the headmaster of the Lanzhou Oil School, while only Mike lived in Peking. The years of political tension and remoteness from their daily lives in post-1949 China put great pressure on Alley's relations with his adopted family. Even in his own 'family' he was always an outsider and, potentially, a liability. In the 1950s and 1960s, Alley tried to keep in touch with his adopted and fostered sons and their families, though he was limited by travel restrictions and regulations managing Sino-foreign interactions. As the political climate became increasingly xenophobic, the connection with Alley became increasingly dangerous for his adopted Chinese family. After 1979, some of them became a liability for him.

Alley was quite unsympathetic to the materialistic demands of the new generation of Chinese youth in the 1980s. In 1983 Alley wrote to Shirley Barton,

This urge to have youth leading is all very well if youth had the experience and ability to be able to make meaningful decisions. It would not be easy to steer a straight course with Deng Xiaoping and Hu Yaobang. Though there are many power lustful in the younger age groups who are keen to step up. . . . The anarchist idea of egalitarianism in everything results in chaos. Power for power's sake not to struggle to push the thing we struggle to attain. It is very common for someone with some developed faculty to look at people without it as fools, just as the literati of old KMT days did. Yet it was the often semi-illiterate who won the war years of Resistance and Liberation.[96]

Alley wrote the poem 'Demonstrate for What?' in criticism of student demonstrations in Tiananmen Square in 1986:

> [. . .] surely to demonstrate in historic Tiananmen
> brings the eyes of the world
> on ambitious youth and a pleasurable notoriety.
> Students are maintained by the State
> to study and to help the masses
> as their servants, not as their masters
> [. . .][97]

Alley was not only unsympathetic to the demands of many Chinese intellectuals for greater freedom in China, he maintained a lifelong anti-intellectualism that was as much a product of his New Zealand upbringing as it was an affinity for Maoist dogma.

Alley's views grew increasingly conservative throughout the 1980s. He wrote in 1984 of his approval for Deng's economic reforms: 'It is a changing world, and China needs all its friends to carry it through. I think that Deng [Xiaoping], Hu [Yaobang] and Zhao [Ziyang] are being very objective, and that their policies fit the needs of the day.'[98] Two years later, however, Alley supported the forced resignation of liberal CCP Party Secretary Hu Yaobang 'so we can now look forward to an insistence on essentials instead of just love the USA and copy her in all. Old Deng is a tough old boy and a good leader.'[99] Like many of China's foreign friends in the Deng era, Alley became increasingly uncomfortable with the rampant consumerism and corruption Deng's economic reforms introduced. But like all the other old resident foreigners whose livelihoods were dependent on the CCP government, he knew better than to make these objections publicly known, saving his bitter asides for a few trusted confidantes.

9

NEW ZEALAND'S ASSET

In the stately old Italian Legation, only a few weeks before his death in December 1987, our group met with the controversial and legendary Rewi Alley (Lou Alley the Chinese call him). Here was a 'grandfather' figure of folklore. As I sat by him in a large comfortable armchair, searching for adequacy of words – in a room so English and Western – my mind debated the New Zealand propaganda that had been put into my head about this man. A communist, no less. Red China, what's worse. It's not what we know, I decided. As usual it was what we didn't know.

On that day, beyond meeting this 90 year-old special person (who had come out of hospital by his own choice to give us time), it was the tears and gifts borne by the Guilin visitors, who were also meeting him for the first time, that left the strongest message for me. Just what had this man done for China to earn such respect, and what future doorway had Rewi Alley opened wide for us? ... In the big-China picture ... Rewi Alley had crafted a respected calling card for New Zealand.[1]

In a 1987 article entitled 'New Zealand's "Calling Card"' Jeremy Dwyer, Mayor of Hastings, described his meeting with Rewi Alley in the deepest awe. To the mayor and many other New Zealanders, Alley was the grand old man of New Zealand–China relations, whose very name opened doors. Though Alley's 'communist' (note the use of lower case) sympathies were noted, this was for background interest only. By the 1980s, the Rewi Alley myth had come full circle and Alley was once again a figure New Zealand politicians were proud to claim as their own. Dwyer's account reflects the change in attitudes towards Alley that came about after New Zealand formalised diplomatic relations with the People's Republic of China. From this time, the government began to realise that Alley's presence and status in China were more an advantage than a disadvantage.

New Zealand's recognition of the PRC in 1972 was a result of changing circumstances in China's domestic and foreign politics. By the end of the 1960s, China's foreign policy began to shift away from the xenophobic excesses of the early days of the Cultural Revolution. Sino-Soviet relations were at an all time low, Sino-Vietnam relations were strained, Sino-Japanese relations were distant. China acted to improve this situation by strengthening existing ties and developing new ones – aiming at countries that had not

Plate 9.1 Rewi Alley, mid-1980s.
Source: Photograph courtesy of Eva Siao.

yet recognised the Communist government. The new initiative was pushed along by a dramatic increase in cultural exchanges and people's diplomacy activities that helped to soften attitudes towards the PRC. The immediate objective of the Chinese government was to break the US circle of containment and to enable China to determine its own relations with the rest of the world.[2]

Rewi Alley's two visits to New Zealand in 1971 and 1973 were part of this initiative, as were reciprocal visits of table tennis teams (what was called ping-pong diplomacy at the time) between New Zealand and China in the early 1970s. China was particularly interested in improving relations with small and middle powers such as New Zealand and Australia because it did not see itself as sharing the same interests as the two superpowers, the USA and the Soviet Union, and hoped to weaken the alliance other smaller powers had with these two giants. In the early 1970s, through its unofficial envoy Rewi Alley, China encouraged New Zealand to adopt 'an independent stance in foreign policy.'[3]

The possibility of recognising the People's Republic of China had been discussed many times by the New Zealand government, but as the then New Zealand ambassador to Washington, Frank Corner, concluded in 1966:

> All New Zealand governments since 1950 have recognised that on this question the attitude of the United States is, and must be, the most important factor. And having in the last few years gone to considerable lengths to strengthen our relations with the United States, it would seem unwise to place those relations in jeopardy by supporting an initiative to which the US was opposed unless our own vital interests required it.[4]

The ambassador's comments reflect the lack of antagonism in the New Zealand government's position on China pre-1972 as well as the lack of ideological bias – non-recognition was simply a policy that New Zealand felt it was required to go along with for the sake of relations with the USA. Numerous despatches from New Zealand officials in Washington reported the intransigence and the extremism of the US position on China in the 1950s and 1960s.[5] Yet in contrast, as early as 1956, a Prime Minister's Department memo commented that the New Zealand public seemed ready to recognise China 'at any time the government wishes to accord it.'[6]

Rewi Alley's influence in China and his usefulness to New Zealand had long been felt by those New Zealanders who campaigned to get their government to recognise the PRC. A letter from the well-known broadcaster Colin Scrimgeour (popularly known as 'Uncle Scrim') to Alley in 1971 shows the naïve belief of many in his ability to get things done in China. Scrimgeour wrote asking Alley to assist him in arranging a medical exchange between the two countries. He told Alley the exchange was significant because 'It would give those of us in New Zealand who are anxious to overcome our image of being "running dogs" for US imperialism a chance to show that not all New Zealanders are of that type.'[7] A copy of the letter and Alley's reply were sent to New Zealand Prime Minister Keith Holyoake, who encouraged the proposal and asked to be kept informed. Unfortunately, at the time and indeed at any time in China post-1949, Alley did not have the power or influence to put such ideas into action and nothing came of it.

None the less it was true that Alley did have extremely good contacts with China's top leadership, especially in the foreign policy arena. In 1967 he informed his brother Pip that the PRC was going to reconcile with the USA, at a time when few people could have been alert to this possibility.[8] In 1968, when many other resident friends of China were arrested on suspicion of spying and held without trial for several years, Alley, George Hatem and Anna Louise Strong were the only ones to be granted the annual privilege of a holiday at the summer resort of Beidaihe.[9] Before Alley's visit to New Zealand in 1971–1972 he met with Premier Zhou Enlai, something he made a point of emphasising to the New Zealand media at the time.[10] Prior to his visit the following year he met with Vice-Foreign Minister and close associate of Zhou Enlai, Qiao Guanhua.[11]

On 22 December 1972, the New Zealand Labour government finally established diplomatic relations with the People's Republic of China. New Zealand's decision to recognise the PRC came about mainly as a result of the USA–China *rapprochement*, but it was also an important part of the election manifesto of the newly elected government. Since Washington had changed its China policy (with very little notice to its allies), New Zealand was free to establish relations with Peking. In the lead up to the 1972 elections in New Zealand and Australia, the Labour Party of both nations not only promised to recognise the People's Republic of China, they also agreed to co-operate with each other on foreign policy. On 5 December 1972 the Whitlam Labor government announced its intention to seek 'immediate negotiations' with PRC representatives in Paris to establish recognition.[12] Soon afterwards the Kirk Labour government in New Zealand instructed its diplomats to do the same with PRC representatives in New York.

In 1972 there was a common view among New Zealand academics and foreign-affairs officials specialising in China that New Zealand had followed US foreign policy far too closely for the last twenty years, to the detriment of its own interests.[13] While the USA had improved its relations with the PRC, New Zealand still treated China like a foe. Academic W. T. Roy argued that New Zealand needed to develop its own working relationship with the People's Republic, separate (but not entirely divorced) from the USA.[14] In the early years after diplomatic relations were established, New Zealand's interests in China were more political in nature than economic. The New Zealand economy was still geared to the demands of the European market and the government wanted peace in South-East Asia and the South Pacific where its vital shipping links were located, so that it could get on with this lucrative trade. The New Zealand government was also concerned about the encroachment of Soviet power into the Asia–Pacific region. China had a similar perspective on the usefulness of relations with New Zealand. The New Zealand embassy in Peking summed up this view in its annual report of 1973. The report stated that China valued its relationship with New Zealand,

> not so much because of our ties with Britain, America or Japan, as for our links with the countries of South East Asia – and perhaps with those of the South Pacific too, though they have not so far shown much interest in that area. Their main aim in South East Asia is to keep the Russians out.[15]

The visit of New Zealand Prime Minister Muldoon to China in 1980 focused on a topic of common concern to both governments: the spread of Soviet influence in the Asia–Pacific region. Both countries emphasised their shared international perspective, such as concern about security of the Asia–Pacific region, Soviet and Vietnam involvement in Cambodia and the Soviet invasion of Afghanistan.[16] Astonishingly, given his profound anti-Communism, Muldoon told Deng Xiaoping 'any support China could give to the island states of the [Pacific] Forum whether political or economic would help maintain political stability in the South Pacific and make it very difficult for Soviet penetration to take place.'[17]

The pragmatic relationship that came to exist between the two countries from the early 1980s on, free of ideological dogmatism, took some time to develop. When diplomatic relations were first established in 1972, the public image of China in New Zealand was dominated by the spectre of ideological extremism. Meanwhile, the public image of New Zealand in China, such as there was, was represented by the figure of Victor Wilcox, chairman of the New Zealand Communist Party and frequent visitor to China in the 1960s and 1970s. Wilcox's writings were published in Chinese (long before Alley's were) and his photo regularly appeared on the front page of *People's Daily*. Until the 1980s, it was Wilcox, not Alley, who was the most famous New Zealander in China.

The year 1972 marked the end of an era, and as diplomats continually reminded the New Zealand government thereafter, New Zealand needed to give some indication that the 'old era' was over and that it was taking a new, 'essentially humanitarian' position on international relations.[18] The honouring of Rewi Alley in some form was seen as an ideal means to demonstrate this.[19] The Australian government seemed even more aware than New Zealand of the usefulness of the Rewi Alley connection. Gary Woodward, former Australian ambassador to China, wrote: 'It is generally accepted that

Australia was not on the Chinese leadership's map when political contacts were opened in 1972. We had no equivalent of Rewi Alley or Dr Norman Bethune.'[20] The Australian diplomat and academic Dr Stephen Fitzgerald told New Zealand foreign-affairs officials in 1972 that he regarded Rewi Alley as 'New Zealand's greatest asset in China.'[21] The notion that Alley was an asset for New Zealand in China rather than a liability led to a further role for him, as symbol of the new New Zealand–China relationship. China was also in need of improving its image in New Zealand and Rewi Alley was the figure selected for this end. To Chinese diplomats, Alley's obedience and loyalty to the twists and turns of CCP politics was a fitting symbol of the style of foreign relations it hoped to have with New Zealand.

From the New Zealand government's perspective, Rewi Alley's new role grew out of recognition of his high standing in China and his stated willingness to assist New Zealand to improve its relations with the PRC.[22] From the Chinese government's perspective, the selection of Alley as a symbol of New Zealand–PRC relations was part of an established strategy for strengthening connections between China and other nations. Particularly from the 1980s, PRC foreign-affairs officials involved in people's diplomacy and foreign propaganda activities were instructed to work on finding common points with foreigners, de-emphasising issues of conflict.[23] Alley and other foreigners such as Canadian doctor Norman Bethune, who had worked with the CCP in the years before 1949, were prime figures to serve as 'common points.' In his history of New Zealand–China interactions from 1792 to 1987, Chinese diplomat Zhang Beihua noted, 'The Chinese like to take some striking foreign figure as a symbol of good relations between China and other nations, and Rewi Alley provided just such a figure.'[24] In its relations with Kenya, China cites the giraffe as a symbol of 'friendship between the Chinese and African peoples.'[25] The Chinese government claims to date the establishment of China–Kenya relations from 1415 AD, when a giraffe arrived at the Ming court from the vicinity of the country now known as Kenya.[26] According to Zhang Beihua, New Zealand–China relations date from 1792, when a sealing expedition came down the New Zealand coast to procure skins for the China market.[27] Technically, therefore, the symbol of China–New Zealand relations should by rights be the seal. Unlike Kenya, however, New Zealand is fortunate in having a suitable human figure to symbolise its relationship with China, namely Rewi Alley.

From the time when the New Zealand embassy was first set up in Peking, Alley was invited to attend official functions there as a living symbol of the relationship between the two countries, and most VIP visitors from New Zealand arranged to meet with him during their stay. In the early 1970s China was still in the grip of Cultural Revolution xenophobia. As a cautionary measure, most Chinese citizens and foreign friends living in China kept their distance from foreign-embassy staff to avoid accusations of being a spy. However, Alley made a point of attending functions at the New Zealand embassy to signal that he supported the development of New Zealand–China relations. Embassy officials also visited him at home on social calls. The diplomats found that Alley was extremely circumspect, and he usually tried to keep conversation to topics concerning matters pre-1949.[28] In private Alley expressed his exasperation at the seeming desire of sceptical Westerners who always hoped to catch him out in a criticism of the Chinese government.

New Zealand diplomats urged the government to find a means to commemorate Alley in order to make the connection more concrete. A Waikato University request for assistance to set up a Rewi Alley scholarship in Chinese Studies was repeatedly turned down by both the Labour government and the National government that followed it in 1975. Both governments were uncomfortable with Alley's Communist Party links, though they acknowledged the value of his connection with New Zealand. Labour Prime Minister Kirk was so anxious about Communism that he kept file cards on members of the various factions of the New Zealand Communist movement, so as to ensure that Labour MPs did not unwittingly become associated with United Front activities.[29] A Ministry of Foreign Affairs report commented on the reluctance of the Kirk government to honour Alley's contribution to New Zealand–China relations: 'The Labour government, still under some fire for the speed and manner of their recognition of the PRC, were not keen to go too far in acknowledging the work of Rewi Alley, still a controversial figure in New Zealand.'[30] A further attempt to elicit support for the scholarship from the government in 1975 and again in 1977 resulted in a similar response.

Nevertheless, even the cautious politicians recognised that it would be advantageous to recognise Alley's role in some way. The reluctance to support the Waikato University scholarship in the 1970s was partly because it had little public support (only NZ$1,500 had been received from the New Zealand public) and because the other half of the NZ$3,000 eventually raised had come from the Chinese People's Association for Friendship with Foreign Countries. The New Zealand government regarded the scholarship as a propaganda tactic to enhance the public image of the PRC in New Zealand. In the Cold War atmosphere of the 1970s, neither the Labour nor the National government was willing to be associated with such an initiative. Yet when the scholarship was finally instituted at Waikato, the government made use of it to promote closer relations. A ceremony was held to mark the occasion at the New Zealand embassy as a means 'to associate the Chinese authorities in Peking with the scholarship.'[31]

New Zealand's first ambassador to the PRC, Bryce Harland, was particularly anxious to see the Rewi Alley connection recognised and exploited for New Zealand's benefit. In 1975 he prepared a report for Prime Minister Muldoon outlining his reasons for supporting a Rewi Alley Chair in Chinese Studies at Victoria University:

(a) Rewi Alley has done more for his fellow man than almost any other New Zealander, and he is well-known internationally, but his work has never been recognised by his own country.

(b) In learning to live with our neighbours, it is essential for us New Zealanders – or at least some of us – to acquire an understanding of countries like China <u>as they are today</u> [sic][32]

Ambassador Harland's plan to establish a Rewi Alley Chair in Chinese at a New Zealand university lacked university support. The main problem seemed to be a lack of funding for such a project. Moreover, both Waikato and Auckland University opposed the initiative, perhaps because it might have taken funding away from their own China-related programmes.[33] New Zealand diplomats continued to search for an alternative means to commemorate Alley. The possibility of publishing some of his letters from China was considered but rejected by Alley's brother Geoff as 'a sticky undertaking.'[34] (What he didn't inform them was that some of the most interesting letters had been burnt in 1968 at Alley's request.) Other suggestions included setting up a teaching exchange in Alley's name, a literary scholarship or a scholarship in Chinese studies separate from the Waikato initiative. All were turned down on the grounds of lack of finances and, it seems, from 1975 until 1984, Prime Minister Muldoon's strong resistance to any official recognition of Alley's activities in China or his potential role in improving New Zealand–China relations. Muldoon turned down a number of attempts to commemorate Alley and unlike later politicians made no mention of Alley in his official speeches during his two visits to China. Though Alley was seated at the top table at banquets hosted by both governments, Muldoon still refused to meet with him in private and refused to be photographed with him.[35] Foreign Affairs officials wrote to the Prime Minister in 1980, 'China has honoured Rewi Alley as it has honoured only a handful of foreigners. It would seem appropriate that New Zealand should do something to recognise his achievements and his peculiar role in our relations with the People's Republic.'[36] Muldoon replied with a terse, 'I have some doubts as things change from time to time.'[37] In 1983, in preparation for the visit of Chinese Premier Zhao Ziyang to New Zealand, diplomats tried once more to persuade the Prime Minister that the time had come to honour Alley as a symbol of New Zealand's improved relations with China. They were told, 'Rewi Alley not a starter.'[38] Muldoon was, however, capable of political expediency if necessary, especially if it was at no cost to New Zealand. In 1977 a letter of congratulation was sent to Alley in Muldoon's name for his eightieth birthday celebrations. The congratulatory message was lavish in praise, if not quite true:

On behalf of the Government and the people of New Zealand, I want to offer you warm congratulations on your 80th birthday. The

work you have done during your fifty years in China has contributed greatly to the development of understanding and friendship between our two countries. We are proud of you.[39]

Muldoon and his scriptwriters' hypocrisy is indicative of the New Zealand
government's general policy on Alley since 1972 and of the attitude
reflected repeatedly in the hefty files on him in foreign-ministry archives.
This stance is characterised in the first place by a deep cynicism towards
Alley's work in China and the esteem in which he is held by the Chinese;
second, by doubt over the intrinsic value of the Rewi Alley connection to
New Zealand–China relations; and, also, by the view that New Zealand will
only remember Alley so long as the Chinese government continues to do so.
The esteem with which Alley had formally been regarded in New Zealand in
government circles in the 1940s and 1950s had ebbed, as those who knew
him or his family personally retired or passed away. Although by 1972
Foreign-Affairs officials recognised that Alley was indeed an 'asset' for New
Zealand in its dealings with the People's Republic, in the eyes of diplomats
of later years, his once-outstanding reputation was tarnished by decades of
apologia for the Chinese Communists. They also tended to be the most
vociferous source of rumours that Alley was a paedophile whose tastes were
catered to by the Chinese government in return for his pro-China work. To
most diplomats, having Rewi Alley as a symbol of New Zealand–China relations became a source of private embarrassment and disdain. It was only per-
petuated because of Chinese insistence on commemorating the role of
foreign friends in the Chinese revolution.

The pressure for the New Zealand government to recognise Rewi Alley's
work in China was partly accentuated by the knowledge that Alley, aged
seventy-five when diplomatic relations were established, could not live for
much longer. In 1980, after reports falsely announced his death, diplomats
at the Peking embassy reminded the government to at least take steps to
have a suitable obituary available.[40] The draft obituary that was prepared is a
testimony to the disingenuous faith of a few people in the Ministry of
Foreign Affairs that the Rewi Alley connection was helpful to New Zealand,
regardless of the reluctance of government leaders to publicly acknowledge
it. The obituary concluded with the statement:

> Rewi Alley symbolised in a very individual way, the friendship
> that can develop between peoples of different countries and differ-
> ent societies. We in New Zealand have been privileged to
> benefit from that friendship as we have sought to develop our
> ties and widen our understanding of that vast land of which
> he became a part. In honouring his memory, we look forward to
> even closer friendship between the people of China and New
> Zealand.[41]

The impression of a 'close' and 'special' relationship between New Zealand and China as a result of Alley's labours was strongly reinforced by comments from Chinese officials. Although at Alley's eightieth birthday celebrations in 1977 speeches merely described Alley as 'an old friend of the Chinese people and New Zealand writer,'[42] in 1982 when Sino-New Zealand contacts were beginning to expand Wang Bingnan, President of the China Friendship Association at the time, described Alley thus:

> Comrade Alley deserves to be called a fine son of the New Zealand people. He carries such fine qualities of the New Zealand people as courage, tenacity, a constant urge to explore truth and daring to get things done. How brilliantly these qualities sparkle when combined with the revolutionary cause of the Chinese people, under the guidance of advanced ideology.[43]

In this speech, Wang, as a representative of the Chinese government, publicly acknowledged Alley's work in China in support of the CCP and deliberately stressed his New Zealand antecedents. This was a broad hint aimed at the New Zealand government that it should maximise the Alley connection in order to strengthen New Zealand–China relations. Yet part of the problem of New Zealand recognising Rewi Alley's contribution to its relationship with China was a reluctance on Alley's part to accept awards from a Western country. The reasons were political; as a foreigner in Communist China, Alley had to be very careful of his connections with foreign countries, including his own. In early 1972, Alley had only agreed to accept an honorary doctorate bestowed on him by Wellington's Victoria University because the New Zealand Communist Party told him it would be 'good for the cause.'[44] After diplomatic recognition was established New Zealand officials and politicians proposed on several occasions that Alley should be granted honours, yet he continually refused to accept them. Alley was always cautious of accusations, both in China and elsewhere, that he sought out personal publicity. He told Shirley Barton in 1984, 'any acceptance would destroy my face here . . . to offer such a thing shows that folk do not understand China very well or my place in it.'[45] Later that year, however, Alley finally agreed to accept an award that was exclusive to New Zealand, the Queen's Service Medal. The New Zealand Ambassador reported that Alley, although unenthusiastic about the award, had agreed to accept: 'If they thought it was a good idea in terms of improving the New Zealand–China relationship [Alley had] no objection to it.'[46]

Alley's eightieth birthday in 1977 marked his official political rehabilitation in China. The late 1970s also marked the beginning of what is called 'reform and and opening' (*gaige kaifang*), when the PRC finally opened its doors to all foreigners regardless of their political beliefs, and actively sought out foreign investment and foreign trade. From this time on, public interest in both Alley and the People's Republic of China escalated rapidly in New Zealand. As travel to China became less restricted, the number of New Zealand journalists who visited China increased and an article on Alley seemed to be an almost obligatory part of their stay. An embassy report noted that there were at least five New Zealand proposals to film documentaries about Alley's life and work in China.[47] The proposal by Geoff Steven's Phase Three Films was eventually accepted, 'partly because Ron Howell [then President of the New Zealand–China Friendship Association] supports it, and partly because it is about China rather than about Rewi Alley.'[48] In 1978 Alley was still reluctant to attract any personal attention. The filmmakers reported that he told them, 'he will not contribute to any film designed to glorify himself but he would be prepared to participate in a film which would tell effectively something of the life in New China and its contrast with the old.'[49] Phase Three Films proposed to use Alley as an interlocutor between New Zealand and China:

> In these documentaries Rewi Alley's unique knowledge and understanding of both China and New Zealand societies could be used to translate some of the important achievements in China into a form easily understood by New Zealanders. In effect he would act as a 'bicultural lens' through which China could be seen and appreciated by New Zealanders not having his benefit of bicultural living.[50]

Peking Television also made a documentary on Alley in 1978, entitled 'Rewi Alley Friend of the Chinese People.' The programme marked the beginning of the Chinese government's initiative to promote Alley as a model figure to the Chinese people:

> At 81, Rewi Alley looks back on half a century of life and work in China, having lived through the many difficult years together with the Chinese people and making invaluable contributions to their revolution. In the meantime he continues to write prodigiously in his unremitting zeal to proclaim to the world the victories of the Chinese revolution and the tremendous achievements of China's socialist construction. . . . 1977 saw the publication of the latest collection of his poems. *The Freshening Breeze* is filled with the author's joy at the continuing forward march of the Chinese revolution to new victories after the smashing of the 'Gang of Four'. . . . His comprehensive knowledge of both countries past and present allows him to make comparisons with the perfect ease which is a characteristic feature of his writing.[51]

Alley's ability to compare favourably the differences betweeen old and 'New' China was particularly valuable in the post-Cultural Revolution era when

China was attempting to rebuild itself after ten years of upheaval. As the government embarked on a radical programme of modernisation, economic reform and opening up to the outside world, China needed to convince both its own people and foreign supporters that Deng Xiaoping's reforms were taking China in the right direction. Alley's comments supporting the reforms and linking them with what had gone before featured prominently in the documentary:

> [The Chinese revolution] has been an important thing for the world, bringing together, as it does, one quarter of the people that exist and bringing them together in the idea of making friendship with all countries, countering the plans of imperialists, new and old, superpowers who threaten the peace everywhere. I feel that it is a very important thing at this time to be able to go on working for friendship with other countries, making China better understood abroad, carrying on with the lessons that we taught at the beginning of the war of resistance of Gung Ho, 'work together'. We think that is a pretty good slogan for the peoples of the world in the next stage.[52]

The documentary listed Alley's contribution in China, from work in the Shanghai underground to adopting Chinese children, noticeably omitting both his factory inspecting and his relief work. Non-Chinese biographical reports on Alley always stressed the significance of this work as marking the beginning of his humanitarian activities. For Alley's Chinese hagiographers, however, since he had worked for the semi-colonial government of the International Settlement it was not worthy of mention. Following the pattern of all Chinese commemorative activities about Alley after 1977, the Chinese documentary made a point of emphasising Alley's association with Deng Xiaoping, showing footage of Deng shaking hands with Alley at his eightieth birthday celebrations.

Alley's changed status was watched closely by New Zealand diplomats. Any attention paid to Alley by senior Chinese leaders was closely monitored by the New Zealand embassy, lists of those who attended his various birthday celebrations from 1977 onwards were noted on file, as were news items on Alley in the print and television media. The 1977 birthday celebrations were perceived by the embassy as very much a Chinese affair and the ambassador planned simply to pay a courtesy call on Mr Alley, 'in order not to intrude on what was clearly to be an essentially Chinese occasion.'[53] Only at the last moment was the ambassador invited to Alley's eightieth birthday celebrations: invitations were received one day before the banquet.[54] In 1977, using Alley as a focus for the *rapprochement* of Sino-NZ relations wasn't a high priority for the Chinese government. As China opened up to the outside world, however, and sought to improve its relationship with other countries, New Zealand began to play a more official role in Alley-related commemorative activities.

In the Deng era, Alley's birthday and the anniversary of his arrival in China always attracted visits from China's current top leaders. Embassy staff were astounded by the honour Rewi Alley was shown by the attendance of such high-profile figures at his birthday and other anniversaries. On the occasion of the fifty-fifth anniversary of Alley's arrival in China, 21 April 1982, Ambassador Tony Small reported:

> with the death of Edgar Snow, Alley must by now be the principal 'old friend of the Chinese people' in residence here; and his formidable contribution to China's social and economic progress make him very much a world figure. . . . It is symptomatic of the degree of regard in which Alley is held that at an initial private meeting held in the Association [for Friendship with Foreign Peoples] grounds . . . the attendance included Liao Chengzhi, Vice-Chairman of the Standing Committee of the National People's Congress, and Huang Hua, Vice-Premier and Minister of Foreign Affairs. Neither stayed very long, but had taken the time, during the busy session of the Standing Committee of the NPC, to come and give their greetings. Our Vice-Minister in the Foreign Ministry – Zhang Wenjin – was also present, but stayed for the entire ceremony.[55]

This high-level attention would continue even after Alley's death. Alley's loyalty to the CCP no matter what happened was respected by CCP leaders and was a model for Chinese citizens to follow.

With the election of the fourth Labour government in 1984, the pace of New Zealand–China relations stepped up as the new government saw hope for export markets in the vast Chinese economy. The Labour government made trade the predominant element in its foreign policy and emphasised this in 1988 by changing the name of the Ministry of Foreign Affairs to the Ministry of External Relations and Trade. Asia, in particular China, was seen as an obvious market for New Zealand products. Consequently, the new government was very willing to make use of Rewi Alley as a symbolic figure to underline New Zealand's so-called 'special relationship' with China if it would help trade prospects.

The formal title for Alley's new role as symbol of New Zealand's renewed relationship with China was not designated until 1985. New Zealand officials were always careful to mirror the vocabulary used by the Chinese to praise Alley. In 1982 Ambassador Small noted in a report, 'Quotable quotes from Wang [Bingnan's] speech: "a fine son of the New Zealand people", "sparking qualities", "a down-to-earth doer".'[56] Three years later Ambassador Watt's speech described Alley as having 'down-to-earth ability and commonsense.'[57] The description of Alley as a 'Bridge builder' (*jianqiaoren*) between New

Zealand and China was first used by Alley's confidante and fellow official friend of China, George Hatem. A dispatch from the embassy in 1985 on the occasion of the presentation of Alley's Queen's Service Medal reported that 'George Hatem . . . made the quite striking observation that Rewi Alley had not only built a bridge between his two countries, but had stood successfully at both ends.'[58] In 1986 Alley described himself as feeling 'privileged' to have helped to 'build a bridge of friendly relations between my homeland, one of the smallest countries in the Pacific, and the land of my adoption, one of the largest in the world.'[59] From this time onwards the term was commonly used by both New Zealand and Chinese officials to describe Alley's role in New Zealand–China relations. In the same year Prime Minister Lange wrote of Alley, 'He is truly a man who has bridged the distance between our two countries.'[60] In 1988 Chinese Foreign Minister Huang Hua praised Alley as 'the great builder of the gigantic bridge of mutual understanding and friend-ship[61] between the Chinese people and other peoples of the world.'[61] The term 'bridge builder' was not unique to Alley, however; it was also used by the Chinese to describe the work of many other foreign friends, such as American journalists Edgar Snow and Anna Louise Strong.

The change in emphasis in New Zealand–China relations was reflected in the 1986 update of Alley's obituary statement from the New Zealand government. Rather than stress the 'friendship' between New Zealanders and the Chinese that Alley helped to foster, which was mentioned in the 1980 version, the new obituary claimed that 'In honouring [Alley's] memory, *New Zealand can look forward to even closer and more broad-ranging friendly relations with the Chinese people from all walks of life*'[62] (italics added). Unlike Muldoon, both Labour Prime Minister David Lange and his Minister of Overseas Trade Mike Moore made a point of being photographed with Alley when they visited China. While speech notes from the visits of minis-ters of the previous National government to China were noticably lacking in mentions of Alley, Labour ministers made a point of drawing attention to his work in China and his connection with New Zealand. Mike Moore's meeting with Madame Chen Muhua, Minister of Foreign Economic Rela-tions and Trade, in 1984 is representative. In his prepared speech, Moore deliberately linked New Zealand's trade interests in China with Alley's work for the Chinese:

> I now have the honour of leading the largest ever trade delegation to leave New Zealand shores, and this Madame Chen is a measure of our intent to boost the level of our involvement in your great and expanding economy to the mutual benefit of both countries.
>
> Of course, New Zealand already has a 'significant' presence in China in the form of our dear friend Rewi Alley who has worked so selflessly in your country and has brought a warmth to our relation-ship that is unique.[63]

Talk of a 'special relationship' with China became increasingly common during the term of the Labour government, particularly in the period 1985–1987. According to the then Ambassador to China, Lindsay Watt, there was euphoria in government circles at the amount of attention China seemed to be paying New Zealand.[64] The enthusiasm of the Labour government for utilising Alley as a symbol of New Zealand–China relations was reinforced by Alley's supporters in New Zealand. The New Zealand–China Friendship Society took pains to link the idea of New Zealand's 'special relationship' with China to Alley's groundwork and pressed for New Zealand companies to recognise this by supporting Alley's own projects in China. In an article headlined 'Rewi Alley's Goodwill Paves Way for China Trade, Companies Urged to Show Thanks,' Jack Ewen, president of the Society, commented that it was in New Zealand companies' interest 'both culturally and economically' to support Alley's projects in China. Beginning in the early 1980s, Alley had beeen working to get the co-operative movement going again in China and to rebuild the Shandan Bailie School. As in the past, both these projects required massive amounts of foreign aid, and Alley naturally looked to New Zealand to provide some of that assistance. In the same article, Garth Fraser, General Secretary of the United Food and Chemical Workers Union and prominent Alley-supporter, criticised New Zealand companies trading with China for 'not giving enough in return for the goodwill Rewi Alley has created.'[65] In a further piece, Tom Newnham, president of the Auckland branch of the New Zealand–China Friendship Society, also made a point of linking the dramatic increase in recent years of New Zealand's exports to China to Alley's work:

> Rewi Alley ... made his life in China some 60 years ago and so identified himself with China's tremendous struggles for independence, dignity and social justice that he is now the most respected foreigner in the country. It is as a New Zealander that he is known to millions of Chinese. His life story itself has helped enormously to boost the confidence of Chinese in their dealings with us, free of suspicions that they might have say, in dealing with a super power.[66]

Certainly the Chinese government was very interested in the election of the New Zealand Labour government in 1984. The grounds for such favourable interest may be seen in a number of articles, published in Chinese political journals, noting the Labour government's firm stance against apartheid, the anti-nuclear policy that resulted in the break up of the ANZUS alliance, efforts to improve relations with Third World countries, assertion of New Zealand's responsibilities as a South Pacific country to the other small island states of the South Pacific, determination to make trade a fundamental aspect of New Zealand diplomacy and, last but not least, a firm commitment to developing friendly relations with China.[67] A further group of articles published in the mid to late 1980s illustrate why New Zealand's commitment to co-operation in the Asia–Pacific region was of interest to China. The articles outline China's interest in forging regional co-operation in the zone. Along with its economic goals of modernising the Chinese economy, the Chinese government was concerned to develop political alliances in Asia and the Pacific, as a counter to US and Soviet power. China saw itself as a natural leader of such a bloc.[68] It was in China's interest as much as it was in New Zealand's to maintain the idea that there was a 'special relationship' between the two countries. What many New Zealanders dealing with China didn't seem to realise at the time was that in the 1980s, China claimed a 'special relationship' with virtually every country it had diplomatic relations with. Not only that, the much vaunted 'friendship' between the two peoples was a standard cliché in China's diplomatic vocabulary.

The Labour government's enthusiasm for utilising Rewi Alley as a symbol of the New Zealand–China relationship was extended to its readiness to spend money to provide tangible evidence of this link. The Labour government paid for such Rewi Alley commemorative activities as a statue by sculptor Anthony Stones for the Peking embassy, renovation of Alley's former cottage in Moeawatea, a sculpture of Alley by Chinese artists for his birthplace, Springfield; donations of books to the reopened, renamed municipal Shandan Bailie Library; as well as substantial donations to the newly constructed Shandan Bailie School. Alley wrote to the Peking embassy of his aims for the new school:

> The great needs of Shandan, lie in improved methods of agriculture, animal husbandry and forestry, But as no existing elementary education teaches these subjects and there is no provision for practical training in such schools the idea began to rise that to cope with the need, a new Bailie School should be set up near the Bailie Farm (the old school farm) and that its students be taken from the existing primary school, and carried through middle school years, in a half-study half-work manner until graduation, when they could help to raise local standards. It was felt that a school of this kind would provide a model to other schools in the North-West, where these subjects are all important.[69]

In 1987 the New Zealand government announced a donation of NZ$150,000 from the 1986–1987 Overseas Development Aid budget to help build the school, as well as an additional NZ$20,000 for associated costs.[70] In 1988 the government announced it was donating a further NZ$60,000 to the school.[71]

Alley's efforts to have the Shandan Bailie school reopen in the 1980s offered new opportunities for New Zealand to deepen relations with

China by targeting aid to projects linked with the school. Gansu, one of China's poorest provinces, was greatly in need of modernisation. While other richer Western nations might be able to lure trade deals with more accessible regions by means of generous loans, Gansu was a province where New Zealand officials hoped that New Zealand had a natural advantage: Rewi Alley's long association with the region. As a small and remote country, New Zealand had to work hard to attract the attention of the Chinese government. The commemoration of Alley and support of his Shandan Bailie School was an important means for this. A Rewi Alley Scholarship was established in 1984 to provide the opportunity for post-graduate study in New Zealand for a student from Gansu in the agro-horticultural sector.[72] Advising the government to support the Bailie school, one official told his superiors in Wellington, 'As you know we strongly favour proposal that there should be an official New Zealand contribution to the new Shandan Bailie School. Rewi himself would greatly appreciate this. Nor would a contribution that was sufficient to be meaningful be unnoticed by the top Chinese leadership in Beijing and in Gansu Province.'[73]

The New Zealand government's emphasis on the connection between Gansu Province and New Zealand came at a cost. In a visit to Gansu and Qinghai to discuss trade prospects New Zealand officials discovered that the Chinese authorities

> were expecting New Zealand to offer low interest finance or tech-nical aid to them and they obviously had not considered that they would have to pay for consulting and equipment provided by us . . . the Gansu authorities told the Ambassador during his visit there that they would like to develop a project with New Zealand *because of Rewi Alley* but whether or not they were prepared to pay money for it was another matter.[74] [Italics added.]

Clearly the Gansu provincial government hoped to take advantage of the New Zealand–Gansu connection to get some low-cost assistance. Chinese officials seem to have realised early on that the utilisation of Alley's name might gain them an extra advantage. A 1982 report of a meeting between embassy staff and Gansu officials noted, 'Mr Zhou welcomed us and referred to Rewi Alley's assistance to the Province of Gansu and a school which he had set up many years ago.'[75] Even Chinese leaders from areas outside Gansu made references to Alley. At a dinner with Wei Chunshu, Chairman of Guangxi Zhuang Autonomous Regional People's Government, held to discuss the development of model farms in the region with the help of New Zealand technology, New Zealand diplomats recorded that 'The Chairman entered with tremendous zest into a discussion about his old friend, Rewi Alley.'[76]

The focus of Rewi Alley commemorative activities was to some extent restricted to Gansu because of Alley's wish that any projects associated with his name should go to the Shandan Bailie School. In 1986 a coalition of private-industry interests that proposed to found the Rewi Alley Cultural Foundation to promote cultural and educational exchange between New Zealand and China was turned down by Alley, who stated, 'the only organisation I trust in New Zealand [to use my name] is the New Zealand–China Society [sic].'[77]

Noticeably, no attempt was made to establish a 'special relationship' between Shanghai and New Zealand, although Alley spent ten years there, three years longer than he was in Shandan. Nor did Alley's thirty-five-year residence in Peking (1952–1987) lead to a 'special relationship' developing between New Zealand and Peking. Neither Shanghai nor Peking had a need to woo foreign investment by such means. The connection with Gansu was maintained because it gave New Zealand more access and influence than it might have had in more prosperous provinces.[78]

Activities associated with Rewi Alley were continually used by the New Zealand government to raise its profile in China. In 1985 the Peking embassy proposed to hold a gathering to formally unveil a Rewi Alley sculpture that had been commissioned by the New Zealand National Library. Embassy officials reported to Wellington that

> Such a function could be expected to attract a wide range of very senior Chinese leaders (perhaps even Deng Xiaoping who, we understand, attended Rewi's last birthday party) and thus would be a useful medium through which to focus attention on New Zealand.[79]

It was not only New Zealand that was keen to exploit the Rewi Alley–China connection in the 1980s. Alley had been described as 'the asset the Australians never had.'[80] In 1987, in an obvious attempt to poach some of Alley's prestige, the Australia–China Council asked the New Zealand government to consider a proposal to establish a Rewi Alley Scholarship for high-school students to attend Chinese schools for six months. If New Zealand allowed the scholarship to be named after Alley, then it would be made open to New Zealand students as well as Australians. Not unsurprisingly, the proposal was firmly rebuffed.[81]

As he did in the 1940s, in the 1980s Alley represented an image that New Zealand hoped to project in its trade relations with China: that of practical experience and knowledge. Prime Minister David Lange in a speech at Guizhou Agricultural College proclaimed:

> the New Zealand farmer, like the Chinese farmers, gets his hands and boots dirty. He is a practical not a theoretical person. He

spends a lot of time out on the land. If something needs to be done he knows how to do it. But he is also a scientific farmer. He is not so much interested in tools and technology as an end in themselves; rather he uses them to achieve particular objectives. If one approach doesn't work, he finds another which will. In other words, the New Zealand farmer is adaptable.[82]

Lange's imagery could be a direct description of Alley, famed for his practical, down-to-earth and above all 'adaptable' qualities. In the rhetoric of the Labour government Alley was used to symbolise New Zealand traditions such as practical egalitarianism and a pioneering spirit of a 'number 8 wire'[83] attitude to problem solving. Alley's work in the co-operative movement and Shandan, focusing on practical knowledge combined with limited resources, reflected the government's own modern-day low-technology offers of assistance to China.

It was in 1987 that the 'special relationship' in New Zealand–China relations reached its peak. The year 1987 marked not only the sixtieth anniversary of Alley's arrival in China (24 April 1927), it was also the year of his ninetieth birthday (2 December) and, as one canny official noted, it was also the fifteenth anniversary of the establishment of New Zealand–China relations (22 December).[84] Rewi Alley commemorative activities burgeoned in this year: memorial meetings were held to celebrate Alley's sixtieth anniversary; Alley's ghost-written memoirs *At 90: Memoirs of My China Years* was re-launched at a ceremony in Lanzhou, Gansu Province; Television New Zealand released a documentary narrated by Prime Minister Lange; Gansu Television also completed a documentary on Alley (which was partially funded by the New Zealand government); and the new Shandan Bailie School opened. In the last year of his life, 1987, Alley's ninetieth birthday celebrations were attended by Zhao Ziyang (then General Secretary of the Communist Party), Li Peng (then Acting Premier), Xi Zhongxun (Senior Politburo member and prominent revolutionary in Gansu Province in the 1940s), Huang Hua (former Minister of Foreign Affairs, and Vice Chair of the National People's Congress), Chu Tunan (former Chairman of the National People's Congress), Chen Xitong (State Councillor, and Mayor of Peking) and Zhu Qizhen (Vice-Foreign Minister). New Zealand, through Alley, gained a lot of favourable press in China in the late 1980s. These were connections that the New Zealand government and New Zealand business people were keen to exploit.

The year 1987 was also a period in which the New Zealand economy boomed. Prospects for trade with China were thought to be particularly good. David Oram, leader of a New Zealand–China trade delegation, commenting on why his group had been met by more senior leaders than ever before, linked it to 'the healthy political relationship between New Zealand and China' and 'the desire by the Chinese to reinforce their open door economic policy message.'[85] A *New Zealand Herald* editorial describing New Zealand's slow start in developing relations with China commented, 'Now we see China as a land whose friendship we need and whose trade we want.'[86] Another writer, in an analysis of why trade prospects seemed to be so good for New Zealand in China, stated, 'Much of the current condition of mutual celebration results from the love borne by the Chinese people for Rewi Alley, for over 60 years an extraordinary one-man volunteer service abroad.' According to this author, a visiting Chinese trade delegation in New Zealand in 1987 'left no doubt that the love shown by Alley to the Chinese people is reciprocated as a living force today. We, as a nation, are the largely unwitting beneficiaries of a legacy that appears unlikely ever to be matched.'[87]

In general, public response in New Zealand to the promotion of Rewi Alley as a symbol of New Zealand–China relations was favourable, although he was still thought of as a 'traitor' in some quarters. The letter of T. R. Louden typifies this attitude:

> The recent letters in praise of Rewi Alley have been truly sickening. New Zealand soldiers fought directly against Red Chinese troops in Korea and against Chinese-armed troops in Vietnam. While Kiwi soldiers were fighting, suffering torture and dying for a just cause, Rewi Alley was openly collaborating with the enemy. While Mao was murdering millions of Chinese, Rewi Alley was helping Stalin's favourite journalist, Wilfred Burchett, with his pro-Mao propaganda.[88]

Some New Zealanders complained at the government's expenditure on a school in China, arguing that it should have been using the money on the New Zealand education system. The Minister of Education gave one writer the official line on why a Chinese school received so much government money when New Zealand schools went short: 'New Zealand is focusing attention on the province of [Gansu]. Rewi Alley's school in Shandan lies within this province thus the government's grant will help to serve our general objectives there. . . . Rewi Alley's very long association with China has been very helpful to the New Zealand government in developing its relationship with China in recent years.'[89] However, most New Zealanders were willing to accept that the renewed interest in Alley was spontaneous and simply as a result of, as one correspondent wrote, 'his long work in establishing small industry and technical colleges, especially in the poorer and more remote areas of China.'[90]

When Alley's memoirs were first published in 1986 diplomats advised the government to adopt a 'positive response [which] would support wider New Zealand efforts to establish a clear identity for ourselves in China.'[91] Alley's comments about New Zealand in the book were of great concern.

With some relief, the Ministry of External Relations and Trade reported that these comments were 'remarkably positive, not least when he refers to the present Government's policies. . . . His book is likely to attract quite widespread attention and will help to raise New Zealand's profile in China.'[92] David Lange was asked by Zhang Wenjin, then the president of the Chinese People's Association for Friendship with Foreign Countries, to write a review of the book in the interests of 'the cause of furthering friendly relations between our two countries.'[93] The republishing of Alley's memoirs in 1987 was part of a joint venture between the New World Press of China (one of China's official English-language publishing houses specialising in foreign propaganda) and the New Zealand Government Printing Office. As the first book to be published jointly by the two governments it was a symbolic choice. The book was the first and last fruit of this curious union.

Alley's death occasioned further opportunities to emphasise the relationship between the two countries. Alley died on 28 December 1987, nearly one month after his ninetieth birthday celebrations. In a letter to Prime Minister Lange thanking him for his condolences, Zhang Wenjin wrote that Lange's statement on Alley's death 'was regarded here as an important document for further strengthening the ties of friendship between our peoples.'[94] The statement had concluded with the words also used in the obituary, 'As we honour his memory, let us look forward to developing even closer and more broad ranging relations between the people of China and New Zealand.'[95]

After Alley's death the New Zealand government took pains to present a roseate picture of Alley's life and work in China, especially his activities in the last forty years of his life. In a letter to Alan Alley, Lange, describing Alley as a 'great humanitarian,' wrote that he was 'a man whose commitment to the principles of humanity and justice remained unwavering throughout his life . . . [his writings on China] have helped interpret Chinese literature and history, not only to New Zealand, but also elsewhere in the outside world.'[96] It was a diplomatic, if not exactly accurate, account of Alley's sixty years in China.

In April 1988, memorial services were held for Rewi Alley in Peking and Shandan. New Zealand was represented by Fran Wilde, Deputy Minister for Foreign Affairs and Trade, as well as Minister for Disarmament. Diplomats were intent on getting as much mileage out of the ceremonies as possible, both from a trade and a foreign-policy point of view. The minister was briefed on the status of the Chinese People's Association for Friendship with Foreign Countries (CPAFFC), Alley's former work unit and sponsor of all Rewi Alley commemorative activities: 'CPAFFC is nominally a non-governmental organisation but it is in effect an arm of the Chinese foreign policy establishment reaching out to develop links with non-official groups in other countries.' The minister was advised to play along with the CCP propaganda line:

[you should] <u>Express</u> the view that cultural exchanges and people-to-people contacts are an important means of building understanding and adding greater substance to the bilateral relationship. <u>Note</u> that you have been impressed with the efforts made by the New Zealand China Friendship Society to raise funds for Rewi Alley's project of rebuilding the Shandan Bailie school in Gansu. <u>Express</u> the Government's support for this project.[97]

Diplomats at the Peking embassy were concerned about the role the New Zealand–China Friendship Society (NZCFS) might take in the commemorative events, anxious that its activities might be linked to those of the New Zealand government and its representatives. Officials reported, 'One practical problem which will be greater when TVNZ come, is that the NZCFS will be here in strength. They are mostly grey-haired, unrepresentative in the New Zealand mainstream but will be assertive in the Peking/Gansu contexts.'[98] Wellington advised that 'there are benefits in drawing a distinction, not least for presentational terms, between the small official government group led by the Minister and the non-governmental group organised by the Friendship Society.'[99] New Zealand diplomats viewed members of the NZCFS with some disdain, though at times their connections and activites in New Zealand and China were useful to the government.

Fran Wilde's speech at the Rewi Alley Memorial Meeting in Shandan linked New Zealand's pioneering ideals (which she claimed Alley typified) with the pioneering activities of the Chinese government to reform China. She also linked Gansu with New Zealand, citing pastureland, animal husbandry, reafforestation and horticultural co-operation. Rewi Alley's peace work (therefore the Chinese government's 'peace work') was given high praise and linked to the Labour government's own policies: 'International peace and disarmament are principal foreign policy goals of the present Labour Government in New Zealand. I know that Rewi was a strong supporter of our policies in this respect.'[100]

The memorialisation of Alley as a symbol of the relationship between New Zealand and China had always necessitated some delicacy in deciding what to commemorate and what to ignore. Depending on the policies of the government of the day, Alley could be, and was, used to symbolise virtually every aspect of New Zealand–China relations. The New Zealand government's earliest obituary of Alley (written in 1980 when Muldoon's National government was in power) reinforced the version it wished to present of the myth: 'Rewi Alley was a man of whom New Zealanders can be proud. . . . Alley never opted out. He did not leave China when things became difficult, he never compromised his views because they were unpopular at home.'[101] This was said despite the fact that Alley had continually compromised his views in China simply so that he might stay on there. A revised 1982 draft obituary preferred to remember Alley's literary output rather than his political work: 'Alley is, in his own way, an ambassador, who through his writing, has made Chinese literature and history known to the outside world. To the outside, these achievements will perhaps be remembered long after his achievements within China (eg. his schools and 'Gung Ho') have been forgotten.'[102] In its statements on Alley the 1984–1990 Labour government found it convenient to link its own anti-nuclear policies and interest in trading links with China to Alley's peace work on behalf of the Chinese government in the 1950s and 1960s. When the Queen's Service Order (QSO) was bestowed on Alley, Prime Minister Lange wrote that it was given 'in recognition of the contribution you have made to world peace and to the development of the warm relations that New Zealanders and Chinese now enjoy.'[103] *People's Daily* reported that the award was to commend Alley for his 'contribution to New Zealand–China friendship'[104] Lange's claim, that the origins of Alley's award were his peace work, was highly unlikely, since the QSO had been nominated by the previous National government, no admirer of Alley's peace activities. The National government that had followed Labour to power in 1991 laid stress on Alley's humanitarian works rather than the peace work and propaganda activities that he engaged in after 1952. Despite the uncertainty over what exactly could be praised about Alley's work in China, the New Zealand government and its representatives continued to participate actively in any Rewi Alley commemorative activities organised by the Chinese government, whether in China or New Zealand. At the celebrations to commemorate the 100th anniversary of Alley's birth, held at the Great Hall of the People in Peking in December 1997, virtually the whole of the New Zealand embassy turned out in support, as did a former New Zealand Governor-General, Sir Paul Reeves.

Nevertheless, it was common sense that the New Zealand government should only mine the Rewi Alley connection so long as there were political benefits in doing so. A report by New Zealand diplomats in Peking in 1988 commented: 'The Rewi Alley factor within the bilateral relationship remains a distinct asset, even though it will fade somewhat. Frankly we are going to need all the assets we have as China more and more plays the field, with its growing array of international connections and multiplicity of suitors, more and more players in the field.'[105] In 1990 New Zealand diplomats addressed the issue of the value of the Rewi Alley connection to New Zealand in a major report entitled the 'Rewi Alley Legacy':

> Alley is well known among Chinese people generally and, as the Ambassador's meeting with the Chinese President in January indicated, he is highly regarded in the Chinese halls of power (although this is expected to diminish as the revolutionary generation passes away). Other than Alley, New Zealand does not have any notable figures in China, which makes his legacy all the more valuable to the relationship.

But we would not like to see the relationship being at all dependent on his legacy nor do we believe our Chinese contacts would like that. Perhaps an appropriate middle ground is to continue to give some small emphasis at the official level to the Alley legacy but leave it largely to private New Zealand interests like the Friendship Society to promote.[106]

A further report, written two years later, is also worth quoting at length for a sense of the cynicism and disdain many officials felt for 'the Rewi Alley legacy' and the necessity of continuing to promote it:

We have to be careful to keep the Rewi Alley connection in the right perspective in the bilateral relationship with China. If we make too much of it we will seem out of touch ideologically with Modern China given his enthusiastic endorsement of some of Mao's excesses, like the Cultural Revolution, which are now totally discredited in China. This kind of consideration points to caution about the Alley legacy at a time when the leadership itself is giving less and less emphasis to ideology and to most of the Maoist ideals for which Alley stood. . . . A lesson from this Gansu celebration, however, is that there is considerable bilateral mileage still to be got out of the Rewi Alley legacy. We should never underestimate the Chinese capaciy to 're-interpret' and Alley is now remembered most for his practical educational achievements, and his support for China's liberation. We tried to help the process along at a seminar discussion on Alley's educational philosophy by asserting confidently that if Alley had been alive today he would 'of course' have been a strong advocate of economic reform and the opening to the outside world. (There is nothing to support this in what is known of Alley's political and economic philosophies – but everyone present was happy to agree with us).[107]

As New Zealand diplomats were well aware, the focus on one figure to symbolise the Sino-New Zealand notions of the New Zealand–China 'friendship' and talk of a 'special relationship' were anomalous in terms of New Zealand's relations with other countries. There were a number of other well-known New Zealanders who had devoted their lives to the service of another country (for example, ophthalmologist Fred Hollow's work in Eritrea, Nepal and Australia; Sir Edmund Hillary's work in Nepal), yet this had not led to the use of Chinese-style people's diplomacy in relations with those countries.[108] However New Zealand diplomats and politicians maintained the fiction of their nation's 'special relationship' with China due to the Alley connection since, they believed, it helped them in their relations with China, which had become one of New Zealand's most important trading partners by the late 1980s. In the first few years after Alley's death there was some concern among officials that as the old guard who had known Alley personally died off, Alley might lose favour with the Chinese foreign ministry. The younger generation in China certainly tended to regard Alley and other old foreign 'friends of China' with considerable disdain. However, as the perennial Alley-related commemorative activities held by various Chinese official organisations demonstrated, New Zealand still had plenty of opportunities to milk the Alley connection if it wished. In 1997 a thirty-two-part series on Alley's life was being produced in China,[109] and in the same year a biography of Alley was included in an eleven-volume set of children's books on China's foreign friends.[110] There was every indication that Alley had not been forgotten in China and would not be allowed to be forgotten. New Zealand diplomats reported optimistically after attending the ceremony to commorate the publication of the book series: 'the Chinese government continues to put great store in the linkages generated by these individuals.'[111]

What New Zealand diplomats and New Zealand journalists reporting on China seemed not to realise is that in the period of dramatic economic downsizing of government bureaucracies from the mid-1990s on, one had to suspect that many official activities relating to the old friends of China were as much to justify the over-padding of staff numbers in organisations such as the Friendship Association – and indeed part of a justification for these organisations' very existence in their competition with rival organisations with duplicate functions – as they were to fulfil any perceived need for such materials. In the 1990s, an entrepreneurial element entered China's 'friendship' work. Rather than there being a specific policy seeking such out materials, it appears that a number of Chinese journalists had realised that writing about foreign friends such as Alley was a sure way to get published in the *People's Daily* and other leading newspapers in China and could lead to other benefits. The same could be said for periodic film projects and news items on Alley and other foreign friends; projects on such safe topics provided a guaranteed buyer in the State-controlled media system. Similarly, one can only suspect financial advantage to be the main motive for the setting up in the 1980s and 1990s of numerous individual organisations, museums, memorials and conferences to commemorate Alley and other less well-known foreign friends of the Chinese revolution. Local authorities in remote areas, obscure writers, underemployed local-level foreign-affairs personnel, and even private business people, all had noted a gap in the market, which had appealing benefits such as financial profit, the possibility of overseas trips, personal fame, opportunities for foreign investment and the virtually guaranteed blessing of central authorities.[112]

In contrast to China, the Alley 'legacy' in terms of the interest of the New Zealand public weakened considerably in the years after his death. New Zealanders' response to the 4 June Massacre in China in 1989 impacted on popular interest in Alley, as diplomats at the Peking embassy noted: 'China is no longer flavour of the month, Alley died two years ago and interest in him is waning.'[113] Great popular interest in China in the mid-1980s contributed to government and public interest in Rewi Alley in New Zealand, yet in 1993 a fundraising dinner organised by the Auckland branch of the New Zealand–China Friendship Society in honour of Alley had to be cancelled due to lack of interest. A few months later a further attempt to raise money in Alley's name, an evening of Chinese dance and music, barely covered its costs. Periodic newspaper articles about Alley and New Zealand and China's attempts to commemorate him kept his name alive to the New Zealand and Chinese public. In 1993 playwright Stuart Hoar wrote *Yo Banfa*, a depiction of Alley's life, which was performed at Auckland University, and in 1998 Jack Body and Geoff Chapple wrote the opera *Alley*, which was performed at the New Zealand Festival of the Arts in Wellington. Both productions were disappointing to many in the audience, not least because they maintained the myth of Alley rather than attempting to get beyond it.[114] At a 1998 academic conference on Sino-New Zealand relations held to commemorate the twenty-fifth anniversary of diplomatic relations between the two countries, Chinese participants repeatedly stressed the Rewi Alley connection and recited the standard line on his life and works in China. New Zealand participants barely mentioned him. During the visit of Chinese President Jiang Zemin to New Zealand in 1999, Jiang also mentioned Alley in numerous speeches and made a point of visiting Alley's former high school in Christchurch.[115] In contrast, the then New Zealand Prime Minister Jenny Shipley understated the Alley connection, noting tactfully in a welcoming speech to Jiang at a dinner in Wellington that Alley was 'well-remembered in China'.[116]

More in keeping with the current popular attitudes towards China in New Zealand in the late 1990s, Jiang's visit was dogged by demonstrations in support of Tibet, Taiwan and Chinese human rights. Whether it was useful or not for New Zealand to stress the Alley connection in its relations with China, it might perhaps have been timely for China to re-consider how useful repeating the old propaganda line was in its relations with New Zealand. New Zealand diplomats and Chinese foreign-affairs officials can rest assured, however, that in the present political climate any changes in tactics are highly unlikely. Celebrating the support of foreign friends for the CCP is regarded as a cost-effective and useful tactic, which it is in no one's interest to let go at present. None the less, throughout the 1990s, as the PRC increased its contact with the outside world, foreigners such as Alley were celebrated ritually much more to symbolise CCP control of the foreign presence in China – a form of political education to Chinese citizens and foreigners alike – than they were to strengthen relations with a politically and economically insignificant country like New Zealand. In this context, stressing the New Zealand connection was an afterthought.

New Zealand had, of course, never had a 'special relationship' with China any more than had any of the other countries for which Chinese officials used this term. And, as New Zealand diplomats recognised, as Sino-foreign inter-actions expanded exponentially throughout the 1990s, the ability of tiny New Zealand to attract the attention of senior Chinese leaders lessened con-siderably. Alley was one of the few means New Zealand had to gain that attention and his legacy will not be given up easily. According to New Zealand diplomat John Carter, in the current era 'Alley is even more of an asset than he was when he was alive.'[117] Although recognition of Alley's work in China is no longer the most prominent aspect of New Zealand–China relations, in the years since his death it has a significance in what another New Zealand diplomat described to me as the 'tapestry' of relations between the two countries. Alley was one of the important 'threads' to which both governments referred in emphasis of their shared interests and the 'warmth' of the relationship between them. In Chinese there is an expression that is frequently used to sum up Alley's role as a symbol of New Zealand–China relations since 1972: 'When you drink from the well, don't forget who dug it.'[118]

10

INTERNATIONALIST

Archetypes have long been a part of Chinese biographical writing. Prominent characters throughout the ages have been set up as models of extreme virtue for others to emulate. Their biographies are idealised to the point of hagiography. In every aspect their character and actions are represented as beyond reproach. In traditional China iconisation took the form of a place in the approved histories, imperial commemoration, an official temple or a commemorative arch. By such means historical figures became part of the Confucian pantheon, in recognition of eternal moral principles that transcended particular political causes. Thus the Ming Dynasty hero Koxinga eventually became apotheosised as a symbol of loyalty by the Qing Dynasty, though the source of his fame had been his fight against the Manchu invasion.[1] Apotheosis was usually conferred from above, although it was not unusual for exceptional historical figures to acquire a position in folklore, fiction and popular religion that also amounted to apotheosis.[2] Asceticism was a necessary part of the image of a model figure in dynastic China. Chinese traditional heroes put love and marriage secondary to public interests. Sexual relations were usually associated with negative models, while romantic love was seen to be in conflict with the status of a hero.[3]

The iconic tradition has continued in the PRC; especially chosen individuals are set up as exemplary models (*bangyang*) from whom the masses are exhorted to learn.[4] Amongst the most well known of these are the mythic Lei Feng, a model soldier, Jiao Yulu, an idealised cadre, and Norman Bethune, the model foreigner.[5] The process of apotheosis is little changed in modern China, though the means may have been updated. Nowadays, instead of the commemorative arches or temples of the past, the government erects commemorative statues. Candidates for iconisation are memorialised in newspaper articles, television and film dramatisations and touring exhibitions. Apotheosis is still conferred from above, as the CCP maintains strict control of propaganda work. The tradition of using historical figures as symbols of eternal moral principles continues, regardless of those figures' original political affiliation.

From the late 1970s, Rewi Alley joined the Chinese pantheon as a symbol of unflagging loyalty to the CCP, a model to Chinese and foreigners alike.

Party propagandists promoted the Rewi Alley spirit (*Aili de jingshen*), which was defined by such qualities as 'loyalty to China's revolution [and] love for the labouring people.'[6] Alley is now remembered in China not as much for the industrial co-operatives, the Bailie Schools or his peace activities – all of which are irrelevant to the political and economic style of China today – but rather for this 'spirit.' It should be mentioned that posthumous iconisation is preferred in both modern and pre-modern China. In authoritarian societies governments like to prevent living individuals from having too much prominence for fear that the general public might mobilise around a living hero and threaten the *status quo*. Hence Lei Feng, Jiao Yulu and Norman Bethune all became model figures after death. That Rewi Alley could become a legend in his own lifetime in China reflects the confidence the Chinese government had in his obedience to its will.

By the end of the Cultural Revolution era, in the late 1970s, the CCP faced a massive crisis of confidence. The re-formed government's solution was to resuscitate former moral heroes such as Lei Feng and Jiao Yulu along with more recent ones such as Alley and his fellow internationalist George Hatem. According to Lu Wanru of the Rewi Alley Research Centre, China's leaders hoped that by promoting Alley they would be able to imbue young people with 'the spirit of internationalism, hard work and simple living' and remind them of what China has been through.[7] Internationalism is commonly defined as the spirit of selfless dedication to revolution as practised by internationalists; those who put their energy into other countries' revolutionary struggles. In China, however, internationalist is the highest-ranking title of China's foreign friends, the foreigners who support CCP rule. Internationalism was first epitomised in China by the Canadian doctor Norman Bethune, memorialised in Mao's famous speech.[8] Bethune died in 1939 in Northern China while working for the Chinese Red Army. Mao wrote of Bethune:

> What kind of spirit is this that makes a foreigner selflessly adopt the cause of the Chinese people's liberation as his own? It is the spirit of internationalism, the spirit of communism, from which every Chinese Communist must learn. . . . We must unite with the proletariat of all the capitalist countries, with the proletariat of Japan, Britain, the United States, Germany, Italy and all other capitalist countries, before it is possible to overthrow imperialism, to liberate our nation and people, and to liberate the other nations and peoples of the world. This is our internationalism, the internationalism with which we oppose both narrow nationalism and narrow patriotism.[9]

Internationalism in the Chinese sense specifically refers to foreigners who dedicate themselves to the *Chinese* revolution. When Mao Zedong praised internationalists, it was not so much to inspire the Chinese people to imitate their devotion to another country's revolution as it was to praise their spirit of 'selflessly adopt[ing] the cause of the *Chinese* people's liberation.' Mao chose Bethune as a symbol of the commitment to the Chinese revolution he required of CCP members. That commitment was characterised by the virtues of self-sacrifice and hard work, serving the people rather than the individual. The article commemorating Bethune was especially prominent during the Cultural Revolution, when Mao was concerned with renewing the spirit of selfless dedication to the revolution amongst Chinese youth. In the era of reform and opening up, the government was less concerned with encouraging revolutionary ardour than a sense of patriotism and loyalty to CCP rule, hence the creation of an updated version of the internationalist tradition, the Rewi Alley spirit.

Rewi Alley's elevation to the Chinese pantheon began in 1977, at the time of his eightieth birthday celebrations. Alley's selective memory was useful in post-Cultural Revolution China, when the government was trying to rebuild after what was officially described as 'ten years of chaos' and to regain its good name in the eyes of the Chinese people and foreign supporters. Alley's loyalty to the CCP was an example to others and was used as such. It was only at the last minute that Deng Xiaoping made his appearance at the birthday celebrations. Yet his presence was a major boost to Alley's political standing. Deng's speech at the event was widely reported, less for promoting Alley, more as a vehicle to signal that Deng had the upper hand in the leadership struggle that was still going on at the time. As a result of the speech Alley became closely associated with the new regime that Deng was forming. The *Xinhua* report on the birthday banquet featured Deng Xiaoping's speech prominently:

> We are joyously gathered here today to extend our warmest congratulations to our veteran fighter, our old friend and our old comrade Rewi Alley on his 80th birthday. Thousands and thousands of foreign friends have helped the cause of the Chinese revolution but it is not easy for Comrade Alley to have done so much for the Chinese people 50 years on end, whether in the years in which we experienced untold difficulty, or when we were fighting for the victory of the revolution, or in the post-victory years. That is why he commands the due respect of the Chinese people.[10]

Deng's remarks signalled the beginning of Alley's new role as a model figure whose deeds would be promoted and 'studied' by the masses. In this one speech, Deng also cleared the political slate for Alley – as well as for most of those associated with him – his Chinese adopted family and ex-Shandan workers, and all past questions about his behaviour were officially resolved.

From this point on, Rewi Alley would be promoted as a symbol of serving the people and following the CCP in everything.

The commemoration of Alley by Chinese officials from then on virtually always included a quote from Deng's 1977 speech. It was also compulsory to mention that Alley's own philosophy was similar to that of Deng. My own interview with the cultural attaché at the Chinese embassy in Wellington was a typical example of this. According to Huang Daozhen (who did not know Alley personally), Alley's views on China were very similar to those of Deng Xiaoping, stressing the economy rather than politics and working to improve the standard of living of the peasants.[11] Speeches at Alley-related commemorative activities were often a useful means for New Zealand diplomats to ascertain the current political line. An embassy report in 1982 of a speech by the then Chinese Association for Friendship with Foreign Countries President Wang Bingnan noted that Deng Xiaoping's leadership role was stressed:

> and care is taken to portray Alley as someone who saw through the Gang of Four and supported Deng Xiaoping. Wang Bingnan claimed that, 'For all the multitude of his works there is not a single article he wrote that extols the Gang of Four. . . . During the so-called campaign to criticise Deng Xiaoping, he turned away in disgust when requested to write an article to criticise Deng Xiaoping. But when in Beidaihe he heard the news of Deng Xiaoping's rehabilitation, he promptly put his rapture into verses.[12]

It was not in fact true that Rewi Alley had never criticised Deng Xiaoping during the Cultural Revolution. In a letter to a friend in New Zealand in 1967 Alley wrote:

> On the last few months. Liu and Deng would have led China steadily toward the revisionists. They will not now be able to do so. There is a much greater understanding on all levels. Some material losses, but one never gets anything good without paying for it. Get someone to run you out to see Vic [Wilcox] sometime, and have a quiet chat with him about it all.[13]

However, in 1976, when Deng was being criticised once more and Jiang Qing wanted Alley and other foreigners to write articles criticising Deng, Alley had the good sense to refuse.[14]

After 1977, numerous articles by or about Alley were published in Chinese newspapers and magazines throughout China in both Chinese and English, beginning with the publication of four of his poems in the *People's Daily* on his eightieth birthday.[15] In 1981, *People's Daily* published Alley's letter of congratulation on the Chinese Communist Party's sixtieth anniversary.[16] This was not meant for foreign eyes; its purpose was to give support to the Chinese Communist Party at a time when public support for the ideals of the Party was low after the Cultural Revolution. In the early 1980s, both Gansu and Beijing Television made documentaries on Alley's life and work in China. A television drama was even made of Alley's work in Gansu during the 1940s. (The original script featured a romance between Alley and an American woman 'Emma,' based on Ida Pruitt. Alley insisted – with some difficulty – that this should be removed from the drama.)[17]

As the power of Deng Xiaoping grew, so too did Alley's role as a model. Alley was useful as a well-known, respectable friend of China whose support lent credibility to Deng's claim that the new economic policies he instituted were consistent with what had gone before. In the late 1970s and early 1980s, Deng's hold on power and on support for his economic reforms were by no means secure. Alley's endorsement of Deng's reforms were useful at a time when other former foreign supporters of the Chinese regime were articulating what many Leftist Chinese felt, that Deng was selling out on Marxism. From the late 1970s, Alley's propaganda activities increased dramatically. He met with scores of foreign visitors, now free to visit China with the new 'Open Door' policy. He accepted numerous interviews, in which he was careful to extol the virtues of the new era, lambasting the old, which he had formerly praised so highly. Though Alley could not travel as easily as before because of old age and illness, he continued to write reportage on the few locations he did visit, such as the area around the resort in Hainan where he spent the winter months. Here he always managed to find some uplifting story about how well the locals were doing now that the oppressive 'Gang of Four' rule had ended, or the successes of the new economic policies. A number of his monographs that had been regarded as politically unacceptable in the Cultural Revolution era were now published. In the 1980s, Alley's publications dominated the small selection of foreign-language books available in Chinese bookshops.

Alley's work in China came to be closely associated with the rule of Deng Xiaoping. It would have been difficult for Alley not to support the regime at this time, given his high profile. As a result of Alley's international reputation and prominence as a foreign supporter of China, he had a guaranteed audience in the Western world of people who wanted to know what he felt about the changes in China in the Deng era. The post-Cultural Revolution period was a time of great disillusionment for many foreign Maoists. Deng's government was now rejecting everything these foreigners had once believed in. While other less prominent foreign friends could express their distaste with the shift in political line by leaving China or keeping silent, Alley's political role and his desire to stay on in China till the end of his days meant that he went along with whatever direction the government chose to take.

While former foreign Maoists were suffering bitter disillusionment, in the 1980s China attracted a whole new group of China-admirers, those who were drawn to the apparent non-ideological line of the new regime and the economic changes that would open up the Chinese economy to the international market. To these foreign supporters, Alley was a soothing, reassuring voice. Alley had a particularly useful ability to compare pre-1949 China with the present day. Although China was poor and backward in the 1980s, Alley could verify that progress had been made since the bad old, pre-Communist days.

The call to 'learn from Rewi Alley' increased in intensity from 1982, the fifty-fifth anniversary of Alley's arrival in China and his eighty-fifth birthday. By 1982 China's Open Door economic policies were well under way and China needed all the technical assistance it could get, especially on 'humanitarian' terms. Alley's ability to attract international attention to China as well as his well-established tradition for humanitarian work were indeed a 'most valuable treasure' for China. Articles commemorating Alley's arrival in China were published in *People's Daily*, *China Daily* and *Xinhua* reports, along with articles in *Beijing Review* and the *Voice of Friendship* (the Friendship Association's official magazine). A similar number of articles appeared around the date of his birthday. In a speech during the birthday celebrations Wang Bingnan (then head of the CPAFFC) styled Alley as a model figure in the Norman Bethune/Lei Feng tradition of Chinese Communist heroes:

> To celebrate Comrade Rewi Alley's birthday is also a call for learning from him. . . . I want to specially mention two points: the first is his spirit of working vigorously despite old age and his devotion to the cause that he believes in. His life has been one of 'work, work and work' coupled with 'learn, learn and learn'. . . . In celebrating Comrade Alley's birthday, we should learn from his spirit of concerning himself with the well-being of the masses, maintaining close ties with them and getting right on the job to work things out.
>
> Comrades and friends, China is now at a critical moment of creating a new situation in all fields of the socialist construction. In order to realise the goal of the Four Modernisations at an early date, we need not only the convergence of arduous efforts of the whole nation under the leadership of the Communist Party of China, but also the assistance of our foreign friends. In this sense Comrade Alley is to the Chinese people a most valuable treasure.[18]

As it once did in the 1940s, Rewi Alley's name in the post-Mao era was utilised to garner foreign aid for China. Wang Bingnan spoke of the external dimension to Alley's role as an internationalist:

> As Comrade Rewi Alley is world famous as an old friend of the Chinese people and for his rich knowledge and excellent

understanding of China's past and present, many foreign visitors to China regard it as a privilege to meet with him. Last year alone he received more than three hundred foreign guests. . . . The number of letters he sent abroad last year amounted to more than 1000.[19]

Rewi Alley's promotion to the role of internationalist was a logical extension of his status as a friend of China. Since the late 1970s, when China established official diplomatic relations with most countries, friendship diplomacy was directed towards encouraging a positive, pro-foreign image of China in the West. In the preface to Alley's *Six Americans in China*, which described the service to the Chinese revolution of six American internationalists, Wang Bingnan wrote:

> Today, with the establishment of diplomatic relations between China and the United States, exchanges between the two peoples have been increasingly expanded. However, it is still necessary to further the mutual understanding and friendship between the two great nations. I believe that the noble sense of justice shared by the six Americans will inspire their countrymen in their hundreds of thousands to show sympathy and love for China and thus enable them to work unswervingly for promoting social progress and safeguarding world peace.[20]

As we have noted, though Alley lived for ten years in Shanghai and thirty-five years in Peking, more than any other area of China, Gansu Province has promoted Alley's image as an internationalist. This is perhaps only partly because Alley often said his happiest years in China were spent there; but, more importantly, Gansu Province, one of the poorest regions in China, needs publicity and Western aid much more than Shanghai and Peking do. Governor Jia Shijie of Gansu Province was one of the most prominent figures in utilising the advantages of the Rewi Alley–Gansu connection. In 1988, reflecting the dual purpose of Rewi Alley commemoration, Governor Jia urged that

> All those living and working in Gansu must learn from [Alley's] great internationalist spirit of pioneering through hardship and danger with self-confidence; must be determined to keep forging ahead so as to deepen the present reform, to make Gansu prosperous at the earliest time possible and to further Gansu's friendship with New Zealand and other countries through down to earth work at our own posts.[21]

Governor Jia wrote that it was useful to learn from the 'Alley spirit . . . at the present time when we are rectifying the party's work style and social morale.'[22] Alley's name was invoked both to lend an aura of morality to the local government and to legitimise current economic policies. Ironically, these new policies were in exact opposition to the view that Alley had expressed so often throughout his life in China, that the collective was the only hope for the people of China. Alley did not support the glorification of his image into an internationalist. In 1982 he wrote to Shirley Barton, 'I'm embarrassed by the newspaper, radio etc. articles on my 55th anniversary of coming to China. But what can I do?'[23] He insisted that the most fitting memorial to him would always be an educational one, in keeping with the ideals he had worked for in China. Alley also opposed the decision of the Lanzhou municipal government to develop a NZ$700,000 park in his honour in the city. The park has a 6 metre statue of Alley surrounded by children as well as a 100 metre mural depicting his life in Gansu Province from 1943 until the early 1950s.[24]

Rather than any special regard for Rewi Alley's contribution to Chinese education, the statue of Alley surrounded by Chinese children symbolised the target group at which Chinese propagandists were aiming when they promoted him. As one Chinese official wrote, 'I am confident that his meritorious achievements will also inspire our younger generation to study industriously and emulate, in particular, his determination for hard work and his spirit of internationalism.'[25] And yet, although young people were enjoined to learn from the 'Rewi Alley spirit,' there was virtually no attempt by the Chinese authorities to elucidate the philosophy and ideals that Alley adhered to. As an internationalist, more than any other role he had been required to perform, it mattered little what Alley as an individual actually thought and did in China. What mattered was that the Chinese Communist Party invoked Alley's name both as a symbol of virtues it wished to instil in young people in China and as a talisman to attract foreign investment in China on favourable terms. Hence, only a couple of Alley's more than sixty published books have been translated into Chinese and little attempt has been made to put his ideas into practice. And yet, despite the fact that Chinese people may not know what Alley believed in, innumerable New Zealand visitors to China since the 1980s can testify that Rewi Alley is currently the most famous New Zealander in China, and probably one of the more widely known foreigners in China over all. The current knowledge of Rewi Alley at grass-roots level throughout China is an indication of the enormous effort put into propagating the myth since the late 1970s.

In any case, however many people actually understood what the 'Rewi Alley Spirit' meant, Alley's altruistic beliefs of working selflessly towards the goal of improving China without material reward were thoroughly out of date in the China of the 1980s, and even more so in that of the 1990s. In 1986, at the opening of a night school in Peking for adult students opportunistically named Bailie University (the original proposal was to call it Alley University, but Alley had disapproved), Alley proclaimed, 'China is a vast land, its people a full quarter of all the people in the world. There are down-to-earth problems everywhere, and if you feel that it is your very own country, and you love it, then you must be prepared to go and work for it, wherever you are needed most.'[26] Then, as now, China suffered from a brain drain of the best and brightest from the countryside to the cities. Many young people came to the cities to be educated and preferred not to return. Alley's idealism fell on deaf ears in the climate of materialism encouraged by the reform policies. The views of many young people I spoke with in China about Alley are summed up by the comments of a Shanghainese student who told me he thought Alley was 'foolish for believing in something that [Chinese] people had long since given up believing in' – the ideals of the Communist Revolution.[27]

Alley's role as a model figure gained even more momentum after his death in 1987, posthumous hagiography being the norm in China. Since 1987 Rewi Alley's deeds have been commemorated in Chinese children's textbooks, photo exhibitions, museum displays, television documentaries, regular newspaper articles and seminars. A Rewi Alley Research Centre was set up at the time when Alley's memoirs were being compiled and it continues to be the focus of annual Rewi Alley commemorative activities. On 21 April 1988, the sixty-first anniversary of Alley's arrival in China, an exhibition was held in his memory jointly sponsored by the Friendship Association and the Peking Museum of Chinese Revolution. A photo album reflecting Alley's activities and contribution during sixty years in China was launched at the same time. In Shanghai a stone tablet was placed in front of Alley's former residence at Number 4, Lane 1315, Yuyuan Lu, and a further television series was made by Gansu Television dramatising Alley's life at Shandan. A number of statues have been erected in honour of Alley: in Springfield, New Zealand, Alley's birthplace; in the Lanzhou Bailie Oil School and in the Shandan Bailie School; in the New Zealand Embassy in Peking; and in New Zealand's National Library. A Ministry of Foreign Affairs and Trade report on Alley's status in China noted ironically, 'It must now be an open question whether there could be more statues of New Zealander Rewi Alley in China than of Mao Zedong himself.'[28] In 1997, the 100th anniversary of Alley's birth and tenth anniversary of his death, a series of books in Chinese and English about Alley were published. A ceremony was held in his honour at the Great Hall of the People, which received extensive coverage on CCTV news that night, as well as a feature article in the English-language *China Daily*. Throughout the late 1990s, periodic articles commemorating Alley continued to appear in the Chinese media aimed at both Chinese and foreigners, keeping his name and work for the CCP alive.

It is easier perhaps for the Chinese to remember a foreigner's contribution to the revolution than it is to remember the contribution of their own people, given the factionalism that has always been a part of CCP politics.

As a foreigner Alley was always an outsider in China and it is easier to make exceptions for outsiders, especially when, as Alley, they have adapted to life in China to the extent that they do not ask awkward questions and are careful to follow whatever is the current line. Praising a Chinese comrade's revolutionary behaviour while he was still alive might be perceived as a challenge to the power structure. Attending Alley's eighty-eighth birthday celebrations in 1985 was Alley's old friend from Shanghai days, Liu Ding, who had a distinguished career as an underground worker in the Communist Party in pre-Liberation days and was sufficiently influential in 1952 to be able to assist in getting the Shandan Bailie School taken over by the Oil Ministry when no other government department would assume responsibility for it. Liu, whose highest title was Vice-Minister of Oil, never achieved the level of national recognition as an upstanding supporter of the Party and veteran revolutionary that Alley did.[29]

Age and seniority within the organisation are all important in China. Alley's prestige grew the longer he stayed alive. Chinese society is intrinsically hierarchical and foreign persons of rank must be met by those who hold equivalent rank within the Chinese system. Hence top political leaders always attended ceremonies in Alley's honour. Senior officials visited Alley on his birthday or when he was sick in hospital and these visits were duly recorded by the Chinese press. In these reports, Alley's work in China was always linked with that of the CCP; he was referred to as a 'veteran fighter in the international cause.'[30] Alley was highly favoured, partly because many of the leaders who became influential at the end of the Cultural Revolution years had known him in earlier times. Foreign Minister Huang Hua had acted as a means of liaison between the CCP and CIC. Other senior leaders in the Ministry of Foreign Affairs, such as Liao Chengzhi, Wang Bingnan and Geng Biao, had also known and worked with Alley in the years before 1949. Alley was on good terms with Deng Yingchao, veteran revolutionary and widow of Zhou Enlai; she regularly attended Rewi Alley commemorative activities. Premier Li Peng knew of Alley from his visit to Yan'an and through his adopted parents Premier Zhou Enlai and Deng Yingchao. President Yang Shangkun had also met Alley at Yan'an, something he made a point of acknowledging to New Zealand Ambassador Michael Powles during Powles's first meeting with him in 1989. President Yang told the ambassador that Alley had been close to Mao Zedong and Deng Xiaoping had been fond of him; 'Not like this Canadian doctor fellow [Bethune] who came here for medical reasons, Rewi Alley got involved with the spirit of the revolution.'[31] In addition to these internationally renowned cadres who knew of Alley there were numerous other influential CCP leaders who knew Alley personally and recognised his work. By the late 1990s, most of these senior figures were out of power or dead. Few of the current senior leadership knew Alley personally, but commemorative activities related to him were still graced by VIPs, if not by the most senior politicians any more.

Alley's writing had always served as a mirror of political trends within the leadership, and in 1987 Alley's public speeches took on the tone of the conservative left in China, emphasising the revolutionary ideals of the 1930s with comments such as 'as long as China's one billion maintain their steady march in the spirit of Yan'an and the old revolutionaries it will not be possible to halt her progress toward national reunification and rejuvenation.'[32] Chinese officials praised Alley for his loyal support of current policies. Closer to the truth were the comments of Alley's good friend George Hatem to a New Zealand diplomat: '[Alley] has been flexible and known when to lie low.' Moreover, as the official added in his report, 'His commitment to the world of solid action has also stood him in good stead.'[33]

Yet, despite the official image of Alley as an unreserved supporter of the Chinese Communist Party, particularly after the Cultural Revolution, Rewi Alley was clearly disappointed by what had come of the New China he had written about so optimistically in the 1950s. Alley's personal doctor and close friend Dr Wu Weiran described Alley as not liking to say anything about this in public, 'not because he couldn't, but because he thought it would serve no particular purpose.'[34] Nevertheless, Alley did not support the student protest movement that developed in China in the 1980s, though he was sympathetic to the desire for greater democracy. He felt that the young people who talked about democracy were not qualified to do so, they didn't know how to endure suffering and weren't hard-working enough. Alley was unsympathetic with the *chuguo re* (leave the country craze) that was an obsession for many young people in China in the 1980s. As we have seen, he refused to give any assistance whatsoever to his adopted grandchildren who wished to go abroad.

From the early 1980s on, Alley's disapproval of the new economic policies of Deng Xiaoping was palpable. While in his writings and speeches he publicly supported the new policies, his private view was very different. He barely disguised this in letters to a Chinese friend describing the bureaucratism and corruption, unemployment and greed for material wealth that came as a result of Deng's policies.[35] In conversations with trusted friends he was sarcastic about Deng's China. Constantly looking back often implies dissatisfaction with the present and in this sense even Alley's promotion of the Yan'an spirit in the late 1980s can be seen as an implied criticism of the corruption of Deng's China. In the 1980s, Yan'an and Shandan became for Alley his totems of a 'Golden Age' when life was much simpler and more morally upright.

The only public sign of Alley's dissatisfaction with the changes in China was his revival of the Shandan school and the Gung Ho movement. By the early 1980s he had enough influence to do this, as well as friends in high places to help him. Gansu Province became the site of Bailie Schools once again, one in Shandan and the other in Lanzhou. The Lanzhou Bailie Oil

School was renamed in 1985 in the hope of attracting foreign aid. School leaders claimed that 'great attention was once again paid to Alley's philosophy of running a school.'[36] However, on the fortieth anniversary of the school no mention was made of the school's former links with foreign missionaries; China had not yet liberalised sufficiently to make this fact either acceptable or useful.

The new Shandan Bailie School was opened in 1987. It was the fulfilment of the dream that Rewi Alley had never given up on after being forced to leave the original school in 1952. Alley's new status as a model figure did have some use for him – it meant that it was easier to get things done. The new school was established with the help of generous contributions from overseas, including the New Zealand government. There were problems with the school from the very beginning. Alley's ideas on the school were out of date and out of touch with the realities of modern China. While Alley tried to recreate the Bailie school of the 1940s, the Chinese authorities wanted a school that would fit in to the existing education system. Alley followed the Jesuit view that moral education for children should begin when they were still young enough to have their thinking influenced. He proposed that the students should start at the school at the age of twelve, two years earlier than the usual age for beginning middle school in China. However, government officials in Gansu wanted the Shandan Bailie School to be a technical high school. Out of respect to Alley the first intake of the school were twelve-year-olds, but after Alley died the age was raised to fourteen.[37]

The school suffered much political infighting amongst members of the school board and disagreement over the direction the school should take. Some leading cadres in the Shandan area were opposed to the school and they did their utmost to obstruct progress there. Rewi Alley's ideas on education were regarded by many as out of date and unrealistic. Jeff Tubby, in a report for the New Zealand Ministry of Foreign Affairs, noted,

> The composition of the [School] Board has given rise to strong political infighting and difficulties of administration. Rewi Alley is in Beijing giving orders. Mme. Li is in Lanzhou giving orders which do not agree with the Beijing orders. Headmaster Ni has the difficult task of being the 'pig in the middle'. The County Director and several of the County administrators do not want the Bailie School at all and do their utmost to be difficult to all parties. Rewi Alley is quite out of touch with reality and this is a source of embarrassment and difficulty.... He has made no attempt to appoint a successor and this will prove a difficult situation on his death. All parties are playing a waiting game in this respect. At this time factions within the County will endeavour to close the school.'[38]

John Hercus, Principal of Christchurch Polytechnic, commented in a 1987 report for the New Zealand government that Alley's philosophy of combining work and study at the school was being virtually ignored. Teachers were reluctant to take part in practical work. A container load of teaching equipment that New Zealand had donated, full of electric fence wire, projectors and whiteboards, had never been used. These practical learning tools did not fit in to the syllabus, which concentrated on the style of rote learning common throughout China. Hercus complained that the official school brochure was misleading: there were no nurseries, gardens, animals, crops or grasslands, since the farm part of the school had not been developed. Moreover, the Shandan library and museum established by Alley for the people of Shandan, which contained most of Alley's collection of Chinese antiques as well as books donated by the New Zealand government, were not open to the general public. Hercus wrote, 'The school brochure states that the philosophy of the school is firmly tied to that which was laid down by Rewi Alley. I have doubts as to whether this is the case in practice; the lack of practical training, including farm-based training, precludes the Alley philosophy from working.'[39]

Since its founding in 1987, the new Shandan Bailie School has moved further and further away from Alley's original plan, actually encouraging the students' desire to take part in the urban exodus by providing them with the skills that would specifically enable them to do so. Ultimately, since the school was set up in 1987, neither Alley's educational theories nor his ideas on the school structure have been set in place. Those who preserve the Alley myth in Gansu have either a complete ignorance of or a complete indifference to his educational philosophy. Amongst the complaints made by foreign supporters of the school is that, while money had been made available for beautifying the school in the form of Rewi Alley statues and other prettifying measures, money for agricultural projects had not been readily available. The school and its association with Alley were used as a means to attract foreign funds and visitors to the area. For this reason, the money spent on beautifying the school was justified by the belief that foreigners should only see the best. A further complaint was that the old Shandan 'boys,' the former pupils, were never consulted on the school, although many of them had stated their willingness to come and work there.

At the same time that the Shandan Bailie School was being set up, Alley was also involved in the revival of the co-operative movement in China. Alley saw the co-operatives as a means to resolve two of China's major problems in the 1980s: that of excess labour and that of disillusioned youth. In Shandan, it was hoped that the co-operatives, some of which were operated by former Bailie students, would work together with the Bailie School. However, according to a report in 1994 from Bill Willmott, president of the NZCFS, the credibility of both the Shandan Bailie school and the new co-operatives were under threat.[40] Neither could be said to be representative of the fulfilment of Alley's ideals. The new co-operatives were not truly worker-controlled; they had developed into a mixture of free enterprise and state-imposed worker ownership. The intrinsic democracy and independence, which a true co-operative necessitates, had never existed because the political and social climate did not allow it; moreover, most workers seemed to prefer outright capitalism to the ideals of the co-operatives. As it had been in the 1940s, Alley's hope for the new Shandan Bailie School was that it would train leaders for the co-ops of the future. However, from the very beginning, links between the new Shandan Bailie School and the Shandan co-operatives were non-existent: while the school trained for agriculture, the co-ops were industrial. The modern co-operatives seem on the whole to have failed in China – the idea of shared profit was incompatible with the trend towards individualistic capitalism.

After Alley's death, New Zealand government spending on projects associated with him declined. Whereas in 1987 New Zealand donated NZ\$150,000 to the Shandan Bailie School and in 1988 a further NZ\$60,000 was spent, such sums have not been equalled in recent years. In 1990 only NZ\$11,500 out of the total NZ\$355,250 spent on the New Zealand–China Exchange Program was spent on Alley commemorative activities: NZ\$10,000 went towards the Rewi Alley scholarship, which allows for a Chinese student from Gansu to come to New Zealand to study agriculture, and NZ\$1,500 to the renovation of Alley's former cottage at Moeawatea. Nevertheless, a report from the same year commented, 'While the Rewi Alley factor is of declining significance in the bilateral relationship, and that is a natural trend, we have so few pegs on which to hang our hat in China that, while the legacy is still alive, so to speak, we need to handle it very carefully.'[41] A Ministry of Foreign Affairs and Trade report on the continuance or not of funding for Shandan Bailie School noted:

> We do not wish to overdo the concentration on Shandan Bailie School/Gansu Province. Economic prospects are not repeat not good and we suspect benefits will become increasingly marginal in the wake of Rewi's death. We must ensure, that at least, the Shandan Bailie School doesn't founder soon after Rewi's death. . . . We do not envisage a large financial commitment over the longer term.[42]

When a Chinese organisation calling itself the 'Rewi Alley Co-operative Foundation' wrote to the New Zealand government seeking money for its activities, it was given a one-off grant of NZ\$10,000 to celebrate the twenty-year anniversary of New Zealand–China relations in 1992.[43] However, the government turned down a request from the Lanzhou Bailie Oil School for funding.[44] At the school's fiftieth anniversary celebrations (fifty years dating from 1942 when George Hogg first set up a Bailie School in Shuangshipu) much was made of the humanitarian origins of the setting up of the school. School officials made a plea for support from overseas to assist in the development of China's oil and petrochemical industries. New Zealand Ambassador Powles attended the celebrations as did a representative of New Zealand company Petrocorp, which had just signed a technology-transfer deal with Gansu Province. In such situations the 'internationalist' Rewi Alley was used as a symbol of international assistance to the Chinese economy, on Chinese terms. From the mid-1990s New Zealand's aid to China tended to focus on projects that had little connection with Alley. By 2000, New Zealand aid to China had moved well beyond the narrow regional focus of the first few years of development assistance to cover a wide range of projects all over China. Instead of receiving special status, Gansu had to compete for funds with other poor provinces in China.[45]

The extent to which Alley's internationalist role will continue to be useful to China is dependent on attitudes in China towards both the Communist ideals he symbolises and China's relationship with the West. In future it would be wise to adopt the view of the New Zealand diplomat who cautioned that with regard to Alley we 'should never underestimate the Chinese capacity to "re-interpret".'[46]

11

EPILOGUE

Like many of China's long-standing foreign friends, Rewi Alley found it difficult to adjust to the shift to a more market-oriented society in the early 1980s. As attitudes towards China in the international community changed, so too did the Chinese authorities' assessment of the importance of its old friends. The privileges to which the friends were entitled were also reassessed. In 1980, Alley lamented that he now had to pay 'foreigners' prices' for his accommodation at Beidaihe and might not be able to go again[1] (though in the last year of his life, the ailing Alley had the use of his own special train carriage on his final trip to Beidaihe).[2]

If we are to believe Alley's doctor of Chinese medicine, Zhao Gaiying, Alley's death in 1987 from cerebral thrombosis and heart failure was a direct result of these economic changes. According to Zhao, Alley died after a fit of rage when he was told at several modern Peking hotels that if he wanted afternoon tea he would have to pay in Foreign Exchange Certificates (FEC), when in the past he had been allowed to pay in *renminbi*, the normal Chinese currency. Alley returned home from the outing overexcited and shouting, '*Wo meiyou waihui*' (I don't have any FEC). He died the same night.[3]

Alley symbolises an era that has all but passed; one in which a beleaguered China was dependent on people-to-people ties to conduct its diplomacy. His work as a publicist and unofficial envoy helped to shape the way in which Westerners perceived China. The activities of Alley and other foreign friends were a conduit along which China's international relations were directed, at a time when Mao divided the world into friends and enemies. In the current era, 'friendship' has a much more muted part to play in Chinese foreign policy, being more of a catchphrase than it was during the 1950s and 1960s when it was one of China's primary tools to influence public opinion in the West. While China still nominates individuals friendly to its interests as friends, the selection criteria and restrictions on the role are much less constrained than they were in Alley's time. Though a few of China's foreign friends from the Cold War era remain in China, their role is insignificant. Unlike most of the other friends, living or dead, however, Alley's name will not yet disappear. His role has shifted to a more spiritual plane: he is today an exemplar of revolutionary virtues for a new generation of Chinese youth and foreigners in China, a generation for whom, however, the notion of revolution seems out of date and even rather strange. Rewi Alley's life epitomises Chinese-style political friendship in the Cold War era; it is a telling example of the ways and means the CCP manipulated foreigners and foreign things for its own ends.

Rewi Alley's close friend Courtney Archer described Alley's decision to stay on in China after 1949 as a 'Faustian choice.' Alley's Faustian choice was that in return for staying in the country that had become his home, he would allow himself to be used for propaganda purposes, even to the point where his personal beliefs dipped completely from view. Though he could not have known it then, the 'covenant' that eventuated between Alley (and other foreigners who became friends of China in the Mao era) and the CCP was that he would not see, hear or speak any evil about China, speaking only the good, and that he would allow himself to become a political tool of the regime. After 1949, Alley suppressed both his sexual identity and his distinctive individualism. In return, the CCP gave him a life vastly superior to that of almost all Chinese people and even allowed him the option of a belief in Utopia.

Rewi Alley left New Zealand in 1927 disillusioned by the failure of his farm. In China he found acceptance, prestige and an opportunity to make his mark in the world. But what happened to the courage and dedication to a cause that was characteristic of his life before 1949? A newspaper article in 1990 described Alley's motives for hiding the evils of the Chinese government as 'complex.'[4] Yet Alley's motives should be understood in terms of the natural human desire for security and safety. In the 1950s, Rewi Alley believed himself to be part of a revolutionary movement and he brushed over or ignored those parts of the new regime that were as oppressive as the former system. In the name of the revolution, he condoned acts that, had they been made by the Chinese Nationalists or the United States, he would have abhorred. Once he had adjusted himself to the system, it became difficult to leave. As George Konrad states, in a totalitarian society 'He who agrees to be controlled exists; he who does not ceases to exist.'[5]

From the 1950s until his death, Alley was a professional friend of China. There are three distinct ranks for China's 'friends': foreign friend (*waiguo pengyou*, sometimes *guoji youren*); friend of China; and the highest accolade, internationalist (*guojizhuyizhe/guojizhuyi zhanshi*). Rewi Alley achieved all three of these ranks in his lifetime. The role of friend of China in the Mao era necessitated absolute obedience to the Chinese government; no public criticism was allowed. The punishment for criticism in politically peaceful times might be total banishment from China; in times of political turmoil, such as the Cultural Revolution, such public criticism resulted in years of imprisonment and suffering for many foreign friends resident in China at the time. In the Deng era, those who could who were unhappy with 'reform and opening up' left, but the majority of the resident foreign friends kept quiet and enjoyed their dwindling retirement benefits. Alley had long ago decided that he would stay on in new China, at any cost. His way of coping with life in the PRC after the idealism and hope of the pre-Liberation days disappeared was to focus on the positive and ignore the negative. This was a self-protective device, not just a political necessity, especially for such an optimistic, positive person as Alley, accustomed to action and getting things done.

Did Rewi Alley object to the myth-making that surrounded him? He might have once, but I believe he came to enjoy it. When you act out a part for so long, eventually you become that part. He enjoyed his lifestyle, luxurious by anyone's standards and far better than he might have expected had he returned to live in New Zealand. He felt he deserved the benefits he had earned and was very proud of his Queen's Service Medal. Although publicly Alley claimed that he felt uncomfortable with the high-level publicity he received late in life as the 'bridge builder' of New Zealand–China relations, to those who knew him he seemed, privately, rather proud of the resurgence of interest in China and himself in the 1970s and 1980s.[6] Modesty was an essential part of the Alley myth; he stated, 'I am not interested in face, fame or fortune.'[7] However, the evidence does not match Alley's claim to humility. Alley was the kind of man who wanted to change the world; he was attracted to power. In the 1950s when given a choice between an obscure retirement in New Zealand or the role as a champion of the Chinese Communists, he naturally chose the latter.

The political myth based on the life of Rewi Alley has been eminently flexible in its uses: as a symbol of Western humanitarianism in China; as a symbol of New China; as a symbol of a new era in New Zealand's diplomatic relations with China; and, in recent years, as a model of moral virtue to Chinese people and a symbol of the Chinese government's quest for Western assistance for China's development and modernisation. These are the positive versions of the Rewi Alley myth, but Alley's mythical presence has also been projected in a negative sense. The eulogisation of Alley was always contiguous with a parallel process of vilification. In the co-operative movement Alley was not only the heroic Westerner: to some he was an imperialist, while to others he was simply 'Screwy Rewi.'[8] Alley's role as peace worker and friend of China lead to his vilification by some in the West who regarded him as a traitor to his country and a toady of the Chinese government. Implicitly, to those in the Western world who disagreed with his public views, Alley's unquestioning support for the Chinese government was seen as a betrayal of the tradition of the Western intellectual as a social critic. Their standards for Chinese intellectuals were not so high. Particularly in the post-Mao era, in the eyes of many in both China and the West, Alley continues to be the prototype of the fellow traveller, an apologist for ideals that others have long since ceased to believe in.

It is important to note that the myth-making about Alley was created by Alley himself as much as it was by others. Alley was by no means a passive witness to his own mythologisation. As a gay man living in an era when sex was not discussed and homosexuality was a punishable offence, Alley had learnt from an early age to play out a role in order to disguise his sexual orientation. Alley's heterosexual role-playing served him in good stead for all the other roles he adopted at different times throughout his life. The outcome of a lifetime of role-playing was that even Alley's closest friends and family members could not claim to know him well.

By the time Rewi Alley died in 1987 at the age of ninety, he was one of the last of a generation of Western men attracted to China for the sexual freedom they found there. Homosexual Westerners were drawn to China in the Republican era for a variety of reasons, which included culture, politics, sex, adventure and travel. China provided a refuge to those fleeing the prejudices of their own societies. Tolerance and acceptance in traditional Chinese society towards same-sex love engendered a climate where sexua ambiguity could flourish. Since homosexuals in China were not peripheral or marginalised, there was no need for a separate and specifically homosexual community to develop. During the Republican era, this began to change as Chinese society became influenced by Western culture, though the chaos of war and extraterritoriality delayed the implementation of these social changes. Prior to 1949, Rewi Alley and other foreigners benefited from this situation. The coming to power of an authoritarian Communist government that viewed homosexuality as a legacy of the feudal past brought this tolerance to an end. The dramatic change in attitudes towards sexuality from the Republican to the Communist era is an example of one of the more unfortunate outcomes of cross-cultural influence from the West to China.

If we contrast the reality of Alley's life with the demands of both the Chinese and Western typology of the virtually asexual hero, we get a better sense of why he might not have objected to being mythologised. Alley's sexuality was one of the important reasons why he came to, and then stayed on in, China. In both the New Zealand and Chinese heroic tradition it would have been impossible for Alley to achieve heroic status had his sexuality been widely known. In Chinese society it is considered a social duty to marry and produce heirs. Even those whose sexual preference is homosexual have traditionally fulfilled these responsibilities. Significantly, one of the most common elements of the innumerable biographical pieces written about Alley is the need to explain why he never married. The authors of such pieces claim that Alley chose not to marry because of his desire 'to do good things for the Chinese people'[9] or because of a failed love-affair. Traditionally, same-sex love was acknowledged in China as a valid sexual preference – one of China's first emperors was responsible for the standard traditional euphemism for homosexuality, 'the cut sleeve.'[10] However, in the

PRC the tolerant attitudes of the past were replaced by more puritanical ones.

After 1949, Rewi Alley was forced to be discreet about his sexuality. This was obligatory in order for him to be allowed to stay on in China. Moreover, as my experiences researching Alley have revealed, this has been a crucial means of maintaining his mythic status in China and New Zealand. After Alley's former work unit, the Friendship Association, learned that I was writing a paper on Alley and other Western homosexuals in China, they instructed Alley's Chinese family members not to speak with me and refused to give me any further assistance with my research. They also told a New Zealand academic, whom I was helping with his own research project on Alley, that they would no longer assist his work if he co-operated with me. In contemporary Chinese eyes, to describe someone as homosexual is to blacken his or her name; no good person could possibly be involved in 'deviant' sexual practices. In New Zealand, the attitude has been similar, at least in more conservative circles. In 1993, when I first presented my research on Alley publicly, at the New Zealand Asian Studies Association Conference, senior figures in the New Zealand–China Friendship Society obtained an advance copy of one page of my conference paper, which happened to have a sentence mentioning Alley's sexuality. On the basis of that one sentence a number of individuals urged the New Zealand government and Victoria University, which was hosting the conference, to have the paper removed from the conference, claiming it was 'not in the national interest' to discuss the topic. I was also approached by members of the society and pressured to remove mention of Alley's sexuality from my work. The attempts in New Zealand to censor my research were finally rebutted by a senior New Zealand foreign-affairs official who, after refusing to suppress the paper, told representatives from the New Zealand–China Friendship Society, 'This is New Zealand, not China.'

More than anything, Rewi Alley was a survivor; the kind of person who would do whatever he had to do to get through the most difficult of times. When I first conducted interviews in China in 1990, slightly over a year after the 4 June 1989 massacre, many people commented that they were sure that Rewi Alley would have spoken out against the massacre, ending his policy of (in public) saying only good things about the regime. Having read Alley's comments in letters during other times of crisis in China, such as the famine years of the late 1950s, the Cultural Revolution and the democracy movement of the 1980s, I sincerely doubt it. Alley was always extremely cautious. Even when he knew his friends and adopted family were being wrongfully accused and persecuted during various political movements after 1949, Alley's main concern at the time always seems to have been his own safety. This is understandable. Alley had witnessed the terrible oppression of the corrupt Nationalist government in the 1930s and 1940s when a man might be buried alive just for supporting a 'progressive' movement such as the co-operatives. To him, perhaps, the excesses of the Chinese Communist government could always be weighed against those times. But when did the balance stop falling in the Communist Party's favour? After the Cultural Revolution there was a marked change in Alley's private views. But by then it was too late to make a change in his lifestyle.

The writings of Orrin Klapp on how heroes are created give an insight into why Alley might have accepted a mythical role. Klapp writes of the way people are 'typed' according to their social role. Individuals define social roles by their friends, lifestyles or conspicuous public roles. A person may create his or her type by manipulating cues, but, once categorised, a person may only change his or her social role by moving on. Klapp defines all types of 'deviant' behaviour as a process of self-typing. He writes, 'Self-typing gives psychological content to the quest for status . . . the deviant may have a status problem (let us say he is a homosexual) because he is typing himself in a manner that causes people to deny him a satisfactory status.'[11] Finding oneself, in Klapp's terms, is a process of building a type for oneself.

The functional needs of a group determine its stock of social types; thus the role typed for Alley by New Zealand's myth-making tradition, the 'man alone' type, tells us as much about New Zealand society as it does about Rewi Alley. Klapp defines public roles as falling into three main social types: hero, villain and fool. These three types help society to maintain its structure and orient its members. To those who see Alley as a villain or a fool his homosexuality is part of that role. In New Zealand and the PRC Alley became a hero – but in both countries heroes cannot be openly gay. In Klapp's analysis, loyalty to a nation is built by identification with hero types and hatred for villains. He tells us a group forms its self-image from social types. These social types provide a national consensus on what it is to belong to a particular country. For those who regard him as a hero, Alley is seen as a do-gooder and a good bloke. Meanwhile, those who see him as a villain portray him as a traitor, a parasite and a suspicious isolate.

Klapp writes that an individual's submission to a particular type can become so successful that depersonalisation occurs and only the type is visible. Perhaps this explains how the man Alley became merged into the mythic Alley. In 1927, when he first moved to China, Rewi Alley was a man in search of an identity, seeking both to re-establish himself and to be himself. Despite the relative freedom he discovered in China to explore his sexuality, Alley always felt a fear of exposure of this aspect of his life, which kept him secretive, playing out roles, even with his own family. This made it easy for him later in life to adapt to the changing needs of his political role.

Though Alley has been useful to the Chinese and the New Zealand governments, it is important to place his significance into proportion. Without Alley, New Zealand would still have been able to maintain good relations with the PRC when it chose to do so. On the same count, it is doubtful that

Alley's sixty-odd books on China, as well as articles, poems and speeches too numerous to list, had any significant impact on the speed at which China was recognised by the Western world. It is safe to conclude that Alley was, in the words of Jacques Marcuse, like other friends of China, 'eminently useable rather than eminently useful.'[12]

New Zealand knows no other symbolic figure comparable to Alley. Never before, and likely never again, has one man come to symbolise New Zealand's relationship with another country. As I have mentioned earlier, there are examples of other individuals who, while New Zealand-born, have made significant contributions in other countries and yet have not been turned into symbols for New Zealand's relations with those countries in the way that Alley was. The primary reason for this is that 'people's diplomacy' relations are not an intrinsic part of New Zealand foreign policy, while they are a fundamental element in the PRC's foreign-relations repertoire. In utilising Alley in its relations with China in recent years, the New Zealand government has mostly responded to Chinese efforts.

Alley is an icon that is quintessentially symbolic of New Zealand, yet at the same time is quintessentially Chinese. New Zealanders tend to identify with Alley's self-deprecation and egalitarianism, his internationalism and humanitarianism. But for the Chinese government Alley typifies qualities of obedience, loyalty and selfless dedication to the cause of China's modernisation. Since 1949 China has been determined to steer its own path without the impact of Western value systems.[13] Rewi Alley has been promoted by the Chinese government because he represented Chinese values that the government would like both Chinese people and foreigners to emulate, rather than Western values. Moreover, to the Chinese authorities Alley was a foreigner who served China first, rather than his own country.

And yet, apart from the opportunism of recent New Zealand governments and the propaganda needs of the PRC government, Rewi Alley has always been a heroic figure to a significant number of New Zealanders. The Rewi Alley myth persisted even in the Cold War era because it symbolised the way many New Zealanders (especially, in the male-dominated culture of New Zealand, New Zealand men) liked to see themselves: active, bold, adventurous pioneers carving a new path where others had failed before; though small in number and limited in resources, still capable of making a difference. Alley's standing in New Zealand has always been directly related to the perception that he was important and famous in other, more powerful, countries. His perceived high standing reflects on New Zealand and has long been a source of national self-satisfaction. In particular, his apparent importance to the post-1949 Chinese government has made New Zealanders feel their tiny country had a significant part to play in world affairs. Every nation needs its myths and the Rewi Alley myth has served New Zealand well: in the 1930s and 1940s it gave New Zealand pride in its humanitarianism; in the 1950s, 1960s and 1970s it was a focus for protest against the conservative views of the New Zealand government and its American ally. Finally, in the 1980s, 1990s and on into the early twenty-first century, it has been a channel for improving relations with China, one of New Zealand's most important trading partners and one of the leading powers in the Asia–Pacific region. In the New Zealand context, the ready acceptance of the Alley myth reflects the deep-seated need of a relatively new nation in the world to establish a unique identity for itself, separate from the colonial past.

The myth that has been created about Rewi Alley has as much to do with his native land as it does with the traditions and norms of his adopted land. While other countries might value genius and excellence, in New Zealand it is the ordinary and everyday that is prized. Ultimately, the greatest term that is used to describe the mythical New Zealand male is his ordinariness. Indeed, one of the highest accolades given to Alley was that he was an 'extra-ordinary, ordinary New Zealander.'[14] When it chose to commemorate him, the New Zealand government always emphasised that Alley was a typical New Zealander, who represented skills and qualities the New Zealand government was proud to claim as unique to New Zealanders. At a meeting to mark the ninety-fifth anniversary of Alley's birth, Michael Powles, then New Zealand Ambassador to China revealed a deep need for being taken seriously in the world scene, which helps explain why New Zealand has gone along with the Rewi Alley myth for so long:

> I would like to think that the combination of qualities displayed by Rewi owed much to the environment of the country in which he was born 95 years ago and grew up in until the age of 30. To the natural beauty of New Zealand, the pioneering spirit prevalent amongst its people, and their commitment to the values of self respect and respect for the worth of others. I would also like to think that this remains as true today as in Rewi's time. . . . It is a matter of pride to New Zealanders therefore that notwithstanding the sixty years that Rewi Alley spent living at one with a culture so rich, powerful and absorbing as that of China, he remained instantly identifiable as a New Zealander. To people of a much younger culture such as ours, coming from a person of Rewi Alley's stature, that is a very important compliment.[15]

On a more popular level, the assertion that Alley was a typical New Zealander was always an important part of his appeal. Alley's biographer Geoff Chapple wrote of his subject:

> To us he remains very much a New Zealander, in speech and in those qualities – the lack of bullshit, the air of easy equality, the belief in work – which New Zealand used to be famous for. He is a

New Zealand hero, having raised these qualities to an epic scale. New Zealand has few enough heroes, and most are officially sanctioned.[16]

Alley was indeed a New Zealand 'hero' and it is, as Hadas writes, the 'authorised image' of this hero status and the 'cult' that has supported it that serve as the theme of this study. Since Alley's death in 1987, the opportunities for further variations on the Rewi Alley myth have increased rather than decreased. Whether the Rewi Alley myth will be maintained for posterity is dependent on the political needs of the future and on the existence of a 'cult', formal or informal, that will ensure the survival of that myth.

APPENDIX

Honours received by Rewi Alley

1945   Offered a knighthood by the British government, Alley refuses.

1947   Nominated for the position of Head of the Far East division of UNRRA (United Nations Relief and Rehabilitation Administration), nomination refused by Chiang Kaishek.

1954   Made Honorary Headmaster of the Lanzhou Oil School (formerly Shandan Bailie School).

1961   Nominated for Lenin Peace Prize, cancelled as the Sino-Soviet split worsens.

1973   Awarded an honorary Doctorate in Literature by Victoria University, Wellington. University of Waikato, Hamilton establishes a Rewi Alley Archive.

1977   Eightieth birthday celebrated at the Great Hall of the People, Peking. Deng Xiaoping attends.

1977   Rewi Alley Scholarship in Chinese Studies established at Waikato University.

1979   Reinstated as Honorary Headmaster at the Lanzhou Oil School, after loosing this title in 1967 during the Cultural Revolution.

1982   Made an honorary citizen of Beijing.

1984   Conferred the insignia of a Companion of the Queen's Service Order for Community Service, in recognition of his work to promote and enhance New Zealand–China relations over many years (this was formally presented at the New Zealand Embassy in 1985).

1984   Became the first foreign member of Chinese PEN.

1985   Rewi Alley Scholarship in Agricultural Science established by the New Zealand and Chinese governments for students of Gansu Province.

1985   Made Honorary President of the Bailie University for Vocational Training in Beijing.

1985   Made an honorary citizen of Gansu Province.

1986   Rewi Alley Exchange Scholarship established as part of the Lanzhou–Christchurch sister city link, for students of Gansu Province.

1988   Exhibition in memory of Rewi Alley held at the Beijing Museum of the Chinese Revolution at the same time as the publication of a photo album, *Rewi Alley*, depicting Alley's sixty years in China.

1988   Alley's former cottage at Moeawatea restored by the New Zealand Historical Places Trust.

1991   Statue of Rewi Alley erected in Springfield, New Zealand, birthplace of Alley.

1997   Centenary celebrations in memory of the hundred years since Alley's birth, seventy years since his arrival in China and ten years since his death held in the Great Hall of the People in Beijing. Alley's autobiography republished in Chinese and English, as are a photo album and a catalogue of the books in his former library, now held in People's University, Beijing.

NOTES

DEDICATION

1 George Konrad, Preface to Miklos Haraszti, *The Velvet Prison: Artists Under State Socialism*, London: Penguin Books, 1983, p. *xv*.

1 INTRODUCTION

1 'Grand Old Kiwi of China Approaching 90,' *New Zealand Herald*, 23 January 1987.
2 For more on this topic see Anne-Marie Brady, 'Making the Foreign Serve China: Managing Foreigners in the People's Republic', Boulder, COL.: Rowman and Littlefield, 2002 (in press).
3 Edgar Snow, 'China's Blitzbuilder Rewi Alley,' *Saturday Evening Post*, 8 February 1941.
4 'Pragmatic Kiwi a Giant in China,' *Auckland Star*, 28 December 1987.
5 Zhao Gaiying, 'Huainian Luyi Aili tongzhi' (Remembering Comrade Rewi Alley), *Renmin ribao* (People's Daily) (Overseas edition), 20 April 1988.
6 'Knighthood had no appeal for Rewi Alley,' *New Zealand Herald*, 6 December 1980.
7 'Rewi Alley in China,' *New Zealand School Journal*, Volume 40 No 9: Part IV: October 1946, p. 284.
8 Colin Morrison, *Visit to Sandan*, CORSO (Coalition of Relief Services Organisations) report, 1947, p. 32.
9 *Rewi Alley Seventy Five*, National Committee for the Commemoration of Rewi Alley's Seventy Fifth Birthday, Hamilton, NZ, 1972.
10 Willis Airey, *A Learner in China*, Christchurch: The Caxton Press and the Monthly Review Society, 1970, pp. 250–251.
11 Rewi Alley, *At 90: Memoirs of My China Years*, Beijing: New World Press, 1987, p. 263.
12 Han Suyin, 'Han Suyin Remembers Rewi Alley,' *New Argot*, 1974.
13 Geoff Chapple, *Rewi Alley of China*, Auckland: Hodder and Stoughton, 1980, p. 210.
14 George Hogg, *I See A New China*, London: Victor Gollancz, 1945.
15 Roland Barthes, *Mythologies*, New York: Hill and Wang, 1972, p. 143.
16 Moses Hadas, *Heroes and Gods: Spiritual Biographies in Antiquity*, London: Routledge and Kegan Paul, 1965, p. 4.
17 *Ibid*, p. 4.
18 Airey, *A Learner in China*, p. 11.
19 *Rewi Alley: An Autobiography* (revised, third edition), Beijing: New World Press, 1997.

2 A NEW ZEALAND CHILDHOOD

1 The correct Maori pronunciation is 'Ray-wi'; however, people of Rewi Alley's generation call him 'Roo-ee', while younger generations have adopted the aberrant 'Ree-wi'.
2 'Rewi Alley,' *Aotearoa*, n.d. approximately 1947, Folder 7, Alley papers, Alexander Turnbull Library (hereafter ATL).
3 *Pakeha* is the term used in New Zealand for non-Maori, especially white, inhabitants.
4 John McLeod, *Myth and Reality – the New Zealand Soldier in World War Two*, Auckland: Reed Methuen, 1986, p. 13.
5 Joy Alley, interview with the author, 23 April 1993.
6 Gwen Somerset, *Sunshine and Shadows*, Auckland: New Zealand Playcentre Foundation, 1988, p. 12.
7 *Ibid*, p. 28.
8 *Ibid*, p. 4.
9 Folder 12, Kathleen Wright Collection, ATL.
10 Pip Alley to Willis Airey, 30 May 1965, 3/2, Alley papers, ATL.
11 Somerset, *Sunshine and Shadows*, p. 21.
12 Rewi Alley to Gwen Somerset, Peking, 1 July 1977, cited in Somerset, *Sunshine and Shadows*, p. 76.
13 Robert Aldrich, *Seduction of the Mediterranean: Writing, Art and Homosexual Fantasy*, London: Routledge, 1993, p. 7.
14 Rewi Alley to Pip Alley, 1 April 1972, Alley papers, ATL.
15 The Plunket Society is an organisation for the care of infants and young children.
16 Joy Alley, interview with the author, 23 April 1993.
17 Somerset, *Sunshine and Shadows*, p. 18.
18 Rewi Alley to Gwen Somerset, 11 August 1977, in Somerset, *Sunshine and Shadows*, p. 81.
19 Alley, *At 90*, p. 41.
20 *Ibid*, p. 41.
21 Courtney Archer, interview with the author, 4 July 1993.
22 Alley, *At 90*, pp. 41–43.
23 See Daryl Klein, *With the Chinks*, London: The Bodley Head, 1919.
24 Alley's copy is now held with the majority of the books of his former library in a special collection at People's University, Peking.
25 Klein, *With the Chinks*, pp. 182–183.
26 Bret Hinsch, *Passions of the Cut Sleeve*, Berkeley: University of California, 1990, p. 2.
27 *Ibid*, p. 4.
28 Aldrich, *Seduction of the Mediterranean*, p. 7.
29 Courtney Archer, letter to the author, 11 May 1994.
30 Harold Acton, *Peonies and Ponies*, Hong Kong: Oxford University Press, 1983, p. 121.
31 Jonathan Spence, *The Memory Palace of Matteo Ricci*, New York: Viking Press, 1984, p. 220.
32 Somerset, *Sunshine and Shadows*, p. 129.
33 *The Frontiersmen*, June 1949.
34 Pip Alley to Willis Airey, 3 May 1965, 3/2, Alley papers, ATL.
35 Alexander Whyte, *Santa Teresa*, London: Oliphant, Andersen and Ferrier, n.d., p. 6. Copy in the possession of Joy Alley.
36 Somerset, *Sunshine and Shadows*, p. 129.

3 SHANGHAILANDER

1 Cited in Willis Airey's notes to *A Learner in China*, Airey papers, Auckland University Library (herafter AUL). The unpublished version differs markedly from the published work, which was heavily censored by Alley; see Willis Airey, *A Learner in China*, Christchurch: Caxton Press and Monthly Review, 1970.

2 Willian Crane Johnstone Jr, *The Shanghai Problem*, Stanford, California: Stanford University Press, 1937, p. 45.

3 *Ibid*, p. 70.

4 *Ibid*, p. 84.

5 1928 letter to family, Sui Wo fires, 6/16, Alley papers, ATL.

6 See Alley, *At 90*, p. 46; Chapple, *Rewi Alley of China*, p. 41; and Airey, *A Learner in China*, p. 65.

7 Rewi Alley to Alley family, n.d. (approximately 1928), 6/1, Alley papers, ATL.

8 Cited in Willis Airey's notes to *A Learner in China*, AUL. The above quotations were omitted and the original letters burnt at Alley's request in 1968.

9 *Ibid*, p. 86.

10 Rewi Alley to Pip Alley, 12 March 1968, 4/13, Alley papers, ATL.

11 Willis Airey, Draft of *A Learner in China*, AUL; and 3/1, Alley papers, ATL.

12 W. H. Auden and Christopher Isherwood, *Journey to a War*, London: Faber & Faber, 1939, p. 237.

13 Courtney Archer, letter to the author, 11 May 1994.

14 Noel Coward, *Noel Coward: Autobiography*, London: Methuen, 1986, p. 219.

15 Henry Champly, *The Road to Shanghai: White Slave Traffic in Asia*, trans. Warren B. Wells, London: John Long, 1937, p. 210.

16 Christopher Isherwood, *Christopher and his Kind*, 1926–1939, New York: Avon Books, 1977, p. 308.

17 Harold Acton, *Memoirs of an Aesthete*, London: Methuen, 1989, p. 1.

18 David Kidd, interview with the author, 30 October 1994.

19 George Kates, *Chinese Household Furniture*, New York: Dover Publications, 1948, p. ix.

20 Alistair Morrison, interview with the author, 9 April 1994.

21 C. P. Fitzgerald, *Why China? Recollections of China 1923–1950*, Melbourne: Melbourne University Press, 1985, p. 152.

22 Archer, letter to the author.

23 Kidd, interview with the author.

24 James Bertram, *Shadow of a War: a New Zealander in the Far East 1939–1946*, Australia and New Zealand: Whitcombe and Tombs, 1947, p. 14.

25 Archer, interview with the author. What Alley calls 'Choshan' is probably Zhoushan Island, a few hours by boat from Shanghai.

26 Hinsch, *Passions*, p. 31.

27 Rewi Alley to Clara Alley, 25 September 1929, Folder 1, Rhodes papers, ATL.

28 Rewi Alley to Alley family, 21 July 1930, Folder 1, Rhodes papers, ATL.

29 See Airey, *A Learner in China*, p. 78; Chapple, *Rewi Alley of China*, p. 44; Alley, *At 90*, p. 54.

30 Willis Airey, notes for *A Learner in China*, Airey papers, AUL.

31 John Bell Condliffe, *Autobiography 1891–1969*, Part One, p. 26, copy held in the Alexander Turnbull Library.

32 Johnstone, *The Shanghai Problem*, pp. 178–182.

33 Dr Joseph Bailie, letter to Rewi Alley, 12 November 1931, cited in Willis Airey, notes to *A Learner in China*, Airey papers, AUL. Not included in the published version.

34 James Bertram, 'Chinese Missions in China,' *Salient*, October 1955.

35 Ruth Weiss, interview with the author, 4 September 1997.

36 See *1932–1934 Daybook*, Box 47, Maud Russell Papers, New York Public Library.

37 Ida Pruitt to Rewi Alley, 25 March 1939, 2/24, Alley papers, ATL.

38 Auden and Isherwood, *Journey to a War*, pp. 235–243.

39 Ruth Weiss, interview with the author, 16 June 1991.

40 *Ibid*, 4 September 1997.

41 On the life and works of Maud Russell see Karen Garner, *Challenging the Consensus: Maud Muriel Russell's Life and Political Activism*, PhD diss., University of Texas at Austin, 1995.

42 Chapple, *Rewi Alley of China*, p. 64.

43 Rewi Alley to Geoff Alley, 12 June 1951, 3/22, Alley papers, ATL.

44 *Dominion*, 12 April 1932.

4 THE HUMANITARIAN

1 Alley, *At 90*, pp. 78–79.

2 K. P. Liu and Frank Lem were among the orginal 'Bailie boys,' young Chinese men whom Joseph Bailie helped to get a Western education so that they might use their careers to help modernise China; Ralph Lapwood was a left-leaning missionary friend of Alley's; Grace and Manny Granich were Comintern agents sent by the Communist Party of America to edit the pro-CCP journal *Voice of China*.

3 'Rewi Alley,' 10 June 1942, China, Economic Affairs: Co-operatives, PM 264/5/9 part 1, National Archives, New Zealand (hereafter NA).

4 Graham Peck, *Two Kinds of Time*, Boston: Houghton Mifflin Company, 1950, p. 193.

5 *Ibid*, p. 194.

6 See R. H. Tawney, *Land and Labour in China*, London: George Allen and Unwin, 1932. J. B. Tayler, *Farm and Factory in China. Aspects of Industrial Revolution*, Student Christian Movement, 1928. Gladys Yang, interview with the author, 27 October 1990.

7 Cited in Barbara Spencer, *China Thirty Years On*, Whangarei, n.p., 1977, p. 49.

8 Edward Said, *Orientalism*, New York: Pantheon Books, 1978, p. 241.

9 Edgar Snow, 'China's Blitzbuilder Rewi Alley,' *Saturday Evening Post*, 8 February 1941.

10 Chapple, *Rewi Alley of China*, p. 117.

11 James Bertram, *Capes of China Slide Away: A Memoir of War and Peace*, Auckland: Auckland University Press, 1993, p. 180.

12 Quoted respectively in 'They Went For A Ride In A Tiger,' *Listener*, 20 June 1947; and 'Lyttleton to Shandan? Sheep Saga with a Sequel,' *Listener*, 14 February 1947. See also 3/13, Alley papers, ATL.

13 'Resignation of Rewi Alley, Noted New Zealander, Built Chinese War Industry,' newspaper clipping, n.d., approximately 1942, Max Wilkinson private papers.

14 See Airey, *A Learner in China*, p. 154.

15 See Peck, *Two Kinds of Time*, p. 164, for an example of Alley using his foreignness to convince a Chinese audience.

16 Jacques Marcuse, *The Peking Papers*, London: Arthur Baker Ltd, 1968, p. 119.

17 George Hogg, *I See a New China*, London: Victor Gollancz, 1945, p. 131.

18 Marcuse, *The Peking Papers*, p. 119.

19 Hogg, *I See a New China*, p. 154.

20 B. Shackleton, Chairman, Waimate Rewi Alley Aid Committee, July 1945, 6/22, Alley papers, ATL.

21 Cited in Airey, *A Learner in China*, p. 179.

22 'Lyttleton to Shandan?' *Listener*. Italics as in original.
23 'Rewi Alley,' *Aotearoa*.
24 'Restoring China Internally,' newspaper clipping, n.p., n.d., approximately 1938, 4/21, Alley papers, ATL.
25 'New Zealand and China,' *Listener*, 9 October 1942.
26 Rewi Alley to Willis Airey, 14 November 1965, 2/21, Alley papers, ATL.
27 Airey, *A Learner in China*, p. 176.
28 George Orwell, *1984*, n.d., n.p., pirate copy of the Penguin edition, purchased in Peking 1996, p. 31.
29 In Chinese '*gu wei jin yong, yang wei Zhong yong*.' This slogan was first cited in a directive to the Central Conservatory of Music in Peking in 1956 and became very prominent after the Sino-US *rapprochement* in the early 1970s.
30 Rewi Alley, 'Some Aspects of Internationalism,' Sam Ginsbourg *et al*, *Living In China* (*Zai Hua sanshi nian*), Peking: New World Press, 1982 (Chinese/English edition), pp. 8–9.
31 Jeffrey Kinkley has commented on this in his introduction to Chen Xuezhao, *Surviving the Storm: A Memoir*, New York: M. E. Sharpe, 1990, p. *xxv*.

5 REWI'S SCHOOL

1 Courtney Archer, interview with the author, 4 July 1993.
2 Peter Townsend, letter to the author, 21 April 1994.
3 *Ibid*.
4 Courtney Archer, letter to author, 11 May 1994.
5 Rewi Alley, 'Some Aspects of Internationalism in China's Struggle,' Ginsbourg *et al*, *Living in China*, p. 2.
6 FAO, 'Training Rural Leaders,' cited by Courtney Archer, letter to the author.
7 Sir Ralph Stevenson, letter to F. J. Case, 'Aid for China Fund,' 23 March 1949, 104/264/9, MFAT. CORSO later included this comment in its annual report 1948–1949, 2/17, Alley papers, ATL.
8 Arthur Menzies, Department of External Affairs, Canada, 8 August 1948, PM 264/5/9, NA.
9 Colin Morrison, Director of CORSO, letter to Department of External Affairs, 2 February 1942.
10 CORSO Annual Report 1948–1949, 2/17, Alley papers, ATL.
11 Wolf Rosenberg, Rewi Alley Aid Group, letter to Mr Bartlett, 30 November 1949, 9/7, Alley papers, ATL.
12 'Lyttleton to Lhasa,' *Listener*, 16 February 1945.
13 G. R. Laking, Secretary for External Affairs Counsellor, New Zealand Legation, Washington, 10 August 1948, China, Economic Affairs: Co-operatives, PM 264/5/9 part 1, NA.
14 CORSO Annual Report 1948–1949, Rewi Alley papers, 2/17, 74-047, ATL.
15 *Ibid*.
16 *Weekly News*, 19 October 1949, Max Wilkinson private papers.
17 'Rewi Alley in China,' *New Zealand School Journal*, Volume 40 No. 9: Part IV: October 1946, p. 284.
18 James Bertram, 'China and You: A Letter to Young New Zealanders,' *New Zealand School Journal*, Volume 41 No. 2: Part IV, pp. 66–71.
19 Archer, interview.
20 Archer, interview.
21 Archer, letter.
22 Archer, interview.

23 Peter Townsend and Mavis Yan, interview with the author, 10 April 1994. Townsend was Executive Secretary of the International Committee of the CIC, successively in Chengdu, Chongqing, Shanghai and Peking from 1943 to the end of 1951, while Mavis Yan worked in the CIC office in Shanghai with Townsend and had earlier worked in the Hong Kong office from 1938 until the Pacific War broke out.

24 Both quotations are from Archer, interview.

25 *Ibid.*

26 Bob Spencer, telephone interview with the author, 19 July 1994. Naireen Masson, who worked at the School from 1948 to 1950 with her husband George, had a similar opinion of homosexual activities there. Naireen Masson, telephone interview with the author, 2 February 1996.

27 George Hogg, *I See a New China*, pp. 131–132.

28 Courtney Archer, interview with the author. Max Wilkinson, interview with the author, 15 May 1993.

29 Wilkinson, interview.

30 'Children Die Naked,' Report from China 1947, Colin Morrison, CORSO, PM 264/5/9, NA. The *kang* is a heated platform used for sleeping on. It is common in peasant households in northern China.

31 Alley, 'Some Aspects of Internationalism in China's Struggle,' Ginsbourg *et al*, *Living in China*, p. 5. From 1949 a handful of girl students also attended the school.

6 THE 'FAUSTIAN CHOICE'

1 Rewi Alley to Shirley Barton, 13 October 1953, Barton papers, ATL.

2 Courtney Archer, interview with the author, 5 July 1993.

3 The revelations of Dr Li Zhisui, doctor to Mao Zedong for twenty-two years, in *The private life of Chairman Mao, the inside story of the man who made modern China*, trans. Prof. Tai Hung-chao, London: Chatto & Windus, 1994, show that the outward puritanism of the CCP was merely superficial, especially in the case of the highest cadres. Interestingly, in Chairman Mao's case, Dr Li not only describes his insatiable appetite for young women, but also (like many Chinese emperors before him) his enjoyment of handsome young men whom he asked to perform for him what Dr Li euphemistically calls 'groin massage' (Li, *Private life*, pp. 358–359). Typically, Dr Li does not classify Mao's behaviour as homosexual (as a Western-trained doctor might); rather, he claims that it is simply a symptom of an over-active sexual appetite.

4 Archer, interview.

5 '*Zhonggong zhongyang guanyu jixu kaizhan kang Mei yuan Chao xuanchuan de zhishi*' (The CCP Central Committee's Directive on Continuing to Unfold 'Oppose America Support Korea' Propaganda), Zhonggong zhongyang xuanchuanbu bangongting, Zhongyang dang'anguan bianyanbu (eds.), *Zhongguo gongchandang xuanchuan gongzuo wenxian xuanbian 1915–1992* (Selected Articles of CCP Propaganda Work, 1915–1992), 4 vols, Beijing: Xuexi chubanshe, 1996, Volume 1, pp. 54–56.

6 17 January 1951, New China News Agency.

7 Rewi Alley to Pip Alley, 9 May 1951, 3/22, Alley papers, ATL.

8 *Ibid.*

9 Rewi Alley to Pip Alley, 18 September 1951, 3/22, Alley papers, ATL.

10 Rewi Alley to Pip Alley, 13 June 1951, 3/22, Alley papers, ATL.

11 'Australian and New Zealander Broadcast to Their Peoples,' New Zealand Army, to External Affairs Dept, 23 May 1951, 104/264/9, NA.

12 'Rewi Alley Tells New Zealand,' *People's Voice*, 25 April 1951.

13 'Conditions in China – Mr Rewi Alley's Comments – *The Press* Criticised,' *Press*, 24 July 1951.

14 'Rewi Alley Not A Communist, Says CORSO Chairman,' April 1951, newspaper clipping, 2/17, Alley papers, ATL.
15 Walter Illsley, *An American in China*, unpublished manuscript, p. 126.
16 *Ibid*, p. 170.
17 Shirley Barton to Arthur Wallbank, July 1950, 3/22, Alley papers, ATL.
18 Rewi Alley to Alan Alley, 8 July 1952, Barton papers, ATL.
19 Rewi Alley to Shirley Barton, 18 June 1952, Barton papers, ATL.
20 Rewi Alley to Shirley Barton, 3 June 1952, Barton papers, ATL.
21 Shirley Barton to Rewi Alley, 20 July 1952, Barton papers, ATL.
22 *Ibid.*
23 Rewi Alley, *Yo Banfa!* (*We Have a Way*), Shanghai: China Monthly Review, 1952, inside cover.
24 Shirley Barton to Rewi Alley, 12 July 1952, Barton papers, ATL.
25 Rewi Alley to Hugh Elliott, 26 August 1952, Barton papers, ATL.
26 Lau Yee-fui *et al*, *Glossary of Chinese Political Phrases*, Hong Kong: Union Research Institute, 1977, p. 326.
27 Rewi Alley to Alan Alley, 19 July 1952, Barton papers, ATL.
28 Hugh Elliott to Rewi Alley, 23 July 1952, Barton papers, ATL.
29 Rewi Alley to Courtney Archer, 8 October 1978, Folder 1, Archer papers, ATL.
30 Alan Alley (Duan Shimou) to Rewi Alley, n.d., approximately 1953, Folder 6, Archer papers, ATL.
31 Mike Alley to Shirley Barton, 23 June 1952, Barton papers, ATL. See also 'Some Notes on the Gung Ho Movement,' Peking, 15 October 1976, Lu Guangmian private papers.
32 Shirley Barton to Mike Alley, 23 June 1952, Barton papers, ATL.
33 Shirley Barton to Courtney Archer, 21 July 1952, Barton papers, ATL.
34 Max Wilkinson to Shirley Barton, 27 May 1952, Barton papers, ATL.
35 Max Wilkinson to Shirley Barton, 1 July 1952, Barton papers, ATL.
36 Rewi Alley to Lao Wei, Kan and Yan, 1 September 1952, Barton papers, ATL.
37 Rewi Alley to Don Kemp, 22 July 1952, Barton papers, ATL.
38 Rewi Alley to Wolf Rosenberg (Rewi Alley Aid Group), 1 August 1952, Barton papers, ATL.
39 See 'Papers on Shandan 1951–53,' Folder 3, Archer papers, ATL.
40 Alan Alley to Rewi Alley, n.d., appropriately 1953, Folder 6, Archer papers, ATL.
41 Courtney Archer to Mike Alley, 3 July 1952, Barton papers, ATL.

7 FRIEND OF CHINA

1 6/24, Alley papers, ATL, also published, excerpted, in *Shanghai News*, 15 June 1952.
2 For example note the following meeting between Australian, New Zealand and UK representatives in Canberra in 1949: 'We felt ... that the price which the Americans are prepared to pay for maintaining Japan as a bastion against Communism – and that probably only as long as it suits Japan – will be at the expense of our security ... recognition would tend to increase the Americans' determination to strengthen Japan at the expense of the security of Australia and New Zealand.' A. D. McIntosh, Notes for file, 10 November 1949, PM 264/3/14 part 1A, NA. Ann Trotter has written extensively on this topic: see Ann Trotter, *New Zealand and Japan 1945–1952: The Occupation and the Peace Treaty*, London: Atlantic Press, 1990.
3 'Organisation for the Propagation of the "Germ Warfare Campaign in New Zealand",' Publicity and Information Division, Department of Tourism and Publicity, 22/1, Marshall papers, ATL.
4 *Press*, 22 January 1951.

5 *Press*, 27 July 1951.
6 Willis Airey to Rewi Alley, 19 June 1966, 2/21, Alley papers, ATL.
7 Shirley Barton to Rewi Alley, 17 June 1952, Barton papers, ATL.
8 Courtney Archer to Rewi Alley, 30 June 1952, Barton papers, ATL.
9 'Rewi Alley's Secretary is having Big Meetings,' *People's Voice*, 27 August 1952.
10 'Note For File,' 3 June 1952, 104/264/9, Ministry of Foreign Affairs and Trade (hereafter MFAT). The New Zealand government department responsible for foreign policy has had several name changes throughout the time period studied. In 1943 it was established as the Department of External Affairs, from 1969 to 1988 it was known as the Ministry of Foreign Affairs, from 1988 to 1993 as the Ministry of External Relations and Trade and it is presently known as the Ministry of Foreign Affairs and Trade. Throughout the text I have maintained the name of the department at the time being cited, although the archival listing is shown as MFAT (Ministry of Foreign Affairs and Trade).
11 'Alley's Work in China Unaffected By New Plans,' 7 March 1951, 104/264/9, MFAT.
12 Foss Shanahan, 2 June 1951, EA 1 109/3/3, MFAT.
13 R. M. Algie, Minister in Charge of Broadcasting, letter to F. P. Walsh, President of the New Zealand Federation of Labour, 14 May 1953, 22/1, Marshall papers, ATL.
14 See 'Deceiving the Deceivers: Moscow, Beijing, Pyongyang, and the Allegations of Bacteriological Weapons in Korea,' *Cold War History Project*, Bulletin 11 – Cold War Flashpoints, 3/99; Milton Leitenberg, *The Korean War Biological Warfare Allegations Resolved*, Center for Pacific Asia Studies at Stockholm University, Occasional Paper 36, May 1998. For an example of scholarship supporting the germ-warfare allegations see Stephen L. Endicott, 'Germ Warfare and "Plausible Denial",' *Modern China*, Volume 5, No. 1, January 1979, pp. 79–104; Endicott and Edward Hagerman, *The United States and Biological Warfare: Secrets from the Early Cold War and Korea*, Bloomington: Indiana University Press, 1999.
15 In the 1950s Russian allegations that the Japanese had also been involved in germ warfare were not widely accepted.
16 Shirley Barton to D. F. Springfield, 19 August 1952, Barton papers, ATL.
17 Shirley Barton to Rewi Alley, 6 July 1952, Barton papers, ATL.
18 For example, see: 'Corso Tells Why Help is Given Work of Rewi Alley,' *Dominion*, 13 May 1952; New Zealand Ambassador, USA, memo to Ministry of External Affairs, 14 August 1951, 104/264/9, MFAT; Memorandum for Mr Shanahan, Ministry of External Affairs, 6 February 1951, 104/264/9, MFAT.
19 Rewi Alley, letter to the editor, *Dominion*, 15 November 1952, 3/21, Alley papers, ATL.
20 *Frontiersman*, 1953, pp. 9–10.
21 'The Germ Warfare Campaign in New Zealand,' confidential report, Publicity and Information Division, Department of Tourism and Publicity, 30 April 1952, Marshall papers, 22/1, ATL.
22 'Courtney Archer,' confidential report, Publicity and Information Division, Department of Tourism and Publicity, 22/2, Marshall papers, ATL.
23 22/1, Marshall papers, ATL.
24 'Organisation for the Propagation of the "Germ Warfare Campaign in New Zealand".'
25 *Ibid.*
26 'A Review of Facts and Opinions Concerning the Communist Challenge to Democracy,' Publicity and Information Division, Department of Tourism and Publicity, p. 14, 22/1, Marshall papers, ATL.
27 Rewi Alley to Pip Alley, 21 March 1952, 3/21, Alley papers, ATL. See also Rewi

Alley, letter to the editor, *Dominion*, 1 June 1952, 3/21, Alley papers, ATL. Alley was protesting an article headlined 'Propaganda From Rewi Alley', which criticised his stance on germ warfare.

28 'Germ Warfare Exposure Was Censored By Daily Paper in Otago Student's Journal,' *People's Voice*, 27 August 1952.

29 Shirley Barton to Nan Green, 6 May 1954, Barton papers, ATL.

30 Rewi Alley to Shirley Barton, 2 July 1952, Barton papers, ATL.

31 Rewi Alley to Shirley Barton, 10 July 1952, Barton papers, ATL.

32 Shirley Barton to Rewi Alley, 17 July 1952, Barton papers, ATL.

33 Shirley Barton to Rewi Alley, 7 August 1952, Barton papers, ATL.

34 Rewi Alley to Shirley Barton, 17 August 1952, Barton papers, ATL.

35 Rewi Alley to Shirley Barton, 23 August 1952, Barton papers, ATL. See Alley, *Yo Banfa!*

36 Rewi Alley to Shirley Barton, 30 August 1952, Barton papers, ATL.

37 Shirley Barton to Rewi Alley, 22 July 1952, Barton papers, ATL.

38 Rewi Alley to Shirley Barton, 23 August 1952, Barton papers, ATL.

39 Shirley Barton to Rewi Alley, 30 August 1952, Barton papers, ATL.

40 Margaret Garland, *Journey to New China*, Christchurch: Caxton Press, 1954, p. 115. Margaret Garland was a New Zealand delegate to the conference; she was a member of the peace movement in New Zealand.

41 *Ibid*, pp. 44–49.

42 *Ibid*, p. 9.

43 Interview with Sir Lionel Lamb, HM Chargé d'Affaires, British Embassy, Beijing, 14 July 1953, PM 264/1/2, MFAT.

44 'China Annual Review for 1952,' HM Government and Foreign Office, PM 264/1/2, MFAT.

45 *Zhejiang sheng waishi zhi* (Zhejiang Foreign Affairs Annals), Beijing: Zhonghua shuju, 1996, p. 223.

46 Hans Magnus Enzensberger, 'Tourists of the Revolution,' *Raids and Reconstructions*, London: Pluto Press, 1976, pp. 224–252.

47 Zhao Pitao, *Waishi gaishuo* (Outline of Foreign Affairs), Shanghai: Shanghai shehui kexue chubanshe, 1995, pp. 1–2. The term *shewai* is sometimes used interchangeably with *waishi*. According to Zhao Pitao, *shewai* is both a synonym for *waishi* and a sub-category of *waishi* activities, usually focusing on administrative matters such as Sino-foreign births, deaths and marriages, Customs, and the police force. For more on the topic of the CCP foreign affairs system see Anne-Marie Brady, 'Making the Foreign Serve China: Managing *Foreigners in the People's Republic.*'

48 Percy Fang, *Zhou Enlai – A Profile*, Peking: Foreign Languages Press, 1986, p. 100.

49 Pei Xiannong, *Zhou Enlai de waijiaoxue* (The Diplomacy of Zhou Enlai), Beijing: Zhonggong zhongyang dangxiao chubanshe, 1997, p. 272; interview with *waishi* cadres, 26 December 1997.

50 Garland, *Journey to New China*, p. 130.

51 Elsie Locke, *Peace People: A History of Peace Activities in New Zealand*, Christchurch: Hazard Press, 1992, p. 100.

52 Rewi Alley to Pip Alley, 27 September 1952, 2/26, Alley papers, ATL.

53 Rewi Alley to Pip Alley, 18 September 1952, 3/21, Alley papers, ATL.

54 Rewi Alley to Pip Alley, 1 June 1952, 3/21, Alley papers, ATL. Rewi Alley told the other New Zealand delegates to the peace conference that he was out of touch with the world beyond China. See Garland, *Journey to a New China*, p. 150.

55 Shirley Barton to Rewi Alley, 24 July 1952, Barton papers, ATL.

56 Rewi Alley to Shirley Barton, 23 October 1953, Barton papers, ATL.

57 In her definitive history of the New Zealand peace movement, *Peace People: A History of Peace Activities in New Zealand*, author Elsie Locke mentions the activities of Rewi Alley twice; once to comment that his fellow New Zealanders had been inspired by his work in Shandan, and the second time with regard to the controversy over the recognition of the PRC, that he had been a New Zealand delegate at the 1952 Asia–Pacific Peace Conference.

58 Yang Xianyi and Gladys Tayler, interview with the author, 27 October 1990. Huang Daozhen, interview with the author, 28 January 1993.

59 Rewi Alley to Pip Alley, 12 June 1953, 2/26, ATL.

60 A tiny number of elderly foreigners in various scattered locations who had no other home to go to and had been cleared of any political problems were also allowed to stay on, but they were not given special status or treated as 'international friends.'

61 Michael M. Sheng, *Battling Western Imperialism: Mao, Stalin, and the United States*, Princeton, New Jersey: Princeton University Press, 1997, pp. 172–173; Yang Kuisong, 'The Soviet Factor and the CCP's Policy,' *Chinese Historians*, Volume 5, No. 1, Spring 1992, pp. 22–25.

62 William G. Sewell, *I Stayed in China*, New York: A. S. Barnes and Co., 1966, p. 127.

63 Andrei Ledovsky, 'Moscow Visit of a Chinese Communist Delegation,' *Far Eastern Affairs*, No. 4, 1996, p. 81.

64 Rewi Alley to Shirley Barton, 10 July 1953, Barton papers, ATL.

65 Rewi Alley to Shirley Barton, 13 October 1953, Barton papers, ATL.

66 This slogan appears prominently in locations frequented by foreigners in China, such as the lobby of the Beijing Hotel. It originates from Mao Zedong's speech to the first meeting of the Chinese People's Consultative Conference on 21 September 1949, published in *People's Daily* the following day. The full version of this quote is 'Our revolution has already gained the sympathy and acclaim of all the people in the world, we have friends all over the world.' Excerpted in *Zui gao zhishi* (Important Instructions), Beijing, n.p., 1969, p. 286.

67 Mao Tse-tung, 'Analysis of the Classes in Chinese Society,' *Selected Works of Mao Tse-tung*, Vol. 1, Peking: Foreign Languages Press, 1961, p. 13.

68 Somerset, *Sunshine and Shadows*, p. 129. Edgar Snow, *Scorched Earth*, London: Victor Gollancz, 1941, p. 94.

69 Rewi Alley, *Travels in China 1966–1971*, Peking: New World Press, 1973, p. 221.

70 Rewi Alley to Shirley Barton, 23 November 1956, Barton papers, ATL.

71 Lu Wanru, interview with the author, 7 November 1990.

72 R. M. Fox, *China Diary*, London: Robert Hale Ltd, 1959, p. 176.

73 Bruce Wallace, 'At Home in Worlds Apart,' *Listener*, 13 December 1971, p. 15.

74 'Time running out for Alley's mission to China,' NZ Press Association report, December 1985, 58/264/6, MFAT, Wellington, New Zealand. Also mentioned by Yang Xianyi and Gladys Yang, interview with the author, 27 October 1990.

75 Lu Wanru, interview with the author, 31 October 1990.

76 Ces English, interview with the author, 2 February 1997.

77 Until 1948, New Zealanders held British passports as British subjects.

78 'Notes on Issue of Passports,' 1955, Passport desk files 1934–1960, IA 69/3 NA.

79 'Banned from Leaving,' *People's Voice*, 8 October 1952.

80 SEATO Security and Anti-subversion Measures, Travel to Communist Countries, Agenda Item 4(c), PM 120/7/18 part 1, 23 September–27 October 1960, NA.

81 'Note for File: Rewi Alley,' 8 June 1956, MERT 104/264/9, MFAT.

82 Alfred Kohlberg to L. K. Munro, New Zealand Ambassador, Washington, 19 January 1953, 104/264/9, MFAT. The poems were 'Bacteria' and 'The Accused,' *Masses and Mainstream*, January 1953, pp. 35–37.

83 New Zealand Ambassador, Washington, 'Memorandum for the Secretary of External Affairs, Wellington,' 23 January 1953, 104/264/9, MFAT.

84 A. D. McIntosh, 'Memorandum for the Ambassador, NZ Embassy, Washington, Publication of Rewi Alley's Poems in *Masses and Mainstream*,' 13 February 1953, 104/264/9, MFAT.

85 'Note for File: Rewi Alley,' 8 June 1956; 'China Annual Review for 1952,' HM Government Foreign Office (PM 264/1/2, MFAT) also mentions the activities of the Peace Committee in China; 'Extract from: Four Power Conference New Zealand Brief,' 16 November 1966, PM 58/11/4, MFAT, details concern about Chinese attempts to influence public opinion in New Zealand towards diplomatic recognition.

86 S. D. Berger, Chargé d'Affaires, United States Embassy, Wellington, New Zealand, Foreign Service Dispatch to the Department of State, Washington, USA, 16 April 1957.

87 Berger, 16 April 1957.

88 *John A. Lee's Fortnightly*, 19 March 1952.

89 Warren Freer to Pip Alley, 1 September 1958, 4/21, Alley papers, ATL.

90 James Bertram, interview with the author, 28 January 1993.

91 A. D. McIntosh to Rewi Alley, 9 March 1950, 104/264/9, MFAT.

92 Joseph Heenan to Colin Morrison, CORSO, MS Papers 1132, Folder 138, J. W. A. Heenan Collection, ATL.

93 Alan Winnington, *Breakfast With Mao*, London: Lawrence and Wishart, 1986, p. 166.

94 See Julian Schuman, *China, An Uncensored Look*, Sagaponack, New York: Second Chance Press, 1979.

95 Ormond Wilson, *An Outsider Looks Back*, Wellington: Port Nicholson Press, 1982, p. 157.

96 The recognition of China was a major issue of contention in Australia too. Note the following extract in a New Zealand government current-events report from Canberra: 'It is interesting to note that, while informed Australian opinion is in favour of the admission of Communist China to the United Nations – whether with or without Formosa is unknown – it is unlikely that the Government would regard this opinion as of such weight that they would take any initiative in persuading the US that such a development is desirable.' 22 June 1953, PM 264/3/14, NA.

97 15 June 1953, Meeting between Ambassador Scott and Minister of Foreign Affairs T. Clifton Webb, PM 264/3/14, NA.

98 Shirley Barton to Rewi Alley, 10 July 1955, Barton papers, ATL.

99 Walter Nash to Pip Alley, 24 October 1958, 2/25, Alley papers, ATL.

100 Walter Nash to Pip Alley, 24 March 1959, 4/21, Alley papers, ATL.

101 Walter Nash to Pip Alley, 15 July 1959, 4/21, Alley papers, ATL.

102 New Zealand Embassy, Washington, to Ministry of Foreign Affairs, 10 November 1966, PM 264/3/14 part 24, MFAT.

103 Rewi Alley to Gwen Somerset and Pip Alley, 11 May 1952, 3/21, Alley papers, ATL.

104 I am not suggesting here that Alley was prematurely pro-Liu; he could not possibly have seen ahead to the differences that were to arise between the two men.

105 Rewi Alley to Winston Rhodes, 24 July 1967, Rhodes papers, ATL.

106 Alley, *Travels in China*, p. 54.

107 Gray Dimond, *Inside China Today: A Western View*, New York: Norton, 1983, p. 93.

108 Tom Newnham, interview with the author, 20 June 1993.

109 Rewi Alley to Dr Joseph Needham, 20 November 1948.

110 Memorandum on 'Stories Out of China,' by Rewi Alley, Courtney Archer papers, ATL. The memorandum seems to have been written to convince Chinese authorities of the usefulness of Alley's writing to the Chinese Communist's quest for international acceptance.

111 Peking: n.p., 1962.

112 Rewi Alley to Pip Alley, 14 February 1961, 4/6, Alley papers, ATL.

113 See, among others, Rewi Alley to Pip Alley, 7 May 1961, 4/6, Alley papers, ATL.

114 Rewi Alley to Pip Alley, 18 July 1969, 8/9, Alley papers, ATL. Alley made veiled reference to his inability to travel for much of the period of the Cultural Revolution in numerous letters to his brother Pip and old friend Shirley Barton. However, in his book on the Cultural Revolution, *Travels in China 1966–1971*, Alley makes no mention of this.

115 York Yang, interview with the author, 18 January 1993.

116 Anonymous informant, interview with the author, 1 October 1990.

117 Rewi Alley, *What is Sin? Poems by Rewi Alley*, Christchurch: Caxton Press, 1967, p. 9.

118 Rewi Alley to Pip Alley, 10 July 1953, 9/3, Alley papers, ATL. Some of the money was given to Shirley Barton so that she could buy books and other materials for Alley.

119 Rewi Alley to Pip Alley, 16 November 1968, 4/13, Alley papers, ATL.

120 Wilfred Burchett, with Rewi Alley, *China: The Quality of Life*, Harmondsworth: Penguin Books, 1976, p. 80.

121 Rewi Alley to Shirley Barton, 13 July 1980, Barton papers, ATL.

122 Rewi Alley to Shirley Barton, 5 June 1979, Barton papers, ATL.

123 Chapple, *Rewi Alley of China*, p. 88.

124 See for example Alley's discussion with Ross Terrill in *800,000: The Real China*, Boston: Little, Brown and Co, 1971, p. 209; Sidney Rittenberg's description of Alley in *The Man Who Stayed Behind*, New York: Simon and Schuster, 1993, p. 209; and Alley's numerous vituperative comments about Mao's sex life, quoted in Harrison Salisbury's *China's New Emperors: China in the Era of Mao and Deng*, Boston: Little, Brown and Co, 1990.

125 *Zhongyang renmin guangbo diantai* (the Chinese Central Broadcasting Station), letter to Pip Alley, 13 February 1951, 6/2, Alley papers, ATL.

126 Rewi Alley to Pip Alley, 7 November 1968, 4/13, Alley papers, ATL.

127 One of the many persistent rumours against Rewi Alley was that he could not read or speak Chinese fluently and that Chinese translators did his translations. Both well-known translators Gladys Yang and Yang Xianyi and Courtney Archer have attested to Alley's Chinese skills. Archer described how he and Alley used to argue over Alley's translations of Tang poetry when they worked at Shandan. Courtney Archer, interview with the author, 4 July 1993.

128 Rewi Alley to Pip Alley, 7 November 1968, 4/13, Alley papers, ATL.

129 *Ibid.*

130 Rewi Alley to Pip Alley, 21 March 1967, 4/12, Alley papers, ATL

131 Rewi Alley to Pip Alley, 13 October 1962, 4/7, Alley papers, ATL.

132 Rewi Alley to Pip Alley, 9 November 1962, 4/7, Alley papers, ATL.

133 Rewi Alley to Willis Airey, 10 July 1968, 3/1, Alley papers, ATL.

134 Alley, *Shandan: An Adventure in Creative Education*, Christchurch: The Caxton Press, 1959, p. 99.

135 Alley, *Travels in China*, p 57.

136 Rewi Alley to Shirley Barton, 20 May 1961, Barton papers, ATL.

137 Rewi Alley, 31 August 1961, Barton papers, ATL.

138 Rewi Alley to Shirley Barton, 17 January 1957, Barton papers, ATL.

139 *Ibid.*
140 Review of *The People Have Strength, Press*, 25 June 1955.
141 Letter from Thomas Cook Travel to NZ MFA, 12 September 1975, 58/264/3, MFAT.
142 MFA Memo to NZ Institute of International Affairs, 19 January 1981, 58/264/3, MFAT.
143 Gordon Amos, 4 June 1975, 58/264/3, MFAT.
144 See the NZCFS website: http://www.nzchinasociety.org.nz
145 Jack Ewen, interview with the author, 27 June 1993.
146 Max Wilkinson, interview with the author, 15 May 1993.
147 NZE-MFA, 12 May 1975, 59/264/11, MFAT.
148 Gould, interview.
149 Bruce Wallace, 'At Home in Worlds Apart,' *Listener*, 13 December 1971.
150 Rewi Alley to Pip Alley, 26 November 1968, 4/13, Alley papers, ATL.
151 Chris Elder, interview with the author, 18 January 1993.
152 Rewi Alley to Pip Alley, 17 September 1965, 4/3, Alley papers, ATL.
153 'Rewi Alley commends N.Zers [*sic*] who beat counter-revolutionaries,' *People's Voice*, 11 November 1970.
154 See 'Communist Party Strengthened By Removal of Small Group of Splitters: Wilcox's Opportunism Exposed,' *People's Voice*, 12 June 1978; 'Tea and Cakes with Governor Reward for Class Collaboration,' *People's Voice*, 28 May 1979; 'Rewi Alley Gives the Show Away,' *People's Voice*, 19 May 1980.
155 Shirley Barton to Rewi Alley, 19 June 1956, Barton papers, ATL.
156 Rewi Alley to Shirley Barton, 14 May 1956, Barton papers, ATL.
157 Rewi Alley to Pip Alley, 15 January 1960, 4/5, Alley papers, ATL.
158 Rewi Alley to Pip Alley, 26 March 1960, 4/5 Alley papers, ATL.
159 SIS 'Rewi Alley,' 30 January 1973, 58/264/6, MFAT.
160 'Rewi Alley Pays Whangarei Visit,' *Northern Advocate*, 26 March 1960, 4/5, Alley papers, ATL.
161 'Alley of Shandan,' *Listener*, 8 March 1960.
162 Wallace, 'At Home in Worlds Apart.'
163 Shirley Barton to Rewi Alley, 7 December 1971, Barton papers, ATL.
164 'The China Beneath the Ground,' *Auckland Star*, 26 October 1971.
165 Rewi Alley to Jim Wong, October 1971, Barton papers, ATL.
166 Jim Wong, 'Around New Zealand with Rewi Alley,' 29 March 1972, Barton papers, ATL.
167 For example: F. B. Dwyer, New Zealand Army Secretary to Secretary of Department of External Affairs, 24 January 1951, 104/264/9, MFAT.
168 Brian Shaw, 'Report on a visit to China,' 5 April 1968, PM 58/11/4, MFAT. Other examples of this type of surveillance on Alley can be found in: New Zealand High Commission, Hong Kong, memo to Ministry of Foreign Affairs, 30 May 1966, PM 58/11/4, MFAT.
169 See Michael Lindsay's book *China and the Cold War*, Melbourne: Melbourne University Press, 1955 for an example of this view.
170 John Fraser, *The Chinese: Portrait of a People*, Toronto: Collins, 1980, p. 177.
171 Paul Hollander, *Political Pilgrims: Travels of Western Intellectuals to the Soviet Union, China, and Cuba*, New York: Oxford University Press, 1981, p. 332.
172 Rewi Alley, 'What China Was and Is,' *Beijing Review*, 10 September 1984.

8 PEKING'S MAN

1 Zhao Gaiying, 'Huainian Luyi Aili tongzhi' (Remembering Comrade Rewi Alley), *Renmin ribao* (Overseas edition), 20 April 1988.

2 Rewi Alley to Pip Alley, 1 April 1972, Alley papers, ATL.

3 Rewi Alley to Pip Alley, 17 April 1972, 8/11, Alley papers, ATL.

4 Zhao Gaiying, 'Huainian Luyi Aili tongzhi.' Alley's younger sister Joy Alley has confirmed that this story is a fabrication. Joy Alley, interview with the author, 23 April 1993.

5 See Andrew B. Kipnis, *Producing Guanxi: Sentiment, Self, and Subculture in a Northern China Village*, Durham: Duke University Press, 1997 for more on the role of *guanxi* and *ganqing* in Chinese political life.

6 I first viewed Alley's library in 1990, where it had been left intact in his former residence in the compound of the Chinese Association for Friendship with Foreign Peoples. Most of his books have now been moved to a special collection in People's University. Library staff informed me that, due to neglect, some of the more valuable books in Alley's collection have been stolen.

7 Rewi Alley, 'Diary,' 3 December 1955, Barton papers, ATL.

8 Rewi Alley, letter to Shirley Barton, 15 May 1955, Barton papers, ATL.

9 David Somerset, interview with the author, 27 January 1993.

10 Alex Yang, interview with the author, 5 November 1990.

11 'Joy Alley Has Few Regrets,' *New Zealand Herald*, 8 August 1985.

12 Edgar Snow, *Red China Today: The Other Side of the River*, Harmondsworth, Middlesex: Penguin (first published 1961), 1971, p. 585.

13 Hewlett Johnson, *The Upsurge of China*, Peking: New World Press, 1961, p. 161.

14 Rewi Alley to Pip Alley, 19 December 1960, 4/5, Alley papers, ATL.

15 Jasper Becker, *Hungry Ghosts: China's Secret Famine*, London: John Murray, 1996, p. 94.

16 Rewi Alley to Pip Alley, 27 January 1962, 3/3, Alley papers, ATL.

17 Rewi Alley to Pip Alley, 22 June 1962, 4/7, Alley papers, ATL.

18 Rewi Alley to Pip Alley, 7 May 1961, 4/6, Alley papers, ATL.

19 Rewi Alley to Pip Alley, 16 February 1962, 4/7, Alley papers, ATL.

20 Rewi Alley to Shirley Barton, 22 December 1962, Barton papers, ATL.

21 Rewi Alley to Shirley Barton, 25 May 1963, Barton papers, ATL.

22 Pip Alley to Willis Airey, 27 January 1966, 3/2, Alley papers, ATL.

23 Rewi Alley, 'Kiwi's Thoughts on Mao's Thinking,' *People's Voice*, 15 June 1966.

24 Anna Louise Strong, an American journalist and lifelong Communist, was famed for her interview with Mao in 1956, published as 'All Imperialists Are Paper Tigers.' She was the most senior member of the community of foreign friends living in China at this time. The meeting with Mao is described in David and Nancy Dall Milton, *The Wind Will Not Subside, Years in Revolutionary China*, New York: Pantheon Books, 1976, p. 106.

25 Sid and his wife Yulin worked at Peking Radio; Israel Epstein was editor-in-chief of *China Reconstructs*; Frank Coe and Sol Adler were US economists who had moved to China in the late 1950s after being investigated by the FBI for treason; Nancy and David Milton were English polishers at the Foreign Languages Press; Chilean artist Jose Venturelli, like Alley, was a 'permanent guest' of the Chinese Peace Committee. The other participants I have already mentioned in the text.

26 The four Americans were Joan Hinton, Erwin (Sid) Engst, Bertha Sneck and Ann Tomkins. Carma Hinton, letter to the author, 4 October 1996.

27 *Ziliao xuanbian* (Selected Reference Materials), Beijing: n.p., 1967, p. 326.

28 'Note of Instruction,' 8 September 1966, Bob Friend (ed.), *Quotations from Chairman Mao Tse-tung on Propaganda*, Peking: Foreign Languages Press, 1967, p. 187.

29 Sid Shapiro, *An American in China*, New York: New American Library Books, 1979, p. 235.
30 Rewi Alley, approximately 1966, 2/21, Alley papers, ATL.
31 Rewi Alley to Pip Alley, 1 May 1968, 4/13, Alley papers, ATL.
32 Rewi Alley to Shirley Barton, 21 March 1969, Barton papers, ATL.
33 Rewi Alley to Pip Alley, 1 January 1967, 3/1, Alley papers, ATL.
34 Rewi Alley to Willis Airey, 10 July 1968, 3/1, Alley papers, ATL.
35 Rewi Alley, 9 October 1968.
36 See *Selected Works of Mao Tse-tung*, Peking: Foreign Languages Press, 1965, Vol. 2, p. 35. Cited in Rewi Alley to Pip Alley, 9 October 1968, 7/8, Alley papers.
37 Rewi Alley to Shirley Barton, 21 March 1969, Barton papers, ATL.
38 Willis Airey to Rewi Alley, 19 April 1967, 3/1, Alley papers, ATL.
39 25 October 1966, 3/1, Alley papers, ATL.
40 Rewi Alley to Pip Alley, 22 May 1969, 4/14, Alley papers, ATL.
41 Rewi Alley to Pip Alley, 4 October 1968, 4/13, Alley papers, ATL.
42 Rewi Alley to Pip Alley, 22 October 1968, 4/13, Alley papers, ATL.
43 Rewi Alley to Willis Airey, 14 August 1966, 2/21, Alley papers, ATL.
44 Rewi Alley to Willis Airey, 2 August 1967, 3/1, Alley papers, ATL.
45 Rewi Alley to Pip Alley, 7 December 1967, 4/12, Alley papers, ATL.
46 Rewi Alley to Pip Alley, 5 May 1969, 4/14, Alley papers, ATL.
47 Rewi Alley to Pip Alley, 24 January 1967, 4/12, Alley papers, ATL.
48 Donald Milne, *New Zealand Herald*, undated article, minus headline, approximately 1983, Courtney Archer papers, ATL.
49 Israel Epstein, *Woman in World History: Song Qingling (Madame Sun Yat-sen)*, Peking: New World Press (second edition), 1995, p. 559.
50 Alex Yang, interview with the author, 13 September 1995.
51 David and Nancy Dall Milton, *The Wind Will Not Subside: Years in Revolutionary China – 1964–1969*, New York: Pantheon Books, p. 301.
52 *Ibid*, p. 372.
53 Han Suyin, *My House Has Two Doors*, London: Jonathan Cape, 1980, p. 496.
54 Brian Shaw, 'Report on a Visit to China,' 5 April 1968, PM 58/11/4, MFAT.
55 1 January 1968, 8/9, Alley papers, ATL.
56 Rewi Alley to Shirley Barton, 5 January 1969, Barton papers, ATL.
57 *Ibid*.
58 Shirley Barton to Rewi Alley, 22 August 1972, Barton papers, ATL.
59 Rewi Alley to Shirley Barton, 3 July 1985, Barton papers, ATL.
60 Rewi Alley to Pip Alley, 1 June 1967, 4/12, Alley papers, ATL.
61 Pip Alley to Rewi Alley, 13 June 1966, 3/2, Alley papers, ATL.
62 Bernard S. Thomas, *Season of High Adventure: Edgar Snow in China*, Berkeley, California: University of California Press, 1996, p. 323.
63 Pip Alley to Willis Airey, 13 December 1967, 3/2, Alley papers, ATL.
64 16 August 1970, Peking, Book 71, Edgar Snow Diaries, cited in Thomas, *Season of High Adventure*, p. 321.
65 Pip Alley to Shirley Barton, 8 April 1974, Barton papers, ATL.
66 Han Xu, 'Mao Zedong de minjian waijiao sixiang he zhongyao juece,' Pei Jianzhang (ed.), *Mao Zedong waijiao sixiang yanjiu* (Research on Mao Zedong's Diplomatic Thought), p. 54.
67 Rewi Alley to Shirley Barton, 4 April 1976, Barton papers, ATL.
68 Rewi Alley to Shirley Barton, 18 May 1976, Barton papers, ATL.
69 Rewi Alley to Shirley Barton, 27 February 1977, Barton papers, ATL. Deng Bangzhen grew up with extended family members in Peking in the 1950s who had

known Alley before 1949. Alley took a personal interest in the boy and regarding him as a foster son, though the relationship was never formalised.

70 Rewi Alley to Shirley Barton, 14 May 1976, Barton papers, ATL.
71 10 February 1976, Barton papers, ATL.
72 Hubbard, 'Rewi Alley: East–West Man,' *Dominion*, 15 January 1985.
73 Rewi Alley to Shirley Barton, 16 October 1976, Barton papers, ATL.
74 Rewi Alley to Shirley Barton, 22 October 1976, Barton papers, ATL.
75 Shirley Barton to Rewi Alley, 28 October 1976, Barton papers, ATL.
76 Rewi Alley to Shirley Barton, 6 August 1977, Barton papers, ATL.
77 Rewi Alley to Shirley Barton, 23 July 1977, Barton papers, ATL.
78 Rewi Alley to Shirley Barton, 27 February 1977, Barton papers, ATL.
79 Rewi Alley to Shirley Barton, 1 May 1980, Barton papers, ATL.
80 Rewi Alley to Shirley Barton, 4 June 1980, Barton papers, ATL.
81 'Rewi Alley's Fifty Years in China,' *New Haven Register*, 14 November 1976.
82 Alley, 'Some Aspects of Internationalism in China's Struggle,' Ginsbourg, *Living in China*, p. 47.
83 Rewi Alley to Shirley Barton, 3 April 1979, Barton papers, ATL.
84 Rewi Alley to Courtney Archer, 8 October 1978, Folder 1, Archer papers, ATL.
85 Rewi Alley to Shirley Barton, 6 August 1981, Barton papers, ATL.
86 *Xinhua*, 2 December 1978.
87 NZE to MFA, 28 July 1977, 58/264/6, MFAT.
88 NZE to MFA, 17 November 1983, 26/1/4.
89 NZE to MFA, 10 September 1985, 26/1/4, NZE.
90 Mao Mao and Bao Bao Li to Rewi Alley, undated, approximately 1978, Barton papers, ATL. (The letter was written in English.)
91 Rewi Alley to Shirley Barton, 26 December 1978, Barton papers, ATL.
92 Rewi Alley to Shirley Barton, 11 July 1979, Barton papers, ATL.
93 Rewi Alley to Shirley Barton, 3 April 1979, Barton papers, ATL.
94 Rewi Alley to Shirley Barton, 3 January 1980, Barton papers, ATL.
95 Rewi Alley to Shirley Barton, 16 April 1984, Barton papers, ATL.
96 Rewi Alley to Shirley Barton, 11 May 1983, Barton papers, ATL.
97 Rewi Alley to Shirley Barton, 6 January 1986, Barton papers, ATL.
98 Rewi Alley to Shirley Barton, 13 February 1984, Barton papers, ATL.
99 Rewi Alley to Shirley Barton, 17 January 1986, Barton papers, ATL.

9 NEW ZEALAND'S ASSET

1 Jeremy Dwyer, 'I Wrote Watch Out World,' *Hawkes Bay Herald-Tribune*, 8 May 1993.
2 Stephen Fitzgerald, *Talking With China: The Australian Labour Party Visit And Peking's Foreign Policy*, Canberra: Australian National University, 1972, p. 43.
3 'Notes of Discussion with Mr Rewi Alley,' 6 February 1973, 58/264/1 Volume 1, MFAT.
4 Frank Corner, NZE, Washington, letter to MFA, Wellington, 10 November 1966, PM 264/3/14 part 24, MFAT.
5 For example see A. D. McIntosh to Frank Corner, MFA, 5 September 1956, PM 264/3/14/1, MFAT.
6 'Communist China,' 18 July 1956, PM 264/3/14/1/11, MFAT.
7 Colin Scrimgeour to Rewi Alley, 14 September 1971, Folder 58, Scrimgeour papers, ATL.
8 Pip Alley to Willis Airey, 13 December 1967, 3/2, Alley papers, ATL.
9 Rewi Alley to Willis Airey, 4 August 1968, 3/1, Alley papers, ATL.
10 'China's Ideals Unchanged,' *Otago Daily Times*, 8 February 1972.

11 'Notes of Discussions with Mr Rewi Alley,' 6 February 1973.

12 John Scott, 'Recognising China,' in Malcolm McKinnon (ed.), *New Zealand in World Affairs Volume Three 1957–1972*, New Zealand Institute of International Affairs, Wellington, 1991, p. 249.

13 See W. T. Roy, *New Zealand's China Policies: a Review and a Prospect*, 31 August 1972, 58/11/1, MFAT. Scott, p. 228, also mentions this.

14 Roy, *op. cit.*

15 New Zealand Embassy, Peking (hereafter NZE), 'China in 1973,' 24 December 1973, PM 26/3/1, MFAT.

16 'Muldoon Visit To China,' 18 November 1980, 59/264/11, MFAT.

17 'Notes from R. D. Muldoon, Prime Minister, meeting with Deng Xiaoping,' 13 September 1980, 59/264/11, MFAT.

18 Bryce Harland, Ambassador, NZE, letter to Frank Corner, MFA, 14 July 1975, 58/264/6 Volume 1, MFAT.

19 For example see Frank Corner, 'Draft Memorandum for Cabinet: Rewi Alley Scholarship in Modern Chinese Studies,' 12 March 1973, 58/264/6 Volume 1, MFAT, and Harland, *op. cit.*

20 Gary Woodward, cited in Lindsay Watt, *New Zealand and China Towards 2000*, Institute of Policy Studies, Wellington, 1992, p. 17.

21 Ministry of Foreign Affairs to Norman Kirk, PM, 30 January 1973, 'Rewi Alley,' 58/264/6, MFAT.

22 'Notes of Discussions,' *op. cit.*

23 'Duiwai bianji jiagong de ABC' (The Foreign Propaganda Editor's ABC), *Duiwai baodao cankao*, Number 2 (1983), p. 29.

24 Zhang Beihua, 'Sino-New Zealand Relations 1792–1987,' M.Phil. Thesis, University of Waikato, Hamilton, 1988, p. 158.

25 Philip Snow, *The Star Raft: China's Encounter With Africa*, London: Wiedenfield and Nicolson, 1988, p. 1.

26 *Ibid.*

27 Beihua, 'Sino-New Zealand Relations 1792–1987,' and C. J. Elder and M. F. Green, 'New Zealand and China,' in Ann Trotter (ed.), *New Zealand and China: The Papers of the 21st Otago Foreign Policy School*, also cite 1792 as the beginning of New Zealand–China relations.

28 Nicholas Bridge, interview with the author, 31 August 1990.

29 Margaret Haywood, *Diary of the Kirk Years*, Queen Charlotte Sound: Cape Catley Ltd, 1981, p. *v.*

30 'Rewi Alley Scholarship,' 1 December 1977, 58/264/6, MFAT.

31 NZE, note to MFA, 3 June 1977, 57/264/6, MFAT.

32 B. Harland, NZE, note to MFA, 14 July 1975, 58/264/6, MFAT.

33 See Frank Corner, MFA to Dr D. B. C. Taylor, Vice-Chancellor, Victoria University, 2 April 1975, 58/264/6, MFAT; Bryce Harland, Ambassador, NZE, to Frank Corner, MFA, 14 May 1975, 58/264/6, MFAT; and 'Note for file,' 2 July 1975, 58/264/6, MFAT.

34 Geoff Alley to Mr Lynch, Ministry of Foreign Affairs, 58/264/6, MFAT.

35 30 July 1980, 59/264/11, MFAT.

36 'Visit to China: Rewi Alley: Visiting Fellowship,' MFA to R. D. Muldoon, PM, 27 August 1980, 58/264/6, MFAT.

37 *Ibid.*

38 MFA, notes from discussion with R. D. Muldoon, PM, 16 February 1983, 58/264/6, MFAT.

39 'Message to Rewi Alley From R. D. Muldoon,' 30 November 1977, 58/264/6, MFAT.

40 See New Zealand Ambassador, NZE, 'China: Rewi Alley,' 25 June 1980, 58/264/6, MFAT.

41 'Draft Obituary,' 30 September 1980, 26/4/1, NZE.

42 *Xinhua* report, 2 December 1977, 58/264/6, MFAT.

43 Wang Bingnan, President of CPAFFC, English translation of 'Meeting to Celebrate the 55th Anniversary of Rewi Alley's Arrival in China,' 21 April 1982, 58/264/6, MFAT.

44 Jim Wong to Pip Alley, 25 March 1972, 8/12, Alley papers, ATL.

45 Rewi Alley to Shirley Barton, 13 August 1984, Barton papers, ATL.

46 'Note for File: New Zealand Honours 1985,' 13 November 1984, 26/4/1, NZE. Alley also wrote to Shirley Barton with a similar response. See Rewi Alley to Shirley Barton, 13 November 1984, Barton papers, ATL.

47 'China Film Proposal – Mr Rewi Alley,' NZE to MFA, 21 March 1978, 58/264/6, MFAT.

48 Bryce Harland, NZE to Geoff Steven, 20 June 1978, 58/264/6, MFAT.

49 Geoff Steven and John Maynard, 'Synopsis of "Rewi Alley's China" by Phase Three Films,' 1978, 58/264/6, MFAT.

50 *Ibid.*

51 'Rewi Alley Friend of the Chinese People,' first shown 27 August 1978, Beijing Television, an English translation of the script is held in 58/264/6, MFAT.

52 *Ibid.*

53 NZE to MFA, 6 December 1977, 26/1/4, NZE.

54 *Ibid.*

55 'China: Rewi Alley,' NZ Ambassador Tony Small, report to Secretary of Foreign Affairs, 23 April 1982, 26/1/4, NZE.

56 *Ibid.*

57 Lindsay Watt, 'On the occasion of the presentation to Mr Rewi Alley, of the Queen's Service Medal,' NZE, 21 December 1985, 26/1/4, NZE.

58 NZE to MFA/Cabinet Office/Ministry of Trade and Marketing/Trade and Industry/London Embassy, 'Rewi Alley and Presentation of QSM,' 27 December 1985, 26/1/4, NZE.

59 Alley, *At 90*, p. 268.

60 David Lange, letter to Zhang Wenjin, CPAFFC, 15 December 1986, 26/1/4, NZE.

61 Huang Hua, 'Meeting to Commemorate Rewi Alley,' 21 April 1988.

62 Secretary for Foreign Affairs, telegram to NZE, 29 December 1987, 26/1/4, NZE.

63 'Minister of Overseas Trade and Marketing's Call on Madame Chen Muhua, Minister of Foreign Economic Relations and Trade,' 10 December 1984, 59/264/11, MFAT.

64 Lindsay Watt, interview with the author, 21 January 1993.

65 Karen Gieseg, 'Rewi Alley's Goodwill Paves Way for China Trade, Companies Urged to Show Thanks,' *Evening Post*, 29 August 1987.

66 'It needn't be a Slow Boat to China,' *Financial Review*, April 1987.

67 For example see Zhou Xisheng, 'Xinxilan Gongdang zhengfu mianlin kaoyan' (The Trials and Tribulations of the New Zealand Labour Government), *Liao wang*, 32, 1984; Erxin Xiaoqian, 'Xinxilan xin ren zongli Daiwei Lasaier Langyi' (New Zealand's Newly Elected Prime Minister David R. Lange), *Shijie zhishi*, 18, 1984; Dai Zengyi, 'Ao Xin Mei lianmeng de weiji' (The ANZUS Alliance Crisis), *Yue tan*, 8, 1985; 'Xinxilan waijiao huoyue de liang nian' (A Dynamic Two Years in NZ Diplomacy), *Guoji wenti ziliao*, 19, 1986; Chen Cuihua, 'Xinxilan zongli Daiwei Langyi' (NZ Prime Minister David Lange), 1986, no bibliographic reference available.

68 Pei Monong, 'Yazhou Taipingyang diqu de xingshi he wenti' (Problems and Circumstances in the Asia Pacific Region), *Guoji wenti yanjiu*, 1985; Gao Heng, 'Yatai

diqu zhanlue xingshi de fazhan qushi' (Developing Trends in the Strategic Terrain of the Asia Pacific Region), *Zhengce yu xiaoxi*, 5, 1989; Liu Jiangyong, 'Taipingyang guoji guanxi de bianqian yu jingji hezuo de xin chaoliu' (The Vicissitudes of International Relations in the Pacific and New Trends in Economic Co-operation), 1989, no bibliographic information available; Hou Ruoshi, 'Yatai diqu de jingji huoli ji hezuo qianjing' (Economic Vitality and Co-operative Prospects in the Asia–Pacific Region), 1991, Fudan University, Shanghai; Cai Penghong, 'Yatai diquzhuyi de guoqu, xianzai he weilai' (Past, Present and Future Asia–Pacific Regionalism), *Xueshu jie dongtai*, 1, 1990.

69 Rewi Alley, 'The New Bailie School Project in Shandan,' 17 November 1984, 26/1/4, NZE.

70 NZE to MERT, 20 February 1987, 58/264/6, MFAT.

71 NZE to MERT, March 1988, 58/264/6, MFAT.

72 'Rewi Alley Scholarship,' February 1986, 26/1/4, NZE.

73 NZE to MFA, 15 October 1986, 26/1/4, NZE.

74 NZE to MFA, 30 September 1982, 264/1/3/1, MFAT.

75 NZE to MFA, 8 September 1982, 264/1/3/1, MFAT.

76 NZE to MFA, 25 February 1987, 264/1/3 Volume 1, MFAT.

77 NZE to MFA, 17 October 1986, 26/1/4, NZE.

78 MERT, 'Gansu Visit: Rewi Alley: NZ Commercial Prospects – Gansu Booming,' 15 September 1992, 58/264/7, MFAT.

79 NZE, outward telegram to Secretary for MFA, 29 March 1985.

80 'It Needn't Be A Slow Boat To China,' *NZ Financial Review*, April, 1987.

81 John McKinnon, First Secretary, NZ High Commission, Australia, 'Note For File: New Zealand/China: Australian Scholarship,' 24 June 1987, 58/264/6, MFAT.

82 David Lange, Speech given at Guizhou Agricultural College, Guiyang, China, 25 March 1986, *New Zealand External Relations Review*, 4/86.

83 'Number 8 wire' is the wire commonly used in fences on farms in New Zealand. The term has come to be associated with a proud tradition in New Zealand of 'do-it-yourself' and the idea that almost anything can be fixed with a piece of 'number 8 wire.'

84 NZE to MERT, 14 April 1987, 58/264/6, MFAT.

85 Tim Donaghue, 'Chinese Show They Want Kiwi Business,' 26/1/4, NZE.

86 'Slow Boat To China,' *New Zealand Herald*, 18 April 1987.

87 Both quotes are from Michael Gifkins, 'Ganbei Cordiality,' *Listener*, n.d., approx. 1987, 26/1/4, NZE.

88 T. R. Louden, *Press*, 7 January 1988.

89 Draft letter, March 1987, Minister of Education, 58/264/6, MFAT.

90 Luke Nottage, 'Cash for Rewi Alley,' Letter to the Editor, *Dominion*, 29 April 1987.

91 H. Francis, 'China: Rewi Alley: Autobiography,' memo to David Lange, 15 December 1986, 58/264/6, MFAT.

92 *Ibid.*

93 Zhang Wenjin, President of CPAFFC, letter to David Lange, Prime Minister of New Zealand, 2 December 1986, 58/264/6, MFAT.

94 Zhang Wenjin, letter to David Lange, 7 January 1988, 26/1/4, NZE.

95 David Lange, PM, letter to Li Peng, Acting Premier of the State Council, China, 30 December 1987, 26/1/4, NZE.

96 David Lange, letter to Duan Shimou (Alan Alley), 30 December 1987, 26/1/4, NZE.

97 'Visit by CPAFFC,' 11 March 1987, 59/264/2, MFAT.

98 'Rewi Alley Commemorative Activities,' NZE, note to MFA, 29 February 1988, 58/264/6, MFAT.

99 MFA, note to NZE, 2 March 1988, 58/264/6, MFAT.
100 Fran Wilde, Deputy Minister for Foreign Affairs, 21 April 1988, 58/264/6, MFAT.
101 'Draft Obituary,' 30 September 1980, 26/1/4, NZE.
102 8 June 1982, 26/1/4, NZE.
103 'Message from PM David Lange, On the occasion of the presentation to Mr Rewi Alley, of the Queen's Service Order,' NZE, 21 December 1985, 26/1/4, NZE.
104 *Renmin Ribao*, 22 December 1985. News of the award was also published in *Guangming Ribao* and *China Daily*.
105 NZE to MERT, 'China: Shandan Bailie School,' 28 June 1988, 58/264/6, MFAT.
106 NZE to MERT, 7 June 1990, 58/264/7, MFAT.
107 'Gansu Visit: Rewi Alley: New Zealand Commercial Prospects: Gansu Booming,' 15 September 1992, 58/264/7, MFAT.
108 Sir Edmund Hillary has devoted himself to improving the living standards of the Sherpa people of the Himalayan Mountains. Unlike Alley, Hillary has always been a respectable figure of the establishment in New Zealand. He was rewarded for his hard work in Nepal by becoming New Zealand Ambassador to India. Fred Hollows devoted his life to working to improve eye care amongst the Australian Aborigines as well as in Vietnam and Eritrea.
109 Greg Ansley, 'Alley Honoured by Chinese Leaders,' *New Zealand Herald*, December 1997.
110 *Zhongguo renmin de pengyou* (China's Foreign Friends), Baoding: Hebei ertong chubanshe, 1997.
111 New Zealand Embassy report, April 1997.
112 For more on the topic of China's foreign friends in the 1980s and 1990s see Anne-Marie Brady, 'Treat Insiders and Outsiders Differently: Managing Foreigners in the PRC,' *China Quarterly*, December 2000.
113 NZE, note to MFA, 'Rewi Alley Biography,' 27 September 1990, about discussion as to whether the NZ government should give further financial support to plans to produce a biography of Rewi Alley aimed at children aged 11–14. The book was to be written by Geoff Chapple, author of *Rewi Alley of China*, and Lu Wanru, ghost-writer of *At 90: Memoirs of My China Years*, and Chen Hong. The book has yet to be published.
114 See for example Tara Werner's comments in 'Operas centuries apart show idealism survives,' *NZ Herald*, 2 March 1998, and Geoff Chapple's comments, '*Yo Banfa* fails to breathe life into Alley,' *NZ Herald*, October, 1993.
115 'Jiang: China, NZ Share Extensive, Significant Common Interest,' *People's Daily Online*, 15 September 1999; 'Chinese President Continues to Visit in New Zealand,' *People's Daily Online*, 16 September 1999.
116 'Jiang: China, NZ Share Extensive, Significant Common Interest.'
117 John Carter, interview with the author, 18 January 1993.
118 In Chinese, '*Yin shui, si yuan*' or the more colloquial '*Yin shui, bu wang wajingren.*' This proverb has frequently been used by the Chinese when mentioning Rewi Alley and his New Zealand connection and is the standard term used to describe the role of foreign friends in China's friendship diplomacy.

10 INTERNATIONALIST

1 For a discussion of the myth-making surrounding the life of Koxinga, and his use by various disparate causes, see Ralph C. Croizier, *Koxinga and Chinese Nationalism: History, Myth and the Hero*, Cambridge, Massachusetts: East Asian Research Centre, Harvard University, 1977.
2 *Ibid*, p. 36.

3 Liao Futing, *Virtues Reflected In Children's Picture Books During the Chinese Cultural Revolution*, Masters thesis, University of Georgia, 1985, p. 54.

4 Donald J. Munro discusses the merging of the Confucian tradition of apotheosis into Chinese Communist social-control theory in *The Concept of Man in Early China*, Stanford, California: Stanford University Press, 1969.

5 Lei Feng was a young Chinese soldier whose name became immortalised after he died in an accident and his diary was discovered. In his diary he is alleged to have wished to be a screw in the machine of socialism, thus demonstrating his loyalty to the party. Lei Feng was first raised as a model to be emulated by Chinese citizens in 1962 and since then has regularly been promoted in numerous campaigns to motivate the Chinese population to revolutionary zeal. Jiao Yulu was a cadre in an impoverished part of Henan, who vowed to turn the area under his control into productive land. Jiao died of cancer before his dream could be realised, but he has been set up as a model from whom other cadres should learn for his dedication to 'serve the people.' Canadian Dr Norman Bethune (1889–1939), who worked as a surgeon with Communist forces behind Japanese lines until he died of septicaemia, was promoted by Mao Zedong as one of the greatest internationalist workers of the Chinese Communist movement.

6 NZE to MFA, 21 April 1982, 58/264/6, MFAT.

7 Lu Wanru, interview with the author, 21 June 1991.

8 Other well-known internationalists include the Indian Dr Kotnis, who, like Bethune, died in the service of the Chinese people; Agnes Smedley and Anna Louise Strong the American journalists; and Dr George Hatem, more commonly known by his Chinese name Ma Haide.

9 Mao Zedong, 'In Memory of Norman Bethune,' 21 December 1939, *Selected Works of Mao Tse-Tung*, Peking: Foreign Languages Press, 1965, p. 337.

10 'Peking Banquet Celebrates Rewi Alley's 80th Birthday,' *Xinhua*, 2 December 1977.

11 Huang Daozhen, interview with the author, 28 January 1993.

12 NZE to MFA, 23 April 1982, 26/1/4, NZE.

13 Rewi Alley to Winston Rhodes, 24 July 1967, Rhodes papers, ATL.

14 Lu Wanru, interview with the author; Deng Bangzhen and Lu Bo, interview with the author, 6 December 1993.

15 NZE to MFA, 6 December 1977, 26/1/4, NZE.

16 Rewi Alley to Shirley Barton, 1 July 1981, Barton papers, ATL.

17 Alex Yang, interview with the author, 5 November 1990.

18 Speech by Wang Bingnan, CPAFFC, 2 December 1982, English text.

19 Speech by Wang Bingnan.

20 Wang Bingnan, preface to Alley's *Six Americans in China*, Beijing: International Culture Publishing Company, 1985, p. *iii*.

21 Jia Shijie, Governor of Gansu Province, Memorial Service for Rewi Alley, 21 April 1988, 58/264/6, MFAT.

22 *Ibid.*

23 Rewi Alley to Shirley Barton, 21 April 1982, Folder 8, Barton papers, ATL.

24 'Alley Opposed to Park Tribute,' *New Zealand Herald* newspaper clipping, n.d., approximately 1987, Joy Alley private papers.

25 Zhang Wenjin, cited in NZE to MERT, 22 April 1987, 58/264/6, MFAT.

26 Lu Guangmian, private papers.

27 Anonymous informant, 13 November 1990.

28 'Gansu Visit: Rewi Alley: New Zealand Commercial Prospects – Gansu Booming,' 15 September 1992, 58/264/7, MFAT.

29 Liu Ding died of cancer in 1986. His highest post was Vice-Minister in the Petroleum Ministry.

30 *Xinhua* describes the visit of Hu Yaobang to Rewi Alley in hospital, 7 March 1982.
31 Michael Powles, interview with the author, 25 January 1991.
32 NZE to MERT, 22 April 1987, 58/264/6, MFAT.
33 NZE to MFA, 23 April 1982, 26/1/4, NZE.
34 Dr Wu Weiran, interview with the author, 22 June 1991.
35 Lu Guangmian, private papers.
36 Lu Wanru, 'Aili de jiaoyu tansuo yu Gonghe shixian' (Alley's educational explorations and the realisation of Gung Ho), paper written for the Gansu Forum on Rewi Alley's Educational Thoughts, 12 September 1992, p. 5. See also 'Lanzhou shiyou jixiao qingzhu jianxiao sishi zhounian' (Celebration of the fortieth anniversary of the Lanzhou Oil School), *Gansu Ribao*, 6 June 1982.
37 Tom Newnham, interview with the author, 20 June 1993.
38 Jeff Tubby, Bay of Plenty Polytechnic, 'Report on the Installation of Equipment at the Shandan Bailie School,' 15 October 1987, 58/264/6, MFAT.
39 John Hercus, Principal of Christchurch Polytechnic and Hon. Dame Anne Hercus, Cabinet Minister, 1987 report, 58/264/6, MFAT. Courtney Archer, interview with the author, 5 July 1993.
40 Bill Willmott, 'New Direction at Shandan,' *New Zealand–China News*, March 1994, p 1.
41 NZE, note to MFA, 'Re: Book Proposal,' 30 October 1990, 26/1/4, NZE.
42 MFA to NZE, 28 June 1988, 58/264/6, MFAT.
43 11 March 1992, 58/264/7, MFAT.
44 Jim Bolger, Prime Minister, letter to Liu Qichiu, Bailie Oil School, 24 February 1992, 58/264/7, MFAT.
45 See www.mfat.gov.nz
46 'Gansu Visit: Rewi Alley: New Zealand Commercial Prospects: Gansu Booming.'

11 EPILOGUE

1 Rewi Alley to Shirley Barton, 24 August 1980, Barton papers, ATL.
2 Geoff Chapple, *Listener*, 28 November 1987, pp. 36–44.
3 Dr Zhao Gaiying, interview with the author, 24 June 1991.
4 'The Myth of Rewi Alley,' *Dominion Sunday Times*, 25 February 1990.
5 George Konrad, preface to Miklos Haraszti, *The Velvet Prison: Artists Under State Socialism*, London: Penguin Books, 1983, p. xv.
6 Nick Bridges, interview with the author, 31 August 1990.
7 A. Hubbard, 'Rewi Alley: East–West Man,' *Dominion*, 15 January 1985.
8 Marcuse, *The Peking Papers*, p. 119.
9 'Women de Ailao' (Our Uncle Alley), *Renmin ribao*, 21 January 1988.
10 Han Wudi (ruled in China 140 BC–86 AD). The 'cut sleeve' in Chinese is *'duanxiu.'*
11 Orrin Klapp, *Heroes, Villains and Fools: the Changing American Character*, New Jersey: Prentice-Hall, 1962, p. 3.
12 Marcuse, *The Peking Papers*, p. 24.
13 Ignoring the fact that Marxist-Leninism is a Western ideology. When China's leaders reject Western value systems they refer to notions of individualism, human rights, democracy and capitalism.
14 Airey, *A Learner in China*, p. 12.
15 Speech by the New Zealand Ambassador, HE Mr Michael Powles, at the occasion to mark the ninety-fifth anniversary of Rewi Alley's birth, People's University, 2 December 1992, 26/1/4, NZE.
16 Geoff Chapple, 'Rewi Alley: A New Zealand Hero in China,' *Listener*, 3 February 1979.

BIBLIOGRAPHY

Books and articles

Acton, Harold, *Memoirs of an Aesthete*, London: Methuen, 1989.

—— *Peonies and Ponies*, Hong Kong: Oxford University Press, 1983.

Airey, Willis, *A Learner in China*, Christchurch: The Caxton Press and the Monthly Review Society, 1970.

Aldrich, Robert, *Seduction of the Mediterranean: Writing, Art and Homosexual Fantasy*, London: Routledge, 1993.

Alley, Alan, 'Memories of my Father Rewi Alley', parts 1–2, n.p., 1996, MS Papers 5792, Alexander Turnbull Library, New Zealand.

Alley, Rewi, *Rewi Alley: An Autobiography* (revised, third edition), Beijing: New World Press, 1997.

—— *At 90: Memoirs of My China Years*, Beijing: New World Press, 1987.

—— *China's Hinterland in the Leap Forward*, Peking: New World Press, 1961.

—— *The Freshening Breeze*, Peking: New World Press, 1977.

—— *Man Against Flood*, Peking: New World Press, 1956.

—— *Oceania; an outline for study* (second edition), Christchurch: Caxton Press, 1971.

—— *Poems for Aotearoa*, Auckland: New Zealand China Friendship Society and Progressive Book Society, 1976.

—— *Sandan: An Adventure in Creative Education*, Christchurch: The Caxton Press, 1959.

—— *Six Americans in China*, Beijing: International Culture Publishing Corporation, 1985.

—— 'Some Aspects of Internationalism', Sam Ginsbourg *et al*, *Living In China* (*Zai Hua sanshi nian*), Peking: New World Press, 1982 (Chinse/English edition), pp. 8–9.

—— *Three Conferences at Cairo, New Delhi and Bandung; being the accounts of journeys to Cairo, then to New Delhi, to attend the World Peace Council Meeting for 1961, and later to attend the Afro-Asian Conference at Bandung in April, 1961*, Christchurch: Caxton Press, 1961.

—— *Travels in China 1966–1971*, Peking: New World Press, 1973.

—— *What is Sin? Poems by Rewi Alley*, Christchurch: Caxton Press, 1967.

—— *Who is the Enemy*, Peking: New World Press, 1964.

—— *Yo Banfa!*, Shanghai: China Monthly Review, 1952 and Auckland: Progressive Bookshop, 1976. The 1976 edition has all mention of Liu Shaoqi erased.

Note: Because Alley's books were so numerous, I have only listed those that were especially useful for my research.

Auden, W. H. and Christopher Isherwood, *Journey to a War*, London: Faber & Faber, 1939.

Barthes, Roland, *Mythologies*, New York: Hill and Wang, 1972.

Becker, Jasper, *Hungry Ghosts: China's Secret Famine*, London: John Murray, 1996.

Bertram, James, *Capes of China Slide Away: A Memoir of Peace and War*, Auckland: Auckland University Press, 1993.

—— *Flight of the Phoenix: Critical Notes on New Zealand Writers*, Wellington: Victoria University Press, 1985.

—— *Return to China*, London: Heinemann, 1957.

—— *The Shadow of a War: A New Zealander in the Far East 1939–1946*, Australia and New Zealand: Whitcombe and Tombs Ltd, 1947.

Brady, Anne-Marie, 'The Curious Case of Two Australasian "Traitors", or, New Zealand, Australia and the Cold War,' *The New Zealand Journal of History*, 2001.

—— 'From Man to Myth: The Iconisation of Rewi Alley,' Conference paper, 10th International Conference of Asian Studies, Wellington, New Zealand, 1993.

—— *Making the Foreign Serve China: Managing Foreigners in the People's Republic*; Boulder, COL.: Rowman and Littlefield, 2002, (in press).

—— 'Man to Myth: Rewi Alley of China,' MA thesis, University of Auckland, 1994.

—— 'Red and Expert: China's "Foreign Friends" in the Great Proletarian Cultural Revolution,' *China Information*, December 1996.

—— Review Article: 'FriendLit,' *Revue Bibliographique de Sinologie*, 1998.

—— '"Treat Insiders and Outsiders Differently": the Use and Control of Foreigners in China,' *China Quarterly*, December 2000.

—— 'West Meets East: Rewi Alley and Changing Attitudes Towards Homosexuality in China,' *East Asian History*, June 1995.

—— 'Who Friend, Who Enemy? Rewi Alley and China's Foreign Friends,' *China Quarterly*, September 1997.

Burchett, Wilfred with Rewi Alley, *China: The Quality of Life*, Harmondsworth: Penguin Books, 1976.

Burchett, Wilfred and Alan Winnington, *Koje Unscreened*, Peking: published by the authors, 1953.

—— *Plain Perfidy*, London: British–China Friendship Association, 1954.

Cameron, Clyde, *China, Communism and Coca-Cola*, Melbourne: Hill of Content, 1980.

Caute, David, *The Fellow Travellers: A Postscript to the Enlightenment*, London: Weidenfeld & Nicolson Limited, 1974.

Champly, Henry, *The Road to Shanghai: White Slave Traffic in Asia*, trans. Warren B. Wells, London: John Long, 1937.

Chapple, Geoff, *Rewi Alley of China*, Auckland: Hodder and Stoughton, 1980.

Chiang King-sui, *Chinese Communists' Smiling Diplomacy and International Intrigues*, World Anti-Communist League, China Chapter, Asian Peoples' Anti-Communist League, Taipei, 1973.

China and the Asian African Conference, Peking: Foreign Languages Press, 1955.

Chow, Rey, *Writing Diaspora: Tactics of Intervention in Contemporary Cultural Studies*, Bloomington and Indianapolis: Indiana University Press, 1993.

Clifford, Nicholas R., *Spoilt Children of Empire: Westerners in Shanghai and the Chinese Revolution of the 1920s*, Hanover, New Hampshire: Middlebury College Press, 1991.

Cohen, Raymond, *International Politics: The Rules of the Game*, London: Longman, 1981.

Coward, Noel, *Noel Coward: Autobiography*, London: Methuen, 1986.

Croizier, Ralph C., *Koxinga and Chinese Nationalism: History, Myth and the Hero*, Cambridge, Massachusetts: East Asian Research Centre, Harvard University, 1977.

'Deceiving the Deceivers: Moscow, Beijing, Pyongyang, and the Allegations of Bacteriological Weapons in Korea,' *Cold War History Project*, Bulletin 11 – Cold War Flashpoints, 3/99.

Dimond, Gray, *Inside China Today: A Western View*, New York: Norton, 1983.

Eberhard, Wolfgram, *Moral and Social Values of the Chinese*, San Francisco: Chinese Materials and Research Aids Service Center Inc, 1971.

Endicott, Stephen, L., 'Germ Warfare and "Plausible Denial",' *Modern China*, Vol. 5, No. 1, January 1979, pp. 79–104.

Enzensberger, Hans Magnus, 'Tourists of the Revolution,' *Raids and Reconstructions*, London: Pluto Press, 1976, pp. 224–252.

Epstein, Israel, *Woman in World History: Song Qingling (Madame Sun Yat-sen)*, Peking: New World Press (second edition), 1955.

Fang, Percy Jucheng and Lucy Guinong Fang, *Zhou Enlai – A Profile*, Beijing: Foreign Languages Press, 1986.

Fitzgerald, C. P., *Why China? Recollections of China 1923–1950*, Melbourne: Melbourne University Press, 1985.

Fitzgerald, Stephen, *Talking With China: The Australian Labour Party Visit And Peking's Foreign Policy*, Canberra: ANU Press, 1972.

Fox, R. M., *China Diary*, London: Robert Hale Ltd, 1959.

Fraser, John, *The Chinese: Portrait of a People*, Toronto: Collins, 1980.

Fromm, Erich, *Beyond the Chains of Illusion*, London: Abacus, 1980.

Garland, Margaret, *Journey to New China*, Christchurch: The Caxton Press, 1954.

Ginsbourg, Sam *et al*, *Living In China (Zai Hua sanshi nian)*, Beijing: New World Press, 1982 (Chinese/English edition).

Hadas, Moses, *Heroes and Gods: Spiritual Biographies in Antiquity*, London: Routledge and Kegan Paul, 1965.

Hall, Richard, *The Rhodes Scholar Spy*, Sydney: Random House Australia, 1991.

Hamilton, John Maxwell, *Edgar Snow: A Biography*, Bloomington and Indianapolis: Indiana University Press, 1988.

Han Suyin, *Wind In the Tower: Mao Tse-tung and the Chinese Revolution 1949–1975*, Boston: Little Brown and Co., 1976.

—— *Phoenix Harvest*, London: Triad Granada, 1982.

Haraszti, Miklos, *The Velvet Prison: Artists Under State Socialism*, London: Penguin Books, 1983.

Hayward, Margaret, *Diary of the Kirk Years*, Queen Charlotte Sound: Cape Catley Ltd, 1981.

Hinsch, Bret, *Passions of the Cut Sleeve*, Berkeley: University of California, 1990.

Hogg, George, *I See A New China*, London: Victor Gollancz, 1945.

Hollander, Paul, *Political Pilgrims: Travels of Western Intellectuals to the Soviet Union, China, and Cuba*, New York: Oxford University Press, 1981.

—— 'Pilgrims on the Run, Ideological Refugees from Paradise Lost,' special pamphlet, *Encounter*, 1986.

Illsley, Walter, *An American in China*, unpublished manuscript, 1953–1954.

Isaacs, Harold R., *Re-Encounters in China: Notes of a journey in a time capsule*, New York: M. E. Sharpe, 1985.

Isherwood, Christopher, *Christopher and his Kind, 1926–1939*, New York: Avon Books, 1977.

James, Bev and Kay Saville-Smith, *Gender, Culture and Power*, Auckland: Oxford University Press, 1989.

Johnson, Hewlett, *The Upsurge of China*, Peking: New World Press, 1961.

Johnstone, Jr, William Crane, *The Shanghai Problem*, Stanford, California: Stanford University Press, 1937.

Kahn, E. J. *The China Hands: America's Foreign Service Officers and What Befell Them*, New York: The Viking Press, 1972.

Kates, George, *Chinese Household Furniture*, New York: Dover Publications, 1948.

Kidd, David, *Peking Story: The Last Days of Old China*, London: Aurum Press, 1988.

Kipnis, Andrew B., *Producing Guanxi: Sentiment, Self, and Subculture in a Northern China Village*, Durham: Duke University Press, 1997.

Klapp, Orrin E., *Heroes, Villains and Fools: The Changing American Character*, New Jersey: Prentice-Hall, 1962.

Klein, Daryl, *With the Chinks*, London: The Bodley Head, 1919.

Leitenberg, Milton, *The Korean War: Biological Warfare Allegations Resolved*, Center for Pacific Asia Studies at Stockholm University, Occasional Paper 36, May 1998.

Li Lien, *The Chinese Communist United Front Strategy and Policy for International Diplomacy*, World Anti-Communist League, China Chapter, Asian Peoples' Anti-Communist League, Taipei, 1977.

Liao Futing, *Virtues Reflected In Children's Picture Story Books During The Chinese Cultural Revolution*, Masters thesis, University of Georgia, 1985.

Lindsay, Michael, *China and the Cold War*, Melbourne University Press, 1955.

Locke, Elsie, *Peace People: A History of Peace Activities in New Zealand*, Christchurch: Hazard Press, 1992.

McCraw, David, *Chinese Foreign Policy*, New Zealand Institute of International Affairs, 1975.

MacKinnon, Janice and Stephen, *Agnes Smedley: The Life and Times of an American Radical*, Berkeley: University of California Press, 1988.

McLeod, John, *Myth and Reality in the New Zealand Soldier in World War Two*, Auckland: Reed Methuen, 1986.

Marcuse, Jacques, *The Peking Papers*, London: Arthur Baker Ltd, 1968.

Miller, William J., *The CCP's United Front Tactics in the US 1972–88*, California: Charles Schlacks Publisher, 1988.

Milton, David and Nancy Dall, *The Wind Will Not Subside: Years in Revolutionary China – 1964–1969*, New York: Pantheon Books, 1976.

Munro, Donald J., *The Concept of Man in Early China*, Stanford: Stanford University Press, 1969.

Olssen, Erik, *John A. Lee*, Dunedin: University of Otago Press, 1977.

Passin, Herbert, *China's Cultural Diplomacy*, New York: Frederick A. Praeger, 1963.

Peck, Graham, *Two Kinds of Time*, Boston: Houghton Mifflin Company, 1950.

Pei Xiannong, *Zhou Enlai de waijiaoxue* (The Diplomacy of Zhou Enlai), Beijing: Zhonggong zhongyang dangxiao chubanshe, 1997.

Perry, Roland, *The Exile: Burchett: Reporter of Conflict*, Richmond: William Heinemann Australia, 1988.

Phillips, Jock, *A Man's Country?*, Wellington: Penguin Books, 1987.

Rewi Alley, Chinese People's Association for Friendship with Foreign Countries and *China Reconstructs*, Beijing, 1988.

Rewi Alley Seventy Five, National Committee for the Commemoration of Rewi Alley's Seventy Fifth Birthday, Hamilton, NZ, 1972.

203

Rittenberg, Sidney and Amanda Bennett, *The Man Who Stayed Behind*, New York: Simon and Schuster, 1993.

Said, Edward W., *Orientalism*, New York: Pantheon Books, 1978.

—— 'Representing the Colonized: Anthropology's Interlocutors,' *Critical Inquiry*, 15 (Winter 1989), pp. 205–229.

Salisbury, Harrison, *China's New Emperors: China in the Era of Mao and Deng*, Boston: Little, Brown and Co., 1990.

Schuman, Julian, *China: An Uncensored Look*, Sagaponack, New York: Second Chance Press, 1979.

Scott, John, 'Recognising China,' in Malcolm McKinnon (ed.), *New Zealand in World Affairs Volume Three 1957–1972*, Wellington: New Zealand Institute of International Affairs, 1991, pp. 227–252.

Sergeant, Harriet, *Shanghai: Collision Point of Cultures 1918–1939*, New York: Crown Publishers, 1990.

Sewell, William G., *I Stayed in China*, New York: A. S. Barnes and Co., 1966.

Shapiro, Sidney, *An American in China*, New York: New American Library Books, 1979.

Sheng, Michael M., *Battling Western Imperialism: Mao, Stalin, and the United States*, Princeton, New Jersey: Princeton University Press, 1997.

Snow, Edgar, *Red China Today: The Other Side of the River*, Harmondsworth, Middlesex: Penguin, 1971.

—— *Scorched Earth*, London: Victor Gollancz Ltd, 1941.

Snow, Helen Foster, *My China Years*, New York: William Morrow and Company, 1984.

Snow, Philip, *The Star Raft: China's Encounter with Africa*, London: George Weidenfield and Nicolson Limited, 1988.

Somerset, Gwen, *Sunshine and Shadow*, Auckland: New Zealand Playcentre Federation, 1988.

Soulie de Morant, George, *Pei Yu Boy Actress*, San Francisco: Alamo Square Press, 1991.

Spencer, Barbara, *China Thirty Years On*, Whangarei, 1977.

—— *Desert Hospital in China*, London: Jarrolds Publishers, 1954.

Sun, Edmond, *The Publications of Rewi Alley, 1960–1972*, Wellington: Library School, National Library of New Zealand, 1973.

Tawney, R. H., *Land and Labour in China*, London: George Allen and Unwin, 1932.

Tayler, J. B., *Farm and Factory in China: Aspects of Industrial Revolution*, Student Christian Movement, 1928.

Terrill, Ross, *R. H. Tawney and his Times: Socialism as Fellowship*, Cambridge, Massachusetts: Harvard University Press, 1973.

—— *800,000,000: The Real China*, Boston: Little Brown and Co., 1972.

—— *China In Our Time: The epic saga of the People's Republic of China from the Communist victory to Tiananmen Square and beyond*, New York: Simon and Schuster, 1993.

Thomas, Bernard S., *Season of High Adventure: Edgar Snow in China*, Berkeley, California: University of California Press, 1996.

Thompson, Leonard, *The Political Mythology of Apartheid*, New Haven: Yale University Press, 1985.

Townsend, Peter, *China Phoenix*, London: Jonathan Cape, 1955.

Trotter, Ann (ed.), *New Zealand and China*, the papers of the 21st Otago Foreign Policy School, Dunedin, 1986.

Van Ness, Peter, *Revolution and Chinese Foreign Policy*, Berkeley: UCLA Press, 1970.

Waldren, Arthur, 'Friendship Reconsidered,' *Free China Review*, April, 1993, pp. 52–57.

Watt, Lindsay, *New Zealand and China in the Year 2000*, Wellington: Institute of Policy Studies, 1992.

Whyte, Alexander, *Santa Teresa*, London: Oliphant, Andersen and Ferrier.

Wilson, Ormond, *An Outsider Looks Back*, Wellington: Port Nicholson Press, 1982.

Winnington, Alan, *Breakfast With Mao*, London: Lawrence and Wishart, 1986.

Wright Arthur F. and Denis Twitchett (eds), *Confucian Personalities*, Stanford: Stanford University Press, 1962.

Xie Yixian, Wei shihua and Song Changmei, *Zhongguo waijiao shi* (A Diplomatic History of China 1949–1979), Kaifeng: Henan renmin chubanshe, 1988.

Yu, Frederick T. C., *Mass Persuasion in Communist China*, London and Dunmow: Pall Mall Press, 1964.

Zhang, Beihua, *Sino-New Zealand Relations 1792–1987*, M.Phil. thesis, University of Waikato, Hamilton, 1988.

Zhang Longxi, 'The Myth of the Other: China in the Eyes of the West,' *Critical Inquiry* 15 (Autumn 1988), pp. 108–131.

Zhao Pitao, *Waishi gaishuo* (Outline of Foreign Affairs), Shanghai: Shanghai shehui kexue chubanshe, 1995.

Zhejiang sheng waishi zhi (Zhejiang Foreign Affairs Annals), Beijing: Zhonghua shuju, 1996.

Zhonggong zhongyang xuanchuanbu bangongting, Zhongyang dang'anguan bianyanbu (eds), *Zhongguo gongchandang xuanchuan gongzuo wenxian xuanbian 1915–1992* (Selected Articles of CCP Propaganda Work, 1915–1992), 4 Vols, Beijing: Xuexi chubanshe, 1996.

Interviews

Alley, Joy, youngest sister of Rewi Alley, interviewed Auckland, NZ, 23 April 1993, 25 June 1993.

Alley, Rod, nephew of Rewi Alley, political scientist, interviewed Wellington, NZ, 20 January 1993.

Archer, Courtney, worked at the Shandan Bailie School 1946–1952, interviewed Rangiora, NZ, 4, 5, 6 July 1993.

Bertram, James, lived in China, Hong Kong and Japan from 1936–1945, involved in the China Welfare League, which helped to fund Indusco, interviewed Wellington, NZ, 28 January 1993.

Bridge, Nick, High Commissioner for New Zealand, Hong Kong, interviewed Hong Kong, 31 August 1990.

Bryan, Derek and Liao Hongying, Derek Bryan worked in the British Embassy in Chongqing during World War Two; he and his wife Liao Hongying were founding members of the Society for Anglo-Chinese Understanding, interviewed Beijing, 27 October 1990.

Carter, John, China Desk, Ministry of Foreign Affairs and Trade, worked at the New Zealand Embassy in Peking 1973–1975, interviewed Wellington, NZ, 18 January 1993.

Deng Bangzhen and Lu Bo, husband and wife team responsible for most of the Rewi Alley statues and portraits in existence in China and New Zealand; Deng is the foster son of Rewi Alley, interviewed Beijing, 24 June 1991, and Auckland, 6 December 1993.

Elder, Chris, former New Zealand Ambassador to China, worked at the New Zealand Embassy in Peking when first set up from 1973 to 1975, interviewed Wellington, NZ, 18 January 1993.

Epstein, Israel, an 'Old Friend of China,' Epstein has lived in China since the early 1940s, interviewed Beijing, 5 November 1990.

Ewen, Jack, former President of the New Zealand–China Friendship Association, interviewed Auckland, NZ, 29 June 1993.

Goddard, Nancy and George, former members of the New Zealand Communist Party; Nancy Goddard is former President of the Wellington branch of the New Zealand–China Friendship Society, interviewed Wellington, NZ, 7 January 1993.

Gould, Flora, ex-New Zealand Communist Party member, interviewed Auckland, NZ, 3 July 1993.

Huang Daozhen, Cultural Attaché, Chinese Embassy, Wellington, NZ, interviewed Wellington, 28 January 1993.

Kidd, David, lived in Peking in the late 1940s, interviewed Kyoto, Japan, 30 October 1994.

Lake, Doug, New Zealanders Doug Lake, his wife Ruth and three daughters Sarah, Jo and Prue lived in China 1963–1969, interviewed (by phone) Wellington, NZ, 11 December 1993.

Lake, Sarah, interviewed (by phone) Nelson, NZ, 4 December 1993.

Lu Guangmian, worked for Chinese Industrial Co-operatives (CIC) in the 1930s and 1940s, helped Alley to revive the co-operative movement in China in the 1980s, interviewed Beijing, 1 and 6 November 1990, 21 January 1991.

Lu Wanru, worked for the Chinese Association for Friendship with Foreign Countries, currently working for Chinese Industrial Co-operatives, ghost-writer of Rewi Alley's memoirs, writer of numerous commemorative articles on Rewi Alley, interviewed Beijing, 31 October 1990 and 7 November 1990.

Mahon, David, New Zealand businessman living in Beijing, visited Rewi Alley regularly in 1985–1986, interviewed Beijing, 22 November 1995.

Masson, Nyarene, George and Nyarene Masson worked at the Shandan Bailie school from 1948 to 1950, interviewed (by phone) 2 February 1996.

Newnham, Tom, regular visitor to China since the 1960s, member of the New Zealand–China Friendship Society, interviewed Auckland, NZ, 20 June 1993.

Powles, Michael, New Zealand Ambassador to China 1990–1993, interviewed Beijing, 31 October 1990 and 25 January 1991.

Roberts, Mary, third cousin of Rewi Alley, lived in China 1977–1980, 1984–1985, interviewed Wellington, NZ, 23 January 1993.

Shapiro, Sydney, 'Old Friend of China,' lived in China since the 1940s, interviewed Beijing, 30 October 1990.

Somerset, David, nephew of Rewi Alley, interviewed Wellington, NZ, 27 January 1993.

Spencer, Bob, worked at the Shandan Bailie School 1947–1950 as a doctor with his wife Barbara Spencer who was the school nurse, interviewed (by phone) Whangarei, NZ, 19 July 1994.

Townsend, Peter, English Promotional Secretary for the Chinese Industrial Co-operatives, Baochi, 1942–1943; Executive Secretary for the International Committee of the Chinese Industrial Co-operatives, successively in Chengdu, Chongqing, Shanghai, Beijing from 1943 to the end of 1951; interviewed (by phone) Melbourne, 15 and 16 February 1994, and (in person) Canberra, 10 and 16 April 1994.

Watt, Lindsay, former New Zealand Ambassador to China, interviewed Wellington, 21 January 1993.

Weiss, Ruth, 'Old Friend of China,' arrived in China 1933, interviewed Beijing, 1 and 20 November 1990, 24 June 1991.

Wilkinson, Max, worked at Shandan 1948–1952, stayed on in China until 1955, interviewed Wellington, NZ, 15 May 1993.

Wu Weiran Dr, personal doctor to Rewi Alley, interviewed Beijing, 22 June 1991.

Yan, Mavis, former CIC worker, interviewed Canberra, 10 and 16 April 1994.

Yang, Alex, Chinese New Zealander, lived in China 1954–1982, interviewed Beijing, 5 and 8 November 1990.

Yang, Xianyi and Gladys, China's most famous translators of classical and modern fiction, interviewed Beijing, 27 October 1990.

Yang, York, Chinese New Zealander, lived in China 1954–1984, interviewed Wellington, NZ, 18 January 1993.

Zhao, Gaiying, Rewi Alley's doctor of Chinese medicine, interviewed Beijing, 24 June 1991.

Newspapers and magazines

Beijing Review, Beijing, PRC
The Dominion, Wellington, New Zealand
Eastern Horizon, Hong Kong
The Listener, Wellington, New Zealand
New Zealand External Relations Review, Wellington, New Zealand
New Zealand Herald, Auckland, New Zealand
The People's Voice, Auckland, New Zealand
Press, Christchurch, New Zealand
Renmin ribao (*People's Daily*) Beijing, PRC

Archives

Alexander Turnbull Library, National Library, Wellington, New Zealand

Rewi Alley papers
Courtney Archer papers
Shirley Barton papers
John R. Marshall papers
Winston Rhodes papers
Colin Scrimgeour papers
Kathleen Wright papers

Chinese Association For Friendship With Foreign Countries (CPAFFC), Beijing, PRC

Rewi Alley papers

Ministry of Foreign Relations and Trade, Wellington, New Zealand

Prime Minister's Department, Ministry of Foreign Affairs and Ministry of External Relations and Trade files

National Archives, Wellington, New Zealand

Prime Minister's department files

National Archives, Washington DC, USA

Department of State files

New York Public Library, New York, USA

Maud Russell Papers

People's University, Beijing, PRC

Rewi Alley Archive

The University of Auckland (Library), Auckland, New Zealand

Willis Airey papers
P. W. G. McAra papers
New Zealand Peace Council papers
Victor Wilcox papers (Vault 35)

Private collections of Rewi Alley papers

Joy Alley
Courtney Archer
Jack Ewen
Lu Guangmian
Max Wilkinson

INDEX